Designed, printed, and bound in Japan
by Kamakurayama Kikaku & Otsuka Kogeisha
Co., Ltd.

6,000 copies for the Museum of Art, Rhode
Island School of Design, Providence, Rhode
Island.

PATTERNS AND POETRY

PATTERNS
AND
POETRY:

Nō Robes from the Lucy Truman Aldrich Collection
at the Museum of Art,
Rhode Island School of Design

Catalogue by
IWAO NAGASAKI
MONICA BETHE

Essays by
MONICA BETHE
SUSAN ANDERSON HAY
IWAO NAGASAKI
HELEN M. NAGATA

Technical Analysis by
PAMELA A. PARMAL

Translated and adapted by
MONICA BETHE

Edited by
SUSAN ANDERSON HAY

PROVIDENCE, RHODE ISLAND 1992

This project was sponsored by
a generous grant from

MITSUBISHI ESTATE CO., LTD.

CO-EDITORS:
Judith A. Singsen and Pamela A. Parmal
(Providence)

PHOTOGRAPHY:
Color plates: Isao Iida*
Microphotographs: Cathy M. Carver

Coordination for publishing by
Bun You Associates, Tokyo.

© Rhode Island School of Design
Library of Congress Catalogue
Card No. 92-53595
ISBN 0-911517-60-X

COVER:
Karaori, Edo period, 1750-1800. Weeping
cherry branches with a key-fret lozenge
background pattern on a ground of alternating
blocks. Lucy Truman Aldrich Collection,
Museum of Art, Rhode Island School of Design.
(Cat. no. 6.)

FRONTISPIECE:
Lucy Truman Aldrich at her home, 110
Benevolent Street, Providence, ca. 1935.
Photograph courtesy of Rhode Island
Historical Society, Providence.

*Japanese names have been cited in Western
fashion, given name first, followed by family
name, except for historical personages. Names
with pre-1868 reference have been cited in
Japanese fashion, family name first, followed
by given name.

Table of Contents

Susan Anderson Hay

THE THEATER of the Kanze Nō troupe in the Shibuya area of Tokyo is a modernist building of post-World War II vintage. Inside there is modern seating in the familiar semicircular arrangement of rows. At the front, however, is a bare cypress surface with pillars and a roof instead of the usual Western stage; a bridge over a gravel path leads off to stage left. At the appointed hour, two groups of men dressed in samurai-gray trousers and black kimono issue silently from doors at stage right. These are the orchestra and the chorus, and they sit directly on the floor of the stage at the back and sides of the roofed structure. A drumbeat breaks the silence, then a single flute. Slowly, very slowly, three men in priestly robes pass through the curtain at left and cross the bridge, progressing gradually across and down to the right front corner of the stage. In their wake follow two servants carrying a huge temple bell.

One of the priests sings and chants a mysterious song. "I am the priest of the Temple Dōjōji. Today we are installing a new temple bell to take the place of one we used to have many years ago. Today we will dedicate the bell – but no women may come to the ceremony," he sings enigmatically, bidding the servants to hang up the bell.

Suddenly on the bridge appears a new character: a woman, a dancer in full brocaded robes with dancer's mask and long-haired wig. She begins a slow, hypnotic dance to the beat of the drum, singing out her wish: by being allowed to dance before the bell, her sins will melt away, and she will find salvation. She pulls her golden kimono tight about her; just visible underneath is another robe – this one with the ominous glint of triangular reptilian scales – but the entranced servants do not notice, and, forgetting their master's words, they allow the dancer to come up to the bell. All at once, she jumps inside, the bell crashes to the ground, and she is hidden beneath.

"Oh, no!" cries the priest, and begins to tell a tale of long ago, of a girl in love, a girl who through a cruel joke was deceived by her lover, a priest of this shrine. She followed the priest to Temple Dōjōji, where he was hidden beneath the bell, and her jealous spirit became a serpent, coiling itself around the bell and melting it with hot breath. Realizing that the dancer is this evil spirit returned to the temple, the priests lift the bell. The dancer beneath has become the demon, the flowered kimono cast off to reveal the serpent robe beneath. Vigorously, she resists the oncoming priests, but by their prayers they subdue her, and she slithers away into the river.

This is *Dōjōji*, one of the best known and most dramatic of Nō plays, always performed in the summer season, always in traditional costume, and, usually, as in this case, acted exclusively by men. The plot, extremely simple, takes only a few lines to summarize, but the action of the play spans three hours. The action is slow but totally engaging; the audience sits entranced through long passages of slow dancing, even the comical servants draw only scant laughter, so absorbing is the experience.

The play is demanding. There is no scenery: only a pine tree painted on the back wall of the stage. There are no props: only the temple bell. The audience must imagine the setting in some imprecise time in the past. It must imagine the temple with its peaceful courtyard and simple buildings, the cherry blossoms, the majestic ringing of the bell. The audience must transform the magnificently costumed but enigmatic characters into people of mood and feeling, the dancer into an unhappy young woman maddened by jealousy. It must allow itself to experience the emotions of sadness, of fury, and the ultimate satisfaction of good overcoming evil that are the heart of the play. The action in *Dōjōji* is dramatic, but in other plays there is less action or even no action at all, and the words of dialogue and song are archaic and obscure, with their allusions to literature, double meanings, and puns. Instead the interest of the play is in the moods and emotions that the actors project. The enjoyment of the audience comes as it is carried, in its imagination, into a distant past where good and evil play out their eternal conflict through love, jealousy, and revenge.

Nō was traditionally practiced in the

courts of the daimyo nobility or performed in shrines patronized by noble families and reflected from an early date the elegant, refined nature of these aristocratic men and women who delighted in the performance of music and the writing of poetry. For these audiences, Nō performances involved five complete plays, ranging from forty-five minutes to two and a half hours in length, interspersed with comedies (*kyogen*), performed by actors specializing in these short, broad intervals between the serious Nō plays. *Dōjōji* in those days came at the end of a daylong performance, and the audience would be electrified by the dramatic defeat of the evil snake.

Historically, Nō plays were organized in a sequence, beginning with one of the "god plays," in which gods and spirits take on human form, blessing the audience and expressing simple themes of goodness, long life, and spiritual love. The second category includes plays about samurai warriors, often those defeated in battle, whose quite human desires for vengeance have relegated them to hell. These warriors, frequently based on historical or legendary figures, return to earth in costumes reflecting their masculine strength to retell the story of their defeat and suffering. A third category, sometimes called "woman plays," includes stories of tragic love. These plays have the most splendid costumes of all, with delicate feminine patterns that symbolize the elegant and tragic court women the actors portray. A fourth category of plays deals with the theme of madness, which may be caused by unrequited love as in *Dōjōji*, by exaggerated emotions, or by possession by the gods. Finally, there are the "demon plays," in which devils symbolize evil and human fears. These plays end with the driving off or death of the demons after a spectacular fight, and this symbolic defeat of evil provided a triumphant ending to the long Nō program.

Because Nō was traditionally performed by men, even in women's roles (today some roles are taken by women actors), because the actors often wear stylized masks that hide actual facial expression, and because direct expression of real emotion is prohibited according to long tradition, costume is of great importance in creating a Nō role. Even today, when customarily only one or two Nō plays appear on a program, the symbolic importance of the costume is still significant, forming a kind of code or language that is particular to the drama. The cut and draping of a robe are particular to the actor's role, while the pattern of the textile from which it is made echoes the season of the year and may indicate age, power, refinement, or other attributes, or, like the triangle-scale underrobe worn by the jealous spirit in *Dōjōji*, a costume may embody the sinister menace of evil. On a more obvious level, sumptuous silks in complex heavy weaves recall the majesty of court life long ago; gold and silver suggest its magnificence; a panoply of colors reflects the richness of court life with its deeply felt emotions and poetic outlook. The robes, like the plays themselves, evoke wonder at the splendor of court life and nostalgia for a more elegant age that is gone forever.

Even an outsider can be captivated. This is what happened to Lucy Truman Aldrich, who collected the robes published in this volume. Although she seems never to have seen a Nō play, she responded immediately to the richness and color of the costumes, which, like Japan itself, appealed straight to her heart. "The gold and lacquer, the beat of the drums... I love it all," she wrote.[1] Acquiring forty-seven Nō costumes between 1925 and 1929, she displayed them in her house in Providence, which, however, never took on an air of Oriental magnificence (see frontispiece), but remained a household of the purest New England restraint. Lucy Truman Aldrich, according to all who encountered her, represented the epitome of upright Yankee character. If anyone might have been impervious to the seductive appeal of these costumes replete with gold and silver, it ought to have been she. It is our good fortune that she allowed her emotions full rein in this case and that she gave these robes to the Museum of Art, Rhode Island School of Design, where they have been admired by so many. The publishing of this catalogue will bring that pleasure to many more people.

The Museum of Art, Rhode Island School of Design, is pleased to thank Mitsubishi Estate Co., Ltd., Tokyo, for their generous support in making this book possible. We wish to express our deep appreciation to Takuji Yamaguchi and Takeshige Osumi of Bun You Associates; and Ryuji Hisama of Otsuka Kogeisha Company, Tokyo. We extend our admiration and gratitude to Isao Iida, who took the beautiful color photographs of the Nō costumes. We also thank Yukiko Aoki and Kazuko Imasaka of *Utsukushii Kimono* (*The Quarterly Magazine of Beautiful Kimono*), published by Fujingaho

Company, Tokyo. Also helpful were the Kajima Foundation for the Arts, Tokyo; Metropolitan Center for Eastern Art Studies, Kyoto; Tokyo National Museum; Hayashibara Art Museum, Okayama Prefecture; Itsukushima Shrine, Hiroshima Prefecture; Kasuga Shrine, Gifu Prefecture; Mōri Museum, Yamaguchi Prefecture; and the Yamaguchi Nō Costume Research Center, Kyoto. Also, we thank Terry Gallagher and Elaine Lipton of Tokyo.

In Paris, we thank the staff of the Association pour l'Etude et la Documentation des Textiles d'Asie under the direction of Krishna Riboud. Alan Kennedy made several important contributions to our research as well.

In the United States, David Rockefeller was of special help in understanding his aunt and her collection, as well as in identifying Aldrich and Rockefeller family photographs in the collection of the Museum of Art, Rhode Island School of Design. We also wish to thank Peter J. Johnson of Mr. Rockefeller's staff, and the staff of the Rockefeller Family Archive, Tarrytown, New York. In Providence, Louise Aldrich Hoge kindly provided insights about her Aunt Lucy. Professor Maggie Bickford of Brown University played an important role in securing funding for the project. We also are indebted to Rita Freed, Money Hickman, and Anne Morse, Museum of Fine Arts, Boston; Philip Bergen and Bridget Knightly, Bostonian Society, Boston; Virginia Hay Smith, Massachusetts Historical Society, Boston; Yutaka Mino and Christa Thurman, Art Institute of Chicago; the staff of the Chicago Historical Society; Dale Gluckman and Sharon Takeda, Los Angeles County Museum of Art, Los Angeles; Milton Sonday, Cooper-Hewitt Museum, Smithsonian Institution, New York; Barbara Ford, Nobuko Kajitani, and Jean Mailey, Metropolitan Museum of Art, New York; Mary Carey, New-York Historical Society, New York; Robert Emlen and Marjory Dalenius, Providence Art Club, Providence; Denise Bastien, Linda Eppich, and staff, Rhode Island Historical Society, Providence; Susan Bean, Peabody Museum, Salem; Leslie Smith, Fine Arts Museums of San Francisco; the staff of the Aldrich Mansion, Warwick, Rhode Island; Louise Cort, Sackler Museum, Washington, D.C.; and Ann Rowe, Textile Museum, Washington, D.C. We also thank Joanne Greenspun and Amanda Stinchecum of New York.

Joseph Gilbert of Gilbert Associates, Providence, provided design advice. Margaret Ordoñez of the University of Rhode Island lent the camera for the microphotographs, which were taken by Cathy M. Carver, our Museum Photographer.

The late Elizabeth T. Casey, former Curator of the Aldrich Collection at the Museum, provided many insights about Miss Aldrich and about her role at the Museum. Pamela A. Parmal, Assistant Curator of Costume and Textiles at the Museum, prepared the technical analysis and helped to develop the vocabulary for this study, entirely new to this country, with the aid of Monica Bethe of Kyoto and Amy Lund, graduate student at the University of Rhode Island. At the Museum we also thank Kathleen Bayard, Cynthea J. Bogel, Michael Brand, Linda J. Catano, Elizabeth Enck, Melody Ennis, Florence D. Friedman, Susan B. Glasheen, Kathy Jellison, Paul Mann, David Newton, Maureen C. O'Brien, Sonali Patel, Debra Pelletier, Louann Skorupa, James Swan, Lora S. Urbanelli, Jean Waterman, Cherie Wendelken, and Arlene Wilson. Additional thanks go to Laurie Whitehead and the staff of the library of the Rhode Island School of Design.

This book could never have been completed without the editorial skills of Judith A. Singsen, in-house editor, nor without the advice and support of Director Franklin W. Robinson, who was closely involved in many stages of the project. Lastly, and above all, we owe a debt of gratitude to our authors, who contributed so much over the six years from the initiation of this project to its completion. Iwao Nagasaki, Curator of Japanese Textiles Section, Tokyo National Museum, suggested the project in 1986 and helped with its every stage. Helen M. Nagata completed her essay after leaving her position as Curator of Asian and Ethnographic Art at the Museum to pursue a Ph.D. at Stanford University. Monica Bethe deserves special commendation, for it was she who organized, wrote, and translated much of the catalogue, developing a new English vocabulary of Japanese terms. To her we extend our special appreciation for the very successful completion of this enormous and time-consuming task.

1. Letter, Lucy Truman Aldrich to Abby Aldrich Rockefeller, May 12, 1919; Rockefeller Foundation Archives, Tarrytown, New York. RG3. 2AA. Box 7. Letter C.

Providence, Paris, Kyoto, Peking:
Lucy Truman Aldrich and her Collections

Susan Anderson Hay

IN 1935, Lucy Truman Aldrich presented
to the Museum of Art, Rhode Island
School of Design, her collection of the
forty-seven costumes from the Japanese Nō
drama that are reproduced in this catalogue.
This outstanding collection was one of several
assembled by the remarkable Miss Aldrich. A
spinster, handicapped by congenital deafness,
she traveled around the world three times
and made nearly fifty journeys to Europe
accompanied by her paid companion, Minnie
E. MacFadden. Calling herself "an old woman
who has traveled,"[1] she accumulated silver,
paintings, furniture, brass and bronze objects,
and an extensive and important collection of
European porcelain figures that she also gave
to the Museum, together with a paneled gallery
in which to display them. However, the most
distinguished of her collections was made in
Asia. In person and on the spot she acquired
most of more than one thousand examples
of textiles and costume from Japan, China,
India, Indonesia, Egypt, and Iran. These tex-

tiles, given to the Museum between 1935 and
her death in 1955, form one of the broadest
and richest single collections of Asian textiles
in this country, and one of the finest in the
world.

The Japanese textiles were her favorites,
and they are the core and glory of the Aldrich
collection. The *kesa*, or Buddhist priests' robes,
are the most numerous, including 104 examples, but the 47 Nō costumes published in this
catalogue form a comprehensive collection of
nearly every type of costume in use in Japan in
the Nō drama in the eighteenth and nineteenth
centuries. Their spectacular colors and patterns, embellished with gold and silver, express
perfectly the splendor of the traditional and
highly stylized Nō theater. In the United States,
only the Museum of Fine Arts, Boston, has a
larger collection of Nō costume; however, it
includes only three varieties of robes. William
Sturgis Bigelow, who collected Boston's robes
in Japan in the 1880's, purchased ninety-five
Nō costumes, all very spectacular kimono-style
robes: elaborate weft-patterned *karaori*, embroidered *nuihaku* stenciled with gold, and
heavy, masculine *atsuita*. The more ethereal
gauze *kariginu, chōken,* and *maiginu*, as well as
other components of the complete costume,
did not seem to appeal to Bigelow, and he did
not collect them. The Metropolitan Museum,
New York, has a collection of twenty-nine Nō
costumes from several different donors, including H. O. Havemeyer, who was an early
Japan enthusiast before moving on to Impres-
sionist painting, but the collection lacks the
wide representation of the Aldrich collection,
and the Metropolitan Museum had to borrow
twelve pieces from Miss Aldrich when it held
its first exhibition in 1935. Sixteen Nō robes
are in the Art Institute of Chicago; the Peabody
Museum in Salem owns ten, four of which were
given by Bigelow; and a handful of other
museums possess one or two examples.

The Aldrich collection has an additional
distinguishing feature, and it is unique.
Yamanaka & Company, the Japanese firm from
which Miss Aldrich purchased her robes,
labeled many of them with their provenance in
major daimyo collections in Japan, writing
descriptions as well as family names on paper
wrappers that they supplied with the robes.
Additional notes on provenance in the bills and
shipping notices, many of which Miss Aldrich
kept, make the collection the best documented
in the United States and of great interest to

Fig. 1
Lucy Truman Aldrich,
about 1920. Photograph
courtesy of Rhode Island
Historical Society.

scholars here and in Japan, where the collection was published in part in the December 1989 issue of *Utsukushii Kimono* (*The Quarterly Magazine of Beautiful Kimono*, no. 150, special enlarged edition).

Not the least of the factors that recommend the Aldrich collection is the personality of Lucy Truman Aldrich herself, who had a singular love of color, a highly disciplined eye, and the intrepid spirit necessary to travel to Asia to acquire the textiles at a time of upheaval and swift change. An experience during her third Asian trip helps to illuminate the difficulties and pleasures of travel in Asia in the early 1920's. Arriving in China in 1923 for a few weeks travel before returning to her beloved Japan, she and Miss MacFadden sailed to Shanghai, where they boarded a special express train for Peking that carried other Western travelers as well as Chinese passengers.

Alone in her compartment, as she later recounted to the press, "I was awakened about half past two in the night... I became aware of the fact that shots were being fired...." She heard a voice out in the corridor say, "Bandits!" and quickly covered her pink crepe-de-chine nightgown with a silk wrapper and a cape belonging to Miss MacFadden, before being taken from her compartment by "a dirty, ragged, barefooted" young man with a grim and determined face and a rifle with bayonet. With windows breaking and bullets flying, Miss Aldrich was dragged out of the wrecked train by the wrists to join a group of Chinese captives (fig. 2). Urged on by the bandits with guns drawn, they marched single file in their night clothes through an extremely cold night, encouraged by the murder of one of the Chinese captives, who had happened to falter. Frightened and separated from her companions, Miss Aldrich noticed thankfully on the second day that the heavy bundles of loot carried by the bandits were forcing a slower and slower pace. Eventually the bandits stopped to examine the bundles, which contained clothing, bed clothes, brass door handles from the train compartments, money, jewelry, and one of Miss Aldrich's trademark floral hats. "This they tried on frontwards, backwards, sidewards and diagonally," their clowning putting them in a better humor and "showing that it was possible for them to entertain other thoughts than murder." Resuming the march, one bandit suddenly took pity on her, directing her to a nearby village and allowing her to

Fig. 2
The wrecked Shanghai-to-Peking express, from which Miss Aldrich, Miss MacFadden, and their maid Mathilde Schoneburg were kidnapped by bandits, 1923. Photograph courtesy of Rhode Island Historical Society.

Fig. 3
Miss Lucy's bandit. Photograph courtesy of Rhode Island Historical Society.

escape. Spending the night warily in a small abandoned hut that she could imagine was a doghouse only temporarily abandoned by its usual fierce occupant, she suffered through a violent thunderstorm, sleeping only fitfully. Fortunately, she was rescued the following morning by friendly villagers, including "her" bandit, who accompanied her to the railway line (fig. 3). From here she was taken to a hospital in Tientsin and reunited with her friends. Legend has it that several years later, when the Chinese government paid reparations, Miss Aldrich spent the money on her collection of Chinese textiles.[2] Certainly the incident sums up Miss Aldrich's character and intentions. Intrepid and resourceful despite her shyness, traveling almost alone, she persisted in collecting regardless of any eventuality. Nothing defeated her; even her hearing improved at times of crisis when she was abroad. Unlike many American collectors of Asian art, she acquired objects on the spot enlisting her own eye and the help of knowledgeable local dealers, enjoying the romantic appeal of her connection with exotic lands and peoples. Textiles were a perfect choice for her. Set apart by her deafness, driven by a Yankee horror of ostentation (and a comparative shortage of cash), she nonetheless had the confidence to collect in an unusual field that satisfied her desire for the finest objects and contributed to her sense of being part of the artistic life of her own family of collectors.

Lucy Truman Aldrich was born on High Street in Providence in 1869, the second child and oldest daughter of Abby Greene and Nelson Wilmarth Aldrich, at the time a partner in the wholesale grocery firm of Waldron and Wightman. Affable and charming, Aldrich believed that he was destined to succeed; although he came from an impoverished branch of the Aldrich family, he traced his ancestry to Rhode Island's founder, Roger Williams, as well as to George Aldrich, the first New England Aldrich, who arrived in Massachusetts in 1631. In the year of Lucy's birth, her father ran for and won a seat on the Providence Common Council as a Democrat from the fifth ward. Six years later, he was elected as a Republican to the Rhode Island legislature, where he sat for only one year, moving in 1876 to Washington, D.C. In 1879 he was elected to the U.S. House of Representatives, and in 1881 to the U.S. Senate, where he remained for thirty years as an exponent of big business, supporting the gold standard, protective tariffs, and a market free from government intervention. Thanks to political connections, he obtained access to capital, lent him by the American Sugar Refining Company, which quickly made him wealthy and allowed him to provide for his family as he believed his heritage required.

Lucy remembered moving in 1876 from the modest High Street house to a larger one on fashionable Broad Street after the death of her older brother, Nelson, Jr., and the births of her brother Edward (Ned) and sister Abby. Here the children were educated in a classroom specially equipped with desks and blackboard. An English tutor, Asenath Tetlow, taught American history, Bible reading, English grammar, arithmetic, and, strangely, German instead of fashionable French. Dancing school began early. After her father was elected to the House, she traveled with the family back and forth to Washington, D.C., where they lived in the Arlington Hotel or in rented houses. In 1890, she was sent to Miss Porter's School in Farmington, Connecticut.

Even before the purchase of the Broad Street house, Nelson Aldrich had begun to collect paintings, prints, and rare books, filling his houses in Washington, D.C., and Providence with fine furniture and handsome objects. Each summer he traveled to Europe, sometimes with his children, sometimes without, purchasing china, silver, and other necessaries of the good life and of good taste as he saw it, as epitomized by his friends Henry Clay Frick, H. O. Havemeyer, and, eventually, the redoubtable J. P. Morgan.

In 1891 Aldrich bought an older house at 110 Benevolent Street, near Brown University on the quiet East Side of Providence, among numbers of wealthy, quiet, and conservative old-guard families. Here, according to her sister Abby's letters, Lucy began to "entertain admirers," young men like Eli Whitney Blake, Jr., secretary of the Providence YMCA and earnest member of the Providence Society for Organizing Charity in the 1890's, and Bostonian Richard Norton. Abby's scrapbook from 1893 describes a life of tea parties, dances, Friday Evening Club meetings, tennis tournaments at Newport, "at home" afternoons, the Yale-Harvard football game. The two sisters were close and shared the same friends: Louisa Metcalf, Edith Richmond, Margaret Dwight, Ellen Dorrance, Frederick Street Hoppin, Jr., William T. Dorrance, Theodora Ledyard Colt, Edith and Charles Merriman, Jr., and many others.[3] Theater parties, bridge parties, costume balls, and pageants were also popular, as evidenced by a charming photograph of Lucy as dairymaid (fig. 4).

In 1896, Nelson Aldrich fulfilled a longstanding dream when he began to build a boathouse on 250 waterfront acres that he had bought over the years. In Warwick, overlooking Narragansett Bay, it was the first building of a planned estate with a mansion suitable for someone of his status. Once the boathouse was completed, it became the origin of boating trips and the scene of social events, its Oriental decoration and myriad books welcoming the girls in Chesterfield suits with leg-of-mutton sleeves that they liked to wear.[4]

In the winter, the family continued to make the Benevolent Street house their headquarters until the completion of the large and opulent mansion on the Warwick estate in

1912. Here, in addition to their whirlwind social schedule, the Aldrich girls could attend the many cultural affairs sponsored by the Providence Art Club, the Providence Athenaeum, and Rhode Island School of Design, and it was here that they could follow and begin to be interested in the world outside the West. Each year the Art Club, of which their father was a founding member, sponsored an exhibition of contemporary American paintings brought from Boston and New York and encouraged its members to collect by holding occasional exhibitions of works of art owned by members. Although the Friday-night lecture series was restricted to men, women had their Thursday-afternoon teas with lectures on subjects ranging from European architecture and art to Dr. Grenfell's Mission at St. Anthony, Newfoundland. Travel narratives were especially popular: Clementina Butler discoursed on "Old and New in Hindoustan" in 1891, while Miss Ruth A. Gaskell entertained in 1896 with "Glimpses of Spain as presented to the Tourist." Maud Howe Elliott came from Boston for five lectures on Rome and classical art in 1892, and in 1894, Egypt, ancient and modern Greece, and Constantinople were on the program.

As early as 1885 the Orient began to appear as a subject for discussion, when Professor Edward Sylvester Morse came from Boston for a Thursday course of lectures on the manners, customs, and household art of the Japanese. Having recently returned from Japan, where he had been lecturing and studying and collecting Japanese art, he was, with Ernest Francisco Fenollosa and William Sturgis Bigelow, one of the greatest exponents of Japonism in the United States, promoting Japanese traditional arts in this country as well as in Japan itself, where modernization had led in part to the abandonment of traditional techniques. A brilliant speaker, he was much in demand as a lecturer and returned to Providence on several occasions until his death in 1926, each time encouraging the appreciation of Japanese art.[5]

In the 1870's the Providence Athenaeum had begun purchasing books on the Orient for its extensive collection on travel and exploration, a collection it saw as reflecting what a gentleman might have in his personal library.[6] The influence of Japonism is evident in this collection as well as an exoticism deriving from earlier interest in the Near East, India, and

Southeast Asia. Books such as A. B. Mitford's *Tales of Old Japan* (London, 1871) were accompanied on the shelves by Mrs. A. H. Lenowen's *The Romance of the Harem* (Boston, 1873) and S. Johnson's *Oriental Religions and Their Relation to Universal Religion in India* (Boston, 1872). By 1900 the collection included nearly every important work on Asia available in this country. In 1878 the Providence Public Library opened with a collection of ten thousand volumes that also included works on the Far East, and the resources of the Brown University Library became more available with the opening of its new building, Robinson Hall, in the same year.

Private collectors were appearing with examples of literature about Japan. Professor Willard H. Munro of Brown University, fellow member of the Art Club, was assembling his own collection, now the nucleus of Brown's Japanese travel collection, and acquired every work about Japan as it was published. Nelson Aldrich himself owned the seven most popular works of Lafacadio Hearn, popularizer of Japanese folk tales and admirer of traditional Japanese ways.

Japanese art itself was also part of the Providence cultural scene. From 1881 on, when Ernest Bigelow exhibited some of his ukiyo-e prints at the Museum of Fine Arts, Boston led the way in gallery and museum exhibitions of Japanese and Chinese art, and these, only an hour away by train, were a magnet for travelers' excursions. In Providence, the Art Club included paintings of Japan by John LaFarge in its annual exhibitions during the 1890's, and in 1901 it exhibited watercolors by the Pacific

Fig. 4
Lucy Truman Aldrich in fancy dress, about 1889. Photograph courtesy of Rhode Island Historical Society

Painting Society, a group of Japanese artists working in the Western style, mostly paintings of tourist sites, which helped to encourage the Westerner's desire to visit Japan. In 1898 the Museum of Art of Rhode Island School of Design held an exhibition of Japanese prints, and in 1904 it exhibited watercolors by Fuji and Hiroshi Yoshida, members of the Pacific Painting Society who had shown their work at the Art Club three years before.[7] These two artists, husband and wife, came to Providence in person several times between 1901 and 1924, becoming well known to members of the Art Club through frequent inclusion of their paintings in the annual exhibitions. It was through their efforts that in 1924, following the Japanese earthquake, the Art Club showed a traveling exhibition that included not only Western-style artists but works by at least one woodblock-print artist, Shinsui Itō.[8]

Finally, encouraging an interest in Oriental art were friends of the family who also collected, such as Frick, the Havemeyers, and Morgan, who were respected for their leadership in the collecting world and in the realm of good taste. Although Frick's major interest was old master paintings – Lucy remembered him giving her a tour of them in his New York home, now the Frick Collection – he also collected Persian and Japanese decorative arts for his house in Pittsburgh.[9] Near at hand and certainly well publicized, although probably not an Aldrich acquaintance, was Bostonian Isabella Stewart Gardner, who had the guidance of William Sturgis Bigelow in Yokohama on one of her collecting expeditions in 1883. Bigelow, in Japanese costume, directed her to his favorite

shop for Japanese art, where Mrs. Gardner bought *objets* for her Beacon Street mansion and "brocades" for herself.[10]

In New York Louis Comfort Tiffany was collecting Japanese decorative arts and freely appropriating Japanese motifs and esthetic principles for his own objects and for his highly publicized and fashionable interior-decoration business. New York collectors of Japanese art included the Vanderbilts, Charles Freer, and the artist John LaFarge, but they were not so bold as to decorate the ceilings of their libraries as Tiffany did for the H. O. Havemeyers with a collage of Nō-robe fragments (undoubtedly not an inspiration for Lucy Truman Aldrich).[11]

In the 1890's, however, the interests of the Aldrich family remained firmly focused on Europe. London, Scotland, Paris, Oberammergau, the North Cape, and Russia, among other destinations popular with privileged Americans, were on the Aldrich itinerary, and in 1898, Lucy and William with Asenath Tetlow spent an entire winter in Europe (fig. 5). The absence of Abby Aldrich on this trip is notable. She remained at home in Providence, in residence at 110 Benevolent Street, where she was receiving continuing visits from a young graduate of Brown University whom she had met in his sophomore year in 1895, John D. Rockefeller, Jr. In 1901, the two were married on the Aldrich estate in Warwick, where a Renaissance-style "teahouse" with a ballroom had just been completed at the water's edge next to the site of the earlier boathouse. Only the two families were present at the ceremony, but fifteen hundred guests were received afterwards on the vast lawns. Lucy was maid of honor.

Gradually, she too was drawn into the Rockefeller orbit, becoming a close friend of her brother-in-law and establishing a relationship which would be characterized by affectionate cordiality all their lives, as their frequent exchange of letters shows. Lucy had often been present at the parties and balls attended by John and Abby during John's college years, and in the early 1900's she visited frequently at the Rockefeller house at 13 West 54th Street and later at the elaborate nine-story mansion built for them at No. 10. In 1903, the Rockefellers' only daughter, Abby, known as "Babs," was born, followed by John D. Rockefeller III, Nelson, Laurance, Winthrop, and David. Lucy became their enthusiastic aunt, entertaining

Fig. 5
The Aldrich family and fellow passenger John D. Rockefeller, Jr., on a trip to the North Cape, 1896. STANDING: back row, left, Lucy Truman Aldrich; back row, right, Abby Aldrich. SEATED: center, Senator Nelson W. Aldrich; right, Abby Greene Aldrich. ON DECK, FRONT: John D. Rockefeller, Jr. Museum of Art, Rhode Island School of Design; Lucy Truman Aldrich Collection.

them in Providence, sending them presents, later receiving them in London and Paris, and she followed with interest the activities of her brother-in-law, John D. Rockefeller, Jr. After graduating from Brown, he acted as assistant to his famous father, becoming a trustee of the University of Chicago in 1898, serving on boards of directors of U.S. Steel, Standard Oil of New Jersey, the National City Bank, and other Rockefeller interests. In 1901 the senior Rockefeller sold his interests in the Mesabi iron range at a favorable price to J. P. Morgan, after a stand-down of the intimidating Morgan by John D., Jr., who enlisted Henry Clay Frick as intermediary. By 1910, he had developed a new role for himself as philanthropist, organizing and administering myriad details as his father established the Rockefeller Institute for Medical Research, eventually to become Rockefeller University; the General Education Board for the education of blacks in the South; and the Rockefeller Foundation. It was these projects that especially fascinated Lucy, and the internationality of these interests was clearly an influence on her future actions, as was the concept of giving in the public interest.

In the early 1900's, public appreciation of these projects, to say nothing of the philanthropic role of both Rockefellers, had yet to develop. Instead, public attitudes had turned against the powerful Standard Oil Company of New Jersey and its monopoly formed through its ownership of many aspects of the oil business, from wells in western Pennsylvania to railroad lines. Practices like preferential rebates and buyouts of small refiners to eliminate "competitive chaos," standard in the 1870's, were giving way to the idea of freer competition, and both John D. Rockefeller and Senator Nelson Aldrich were suffering because of this change in public conviction.

In 1911 the Supreme Court decided that the huge Standard Oil of New Jersey, which had in the 1890's controlled more than eighty percent of the petroleum business, violated the Sherman Antitrust Act. Before and during the controversy that led to the Supreme Court decision, "the Rockefeller crowd" was continually vilified in public and in the press by progressives like Theodore Roosevelt, Ida Tarbell, and Robert LaFollette. John D. Rockefeller, Jr., came in for his own share of abuse when the classes he taught at the YMCA, a longstanding interest of his own and of his wife, who had been a director in Providence,

were attacked as self-serving. Similarly, Senator Aldrich, whose own peculations had been just as acceptable in the 1870's, came under attack by Lincoln Steffens and others for being "the Boss of the U.S.," and "the chief exploiter of the American people." The Warwick estate became "the house that sugar built." Undaunted by the attacks, Aldrich continued to build the enormous Warwick mansion, collect rare books and paintings, and travel abroad, taking Lucy to Egypt in 1913.

His family did suffer greatly under these attacks, which helped to magnify Lucy's shyness, turned both sisters against the idea of display of their wealth, and, at the time that they were both beginning to collect works of art, inspired them to a certain frugality not in the nature of their father. Abby Aldrich Rockefeller was already beginning to acquire Japanese prints of birds and flowers, which she regarded as inexpensive as well as beautiful, and her first purchases of modern art after the Armory show in 1913 reflected just these considerations. Even in 1936, according to an article in *Time* magazine, the highest price she would pay was only $1,000, which she took out of her own Aldrich money.[12]

In 1915, Senator Aldrich died. According to Warwick tax records of 1914, his personal estate was worth $1,000,000, while his real estate amounted to $613,000, not counting the house and furnishings in Providence. This figure also does not include his investments elsewhere, which amounted to from $8,000,000 to $28,000,000, according to various biographers. To his wife he left the house at 110 Benevolent Street and all his household goods, both there and at the Warwick Neck estate, which the children, except Abby, were to own jointly. To Abby Aldrich Rockefeller, he left $100,000, no doubt believing that she had enough already. Lucy was to receive $8,000 per year from a trust fund drawn from the rest of the estate, as were each of the other children: Ned, Stuart, William, Richard, Winthrop, and Elsie.[13]

Lucy continued to live with her mother at 110 Benevolent Street during the winters and in Warwick each summer. Although she now had the wherewithal to support her own travels, World War I prevented the usual summers in Europe, and she occupied herself in Red Cross work, to which John D. Rockefeller, Jr., contributed with money sent to her. In 1917, Abby Greene Aldrich died, leaving the house to Lucy

and Abby and the trust fund to be divided outright among the surviving children. One year later, Lucy began to make plans to visit Asia, where John D. Rockefeller, Jr., and the Rockefeller Institute were deeply committed to the support of medical education in China. Lucy would go first to Japan, then to China, where she would visit the Rockefeller-funded building of Peking Union Medical College now rising for the education of Chinese doctors in Western medical techniques.

In April of 1919, she and her companion, Miss MacFadden, sailed on *The Empress of Russia* from Vancouver to Yokohama. Because the trip had been arranged through the office of John D. Rockefeller, Jr., the two women were escorted throughout by Standard Oil executives and their wives. From their headquarters at the Grand Hotel, Yokohama, trips were arranged to Tokyo (lunch at Frank Lloyd Wright's Imperial Hotel) and Kamakura (the great Buddha and cherry blossoms), then to Miyanoshita in the mountains.

By May 12, they were in Kyoto, where Miss Aldrich made her first visit to Yamanaka & Company, from whom she would acquire so much of her future collection. Although she was probably familiar with this firm, which had offices in Boston as well as in Japan, she had no experience collecting Asian art and was nervous about her purchases. At the request of her sister Abby, and upon the receipt of a check to pay for them, Miss Aldrich bought for Abby three small screens and a Japanese print. Afterwards she wrote apologetically to Abby that she knew "absolutely nothing about Orien-

tal things," and that she was afraid of making mistakes, but that she was "learning fast."[14] In this tentative way Lucy Truman Aldrich began the purchase of many of the Japanese prints that form the nucleus of the Abby Aldrich Rockefeller collection of bird and flower prints at the Museum of Art, Rhode Island School of Design, and of the textiles that make this Museum's collection one of the finest in the world.

Her confidence did not take long to develop. Declaring herself possessed of a good eye if not good ears, she had already begun to love Japan and things Japanese. "The more I see of Japan the better I like it," she wrote to Abby. The "curious and beautiful" things she saw also included running sewers and children with appalling diseases, but overall she was charmed. "I'd much rather be a Buddhist than a Baptist anyway – the whole thing appeals so much more to my temperamental, or is it emotional, love of color: the gold and lacquer, the beat of the drums and even the smell of the incense. I love it all," she enthused.[15]

After a short trip to Korea in hot and steamy July weather, the women returned to Japan to spend four weeks in Nikko, staying in the Kanaya Hotel at the top of the hill, window-shopping at the shop of Sasaya Kobayashi for prints and fabrics, enjoying the people and the scenery along the steep streets and at the gilded and ornate shrine of Toshogu, and at Lake Chuzenji (fig. 6). At every turn they enjoyed the romantic sensation of seeing Japanese prints come to life. Miss Aldrich became more confident in her shopping, gradually realizing that she could count on dealers like Yamanaka and Kobayashi to find her good things, albeit things that struck her as very expensive. Feeling extremely extravagant, she returned to Yokohama at the end of August with twenty-one prints for Abby, some Imari plates and bowls, and four "pieces of old curios" purchased for 188 yen from Shojiro Nomura, the famous dealer and collector of *kosode* (antique kimono for street wear), from whom she would in later years purchase several *kesa*. For herself she had bought "brocades" including two *kesa*, the first pieces in what would be an incomparable collection of the beautiful but, in the West, little-known Buddhist priests' robes.

In September she and Miss MacFadden were off by steamer to China, where a house had been lent them for a month by George E. Morrison, an Australian (fig. 7). A former

Peking correspondent of *The London Times*, Morrison was currently in Europe serving as a political adviser to the representatives of the Chinese government at the Versailles Conference that ended World War I. From this large house of four courtyards and many gates, the two women planned to visit the Rockefeller Foundation's headquarters and the Peking Union Medical College, but mainly, by Lucy's own account, they shopped – that is, Chinese merchants came to the house with bundles of tapestry cushions, Taoist priests' robes, embroidered hangings, and hundreds of examples of court robes of the Ching dynasty, only recently dispatched. It was a superb time to be buying imperial textiles in China; never again would they be so available or so inexpensive (in spite of Miss Aldrich's complaints), as old families fell from power, were impoverished, and sold off the elaborate robes that they would never wear again. Miss Aldrich succumbed to a *kossu* (tapestry) cover, one or two robes, and a mandarin hat with which she returned to Providence in December.

By the following November (1920), she and Miss MacFadden were off again, this time to India, taking with them Abby's seventeen-year-old daughter Babs. Leaving from Vancouver on the Canadian Pacific's *R.M.S. Empress of Asia*, they touched only briefly at Yokohama and Nagasaki and had time for one shore visit in Shanghai and one in Manila before landing in Hong Kong. Sailing up the Pearl River to Canton, the youthful Babs and her impressionable aunt were enchanted with little towns, bridges, boats, and pagodas, which reminded Lucy of the chinoiseries of European chintzes. Gone utterly were the fears and insecurities of the previous year.

Led by Mr. Graybill of the Canton Christian College, "there followed a wild week of shopping which was really sightseeing too," rationalized Lucy to Abby, as the group persuaded merchants to get out their wares from boxes in which they were packed away for safekeeping.[16] In contrast to the previous year, which was spent largely in peaceful, urban Peking, Lucy and her entourage were now experiencing the aftermath of the chaos and fighting that characterized the country in the late teens and early twenties. While the central government tried to exert pressure on the warlords who had traditionally held power in the countryside, even during the Ching dynasty, bandits and counterrevolutionaries were con-

stantly threatening Chinese and foreigners alike, as Lucy would find to her regret two years later. For now, she imagined that the violence was over, and realizing that people were selling off their treasures because of impending famine and from fear of losing them in further fighting, she bought nearly $3,000 worth of textiles, furniture, and jade to decorate her homes in Providence and Warwick.

From Canton they went to Java, where they visited Djakarta, Borobodur, and Solo (Surakarta), where the sultan's palace was. Although shopping was undoubtedly on the itinerary, all in the party were tired, and Babs had become ill. Canceling a trip to Sumatra and bypassing Ceylon, they took a steamer to Calcutta (fig. 8), where they were greeted by an

Fig. 7
The George Morrison house, Peking, where Miss Aldrich lived in September 1919 and where she purchased her first Chinese textiles. Museum of Art, Rhode Island School of Design; Lucy Truman Aldrich Collection.

Fig. 8
Miss Aldrich (right), Miss MacFadden (center), and Babs Rockefeller (?) arriving in India, late 1920 or early 1921. Museum of Art, Rhode Island School of Design; Lucy Truman Aldrich Collection.

unexpected shortage of hotel rooms, not only in Calcutta but everywhere they intended to visit. Facing cancellation of the whole trip, Lucy decided to use the $7,500 letter of credit from John D. Rockefeller, Jr., that had been intended for Babs's expenses to hire a railway car with restaurant car attached. In this unexpectedly luxurious manner the group proceeded to Delhi, Agra, and Kashmir, where they had been urged to go by Lucy's Providence friend Louisa Metcalf. Here they went up to Darjeeling, where at the sight of Mount Everest at dawn Babs thoroughly recovered. When Lucy herself came down with dysentery, however, they decided to abandon a proposed trip to Southeast Asia, leave India at once, and return by way of France, but not before Miss Aldrich had recovered enough to order brass boxes, enamel work, an antique Kashmir shawl, and a small stone sculpture shipped home from Ganeshi Lall and Son, Manufacturing Jewelers, Embroiderers, and Shawl Merchants, before departing from Bombay on February 19.

That summer Miss Aldrich remained in France and England, returning late in the year to spend the winter in California. To her great surprise and elation, Abby sent her the deed for her half of the house as a birthday gift, and Lucy returned to 110 Benevolent Street as its sole owner, joyful to be on her own in the old house. "I could never get really interested in planning a home anywhere else," she confessed to Abby, inviting her to come see the "few" things she had bought in India.[17]

In June Lucy set off again, enthusiastically planning to travel around the world a second time, but in reverse, beginning with Paris in June of 1922 and London in August, where she stayed at the Connaught Hotel and bought sweaters from Jaeger. Fully equipped with these, dresses from Worth in Paris, and jewelry she purchased at Cartier, she and Miss MacFadden sailed for Ceylon from Marseilles in November on the *André Lebon*, spending the winter months in India, again renting a special railroad car. On this trip she purchased many of the Indian costumes and textiles now in the Museum's collection, which were described by the dealer as "old old times." These include embroidered, brocaded, and tie-dyed saris, Mogul *patkas* (sashes), and some of the most unusual Indian shawls in any American collection today – unusual because they include traditional Indian designs, as well as the types of "Kashmir" shawls preferred in the West.

Having missed Japan on the previous excursion, they spent the spring "doing" Japan and planning a brief trip to China for the summer. On April 15, Lucy wrote to Abby that they would be sailing to Shanghai, then going by train to Peking "to stay as long as the heat will let us." However, it was bandits who ultimately spoiled the trip, as we have seen, attacking the Shanghai-to-Peking express and holding the travelers for ransom, causing Lucy to lose her Cartier jewelry and her interest in traveling further in China. In the end, no ransom was paid, and the release of all the captured travelers was negotiated after threats of force by the Western powers if treatment of their nationals did not improve. After her recovery from the sprained back she sustained in what became a major international incident, she acknowledged that travel in China was not the romantic idyll she had experienced on her two earlier trips; indeed, a much less pleasant reality lay just beneath the surface comforts offered to the first-class traveler. The experience taught both Miss Aldrich and Miss MacFadden much about the reality of life in China, to a degree they had never expected to know. "At no time since the Boxer trouble has there been so much unrest throughout China," wrote Miss MacFadden to Abby Rockefeller.[18] "All the Europeans living in China are frightened," Lucy informed her sister.[19] Having come face to face with brutality and murder, they were both humbled and grateful to have emerged alive. Praise for the kindness of villagers and helpful expatriate Americans fell from their lips, but they would never return to China.

From safe haven in Kyoto, they prepared to return to Providence directly, giving up once again the hoped-for trip to Southeast Asia. In the five weeks in Japan prior to the disastrous trip to China, Miss Aldrich had visited Yamanaka & Company in Tokyo and Kyoto and Shojiro Nomura at his Kyoto shop. Her collection of priests' robes was now a real collection, with additions purchased from both dealers. "I have spent millions," she wrote to Abby.[20] Some jewelry and two pieces of antique Chinese brocade purchased in Shanghai had been lost to the bandits, but the Japanese screens, ceramics, bronze Buddhas, and netsukes she had purchased before leaving were being shipped to Providence and so were safe. Nomura was sending her two cases of "curios" containing nineteen bronze Buddhas, lions, and incense burners, together with prints by Hokusai, Yoshitoshi, and Toyokuni for the house on Benevolent Street and for Abby's collection of bird-and-flower prints.

The misfortunes of the year 1923 did not end with the departure of the women for home. In November came word of what was called "the worst disaster of all time," a tremendous earthquake that leveled Yokohama, Tokyo, and Nagoya, where they had just been sightseeing, but fortunately spared many of the ancient sites of Kyoto. Providence joined in the unprecedented Western rescue effort when the Art Club exhibited and sold works assembled from artists all over Japan for the benefit of the refugees.

Fourteen months' respite in Providence was enough, and in August of 1924, Miss Aldrich and Miss MacFadden were off again to Paris to begin the oft-postponed trip to Southeast Asia, stopping in Cairo briefly, then on to Ceylon, Cambodia, Siam, and Java, before going to Calcutta for the months of December 1924 and January 1925. At each stop Lucy bought bronzes, decorative wooden objects, and textiles for her now rapidly expanding collection: Cambodian and Indonesian *ikat*-dyed silks; brightly colored silk plaids in Siam; saris and shawls in India.

Her collection of Japanese textiles remained the most extensive. Once again she purchased *kesa* and other textiles from Yamanaka & Company in Kyoto, and receipts indicate that these included her first Nō robes, thirty of them, described as "old Japanese 'Nō' dance costumes," for $10,000 or 24,242.40 Japanese yen.[21]

Although the Nō costumes immediately attracted her interest by their colorful splendor, there is no evidence that she ever attended a performance of this highly sophisticated, intensely exotic art. Whether this was because of her deafness – although this would not have been a tremendous barrier – or because of the reputation of the Nō drama as a difficult art, unapproachable for Westerners, or because it was simply impossible for a Western woman to attend a performance in those still tradition-bound days (Tokyo and Kyoto had been open for Western tourism for only twenty years) is not known. For many years she continued to call her collection "Nō dance costumes," a designation given them by the dealer Yamanaka; however, attendance at a performance would have revealed the true character of Nō as an

elusive combination of opera, drama, and stylized motion that can only vaguely be called dance in the Western sense. When she was preparing for the exhibition of the robes at the Museum of Art, Rhode Island School of Design, in 1937, Miss Aldrich's curator, Elizabeth T. Casey, had to request from Kojiro Tomita, Curator at the Museum of Fine Arts, Boston, a definition and description of Nō in order to write labels and give explanatory talks. Be that as it may, the thirty pieces that she acquired in Japan in 1925 represent nearly every type of Nō costume, which can be attributed to the astuteness of the dealer in placing the best robes in a comprehensive collection that would truly represent the reality of Nō. Yamanaka & Company also took pains to see that Miss Aldrich's collection was not only wide-ranging but adequately documented and stored, supplying wrappers with each robe and provenance when available and advising her how to display and house them, even visiting her in Providence.

Yamanaka & Company was a family-owned firm dealing in Japanese and Chinese objects. Based in Osaka, the firm had moved to establish branches all over the world in the 1890's. In the wake of Japonism and the great dealers Siegfried Bing and Tadamasa Hayashi, Yamanaka opened a store in Paris and by 1916 had become an influential part of the French art world. Haru Reischauer recounts how her great-uncle, Kojiro Matsukata, oil magnate and shipyard owner, was approached by Yamanaka's European representative Yuji Okada in London in 1916 with an offer to sell him the famous Japanese print collection of Henri Véver, the Parisian jeweler who had been among the first great collectors of these prints in France. The Battle of Verdun was taking place, France was under German siege, and Véver was desperate to sell the more than eight thousand prints he had purchased – one of the finest collections in the world. Matsukata bought them all, sight unseen, and returned them to Tokyo after the war, where they eventually became the core of the ukiyo-e collection at the Tokyo National Museum.[22]

In 1895, again following in the footsteps of Siegfried Bing and Japanese dealer Shugio Hiromichi, Yamanaka & Company opened a gallery in New York at 20 West 27th Street, and by 1900 had a store at 254 (later 680) Fifth Avenue. A Boston branch opened at 324 Boylston Street in 1897, and by 1924, when Yamanaka & Company opened its doors in the fashionable Casino in Newport, Rhode Island, it had branches in London, Peking, Washington, D.C., and Atlantic City, and would soon open in Chicago, Cleveland, and Bar Harbor, remaining on the American scene until just before World War II. A Chicago publication commented in 1928 that the new company, which had located on North Michigan Avenue because it was the most fashionable address in Chicago, was "beautifully finished" and pictured a gallery lined with dark, built-in wooden cases displaying paintings, sculpture, porcelains, ivories, and Chinese and Japanese lamps and furniture.[23]

The company, which had existed for more than four hundred years in Japan, could, through its connections and because of its reputation, sometimes obtain objects for sale from daimyo collections, and in 1935 it offered for sale in Boston some eighth-century silk fragments.[24] That the directors of Yamanaka & Company cared deeply about the objects they sold and the careful and authentic presentation of Japan and of Japanese art is shown not only by their care in assembling Lucy Truman Aldrich's Nō robe collection with its breadth of examples, but also in their involvement in publicizing Japanese architecture and gardens through public projects that they sponsored. In 1916 the firm sponsored a competition for a house in Japanese style that could be built on the Hudson river, specifying young Japanese architects and draftsmen as competitors. The prize-winning design was typically Japanese, on two floors around a square stairwell with verandas and balconies, and was designed by Iwao Shimizu of Tokyo; however, it was never built.[25] In another effort, the firm sponsored and built a large model of a representative Japanese landscape, complete with farmyard, lagoon, and pagoda, designed in 1915 by Japanese garden expert Takeo Shiota for the Newark Public Library.[26]

The galleries became a respected source not only for art objects but for information about the works sold there; branch managers found themselves helping with display installations for their patrons, as well as advising collectors on what and when to buy. Lucy Truman Aldrich's purchases were not the only objects from Yamanaka & Company to find their way into museum collections. Henry Walters bought most of the important early Buddhist scrolls, stone carvings, and wood sculptures in his collection from Yamanaka &

Company in New York between 1919 and 1931; these are now in the Walters Art Gallery, Baltimore.

From 1925 on, Yamanaka & Company clearly considered Miss Aldrich to be one of their best clients. In October of 1925, back in Providence, the Japanese owner Sadajiro Yamanaka visited her at 110 Benevolent Street, and in November, the Yamanaka store at 456 Boylston Street in Boston was sending her textiles on approval. *Obi* (sashes for priests' robes), *fukusa* (gift-wrapping cloths), *uchishiki* (silk squares), and more *kesa* came on approval from Boston, and another collection of similar textiles was forwarded from the Bar Harbor branch of the Yamanaka empire.

In January 1926, Miss Aldrich and Miss MacFadden set out once again, this time for Egypt, where there was another important Rockefeller project under consideration. Four years after the discovery and opening of King Tutankhamen's tomb by British archeologist Howard Carter, public interest in the area was still high. Although the widely publicized opening of this tomb with its incredible hoard and the intense newspaper coverage of the sensational aspects of the story of its discovery monopolized public attention, other Western scholars were also at work in the area. One organizer of scholarly investigation in Egypt was the Oriental Institute of the University of Chicago, established in 1919 by John D. Rockefeller, Jr., at the university his father had founded in 1893. Its director, Professor James Breasted, had been working on materials from the area since 1905, collecting, translating, and publishing ancient inscriptions, and was justly famous for this extraordinary work. The brilliant and charismatic Breasted saw much more of value than inscriptions in the area, however, and in 1919 had approached the junior Rockefeller with a plan for a permanent University of Chicago expedition to Egypt, which would result in new discoveries about the development of civilization itself. Breasted wanted no less than to collect as many as possible of the objects and writings of the Near East in "systematically arranged archives" that could support the study and publication of the history of the rise and development of civilization, a project he himself wanted to undertake. Rockefeller responded with a gift of $10,000 per year for five years to get the project started and to enable Breasted to locate and purchase as many artifacts as he could find.

In 1926, after the renewal of funding of the Oriental Institute with a budget of $50,000 per year by the enthusiastic Mr. Rockefeller, an even more ambitious project was being debated. Breasted had been purchasing artifacts for the seven years of the Oriental Institute's operation, but much of his study had been conducted in the Egyptian National Museum in Cairo, and for years he had labored over the transcription of the religious texts stored there. He had been appalled by conditions in the exhibition rooms and especially the basement storage areas, which flooded every time the Nile rose above its banks, destroying valuable artifacts. In 1924 he had approached the Rockefeller Foundation with the idea of obtaining sponsorship for a new museum for Cairo in the abandoned British barracks next to the old museum. Rockefeller was thoroughly captivated by the energetic and ambitious Breasted. He had responded to Breasted's proposals not only with a figure of $10,000,000 as a proposed gift to Egypt for the construction of the new museum and an offer of the services of his own architect, but he had also volunteered to sponsor the excavation of the ancient site of the battle of Armageddon in the great Megiddo plain between Haifa and the hills of Nazareth in present-day Israel.[27]

Miss Aldrich arrived in Egypt at a time of crisis for the Cairo museum project, which on January 6, 1926, was rejected by King Fuad as interference in Egyptian affairs. Breasted immediately enlisted her help. Would she contact her brother William, a Boston architect (he was currently building an expanded museum for Rhode Island School of Design) who served as a Trustee of the Museum of Fine Arts, and ask him if he might persuade their agent in Cairo, George A. Reisner, who was opposing the building of the museum, to change his mind in favor of the project?[28] This she did forthwith, but the effort proved fruitless, partly because the Minister of Culture, the Frenchman Pierre Lacau, continued to represent the project as an American attempt to take over direction of all Egyptian antiquities. Late in the year, the offer was rejected altogether. Disappointed, but losing no time in recrimination, Breasted offered another proposal: a museum in Jerusalem for the antiquities being found in archeological investigations in Syria, Israel, and Jordan, then under British rule.

Thoroughly caught up in these events, Lucy returned to Providence for the summer,

but by late 1926 was back in Egypt, traveling again to visit Breasted and his family in Luxor. As he had done earlier, he took her to his favorite monument, the tomb of Seti at Abydos

Fig. 9
James Breasted in the Ramesseum at Thebes, 1926. Photograph probably by Lucy Truman Aldrich. Museum of Art, Rhode Island School of Design; Lucy Truman Aldrich Collection.

Fig. 10
Lucy at the rock temple of Rameses II at Abu Simbel, Egypt, 1926. Museum of Art, Rhode Island School of Design; Lucy Truman Aldrich Collection.

with its painted wall reliefs, which Rockefeller money was helping to publish, and to Thebes (fig. 9) and Abu Simbel, where she was dwarfed by the huge rock monuments (fig. 10). Following Breasted's advice, she went on to Jerusalem to sightsee and to look at the site of the proposed museum. Apparently, however, she refused his counsel that she should buy a collection of Egyptian textiles, possibly Coptic pieces that had appeared on the market as thieves and scholars vied for antiquities in the many-layered sites all over Egypt.

The summers of 1927 and 1928 again found Miss Aldrich in Europe. In 1927 the entire Rockefeller family was systematically visiting French cathedrals in anticipation of the design and construction of Riverside Church, which they had agreed to fund in New York. In February 1929, following a trip on the Nile, the family was received in Paris by an enthusiastic Lucy who saw that the children enjoyed themselves by taking them to traditional spectacles like the Cirque d'Hiver.

In 1929, after spending most of the year in Europe, Lucy made one final trip to Japan, spending time in the months of October and November in Tokyo and Kyoto. By now a seasoned textile collector, she concentrated on her favorites: *kesa*, which she would continue to collect until 1941, and sixteen additional Nō costumes, including the finest robes in the collection. Receipts from Yamanaka & Company show *karaori*, *atsuita*, and *chōken* from collections made by the great daimyo families Ikeda, Hirase, and Maeda in Japan before 1868, when the Nō drama was still an important part of court life.

Although Nō, like other traditional Japanese arts, had suffered in the 1860's as Japan struggled to give up its traditional ways in favor of Western development, it enjoyed a revival in the late nineteenth century. In spite of this, several branches of the noble families were impoverished, and some of the great family collections were being dispersed. Yamanaka & Company were able to obtain examples from several daimyo collections for Miss Aldrich. Most of the costumes purchased by her in 1929 came from known sources, recorded by Yamanaka & Company on the receipts and on paper wrappers that they supplied for all the robes. According to their receipt of January 20, 1930, seven of the robes came to Yamanaka & Company through Mr. Yamada, Nishijin, Kyoto, probably another dealer who had collected the robes from various daimyo sources.

Thanks to the existence in the Aldrich records of the shipping receipts, which were required to state the source of each object being imported into the United States, we know not only the name of the source in Japan but the address of each dealer or private person from whom the rest of the robes, as well as *kesa* and other objects, had been obtained. For the remainder of Miss Aldrich's 1929 Nō-costume purchases, two different names appear, the most prominent among them the Bijutsu-club ("Art-Club") in Teramachi, Oike, Kyoto, from which the dealer acquired six of the robes. Another robe came from K. Tsuchihashi of Sakaimachishijo, Kyoto, possibly another small dealer, and the last two robes from an unidentified source.[29]

As a result of this complete documentation, the robes acquired in 1929 have international importance apart from their beauty. Because their provenance is known, Monica Bethe has been able to compare them with other documented robes in Japan, finding similarities of design and construction that suggest a close relationship among certain "sister robes" possibly woven on the same looms or from the same designs (see pp. 40-42).

Her Asian textile collection now nearly complete, with examples from many different countries encompassing superb collections of Chinese, Indian, Indonesian, and above all Japanese textiles, Miss Aldrich's attention turned in the 1930's to a new field completely, that of porcelain figures. Apart from a trip to Egypt in 1931, she spent most of her time traveling in Europe purchasing English Bow, Whieldon, Chelsea, and Derby figures; figures from the Frankenthal, Nymphenburg, Ludwigsburg, Höchst, and Dresden factories in Germany; figures from Copenhagen and Vienna; and an occasional Chinese example.

As was her custom, she got the best advice she could, consulting Sir Joseph Duveen in London. He sent her to the great dealer Alfred Thomas, whose collection for the Ashmolean Museum was one of her inspirations, and the dealers Hyman and Partridge.[30] She continued to buy *kesa* by mail from Yamanaka & Company of Boston, but her interest in other Asian textiles had waned.

In Providence briefly in 1933, she was appointed by the Rhode Island School of Design to its Museum Committee. In 1931, encouraged by her friend Helen Danforth, the new President of the School, she had begun to lend certain of her objects to the Museum. She was perhaps also motivated to do so because her brother William, the Boston architect, had recently completed a large and elegant building for the expanding collections. Soon after she took her seat on the committee, she began to think about future donations. In 1934 she persuaded Abby, whose attention was now consumed by the Museum of Modern Art and the Rockefeller restoration of Williamsburg, to donate to the Museum her collection of

Japanese prints that both of them had bought in previous years, a collection that had grown to more than seven hundred prints of birds and flowers by Hiroshige, Hokusai, and other masters. It is today unique in the world: no other museum, not even in Japan itself, has such a comprehensive collection of bird-and-flower prints, and it is attracting worldwide interest through its exhibition and publication in Japan as well as in this country.[31]

Meanwhile, Miss Aldrich's Nō robes hung in her house, decorating walls, or draped over stands in the new "Museum Room" she had added at the back, or were stored in closets and drawers, which amused her Rockefeller nephews by being full to bursting (fig. 11). Even she began to be bothered by the crush of objects – furniture, silver, china, linens, prints, paintings, Asian textiles, and bronzes everywhere – complaining that the house was getting full of clutter. She even went so far as to contemplate selling things at auction. Fortunately for posterity, the decline of the market during the Great Depression prevented her from doing so. One of her friends wrote of her admiration for the house: "What I have always liked about your collection is its miscellany… all forms of beauty of all Nations and lands… Oriental and occidental and native – Winslow Homer, Aubrey Beardsley, gold Buddhas and old Paris."[32] Certainly it was one of the most admired in Providence, and Lucy was famous for having created it.

In 1934, Alan Priest, Curator of Asian Art at the Metropolitan Museum of Art, approached Miss Aldrich with a proposal for an exhibition of Japanese textiles in New York. Immediately she agreed to lend twelve robes, with representation from her fine groups of *karaori, suihaku, kariginu, atsuita,* and *nuihaku* (cat. nos. 15, 18-21, 24, 25, 31, 38, 39, 41, 42).[33] Miss Aldrich asked Kinsei Nakagawa from Yamanaka & Company, Boston, her longtime adviser, to visit the Metropolitan Museum to handle the robes while they were being photographed for the catalogue and to appraise them for insurance purposes. This he did, giving the prices he thought he could get for them if they were being sold in his store. Ten years after she had bought her first thirty pieces of Nō costume for $10,000 and at the depths of the Great Depression, twelve of them were valued at $13,300. "I had a glimpse of the Nō robes which came from Japan [for the exhibition]," added Nakagawa. "There are

Fig. 11
The house at 110 Benevolent Street, with cat. no. 23 displayed on a bamboo stand and a *kesa* on the wall behind, about 1930.

some good ones, but your collection is very fine." As for the robes from the Metropolitan Museum, "none of them can compare with yours," wrote this talented and redoubtable Japanese spokesman for the arts of his country.[34]

Kinsei Nakagawa also served as the chief source of information both for Miss Aldrich and for Alan Priest. Her collection was unusual, Nakagawa told her, in that it had a number of examples of many different types of robes, unlike the collection made by Bigelow for the Museum of Fine Arts, Boston, which contained only *karaori, nuihaku,* and *atsuita.*

At the end of the Metropolitan Museum exhibition, Miss Aldrich decided to donate the Nō robes and also her Ching-dynasty Chinese

Fig. 12
Nō robes on display in the "Silk Room," 1937. Museum of Art, Rhode Island School of Design.

costumes to the Museum of Art at Rhode Island School of Design. One of the galleries on the top floor of the new building was made over with blue wallcoverings, shoji window screens, and new lamps into a gallery for the textiles, where they immediately went on display (fig. 12); Abby's prints were to be shown in an adjacent gallery. At the same time, a storeroom was equipped with specially designed wooden cases of large drawers where the textiles could lie flat, folded as little as possible. Miss Aldrich, not trusting the Museum staff, came to care for the textiles herself or with Miss MacFadden. When these arrangements had been made, Miss Aldrich also deposited her Japanese *kesa* on loan, giving at the same time a number of Indian saris and an elaborate robe worn in the performance of the Japanese court dance *bugaku*.

Miss Aldrich and Miss MacFadden inaugurated a series of month-long displays on the top floor, next to the gallery containing the great Dainichi Buddha (purchased by the Museum in 1936). Together with the room that had been set aside for Abby Aldrich Rockefeller's Japanese prints and a gallery containing Chinese sculptures in part collected by Abby with John D., Jr., more than half of the top floor had been transformed into a distinguished Asian section, thanks to the inspiration and philanthropy of Lucy Truman Aldrich. It is a great tribute to her that she saw the need for this and was able to mobilize her generous family to bring it about.

In 1937, the Museum decided to present all of Miss Aldrich's Japanese gifts and loans in

a five-gallery exhibition in every available space (fig. 13). Again, Kinsei Nakagawa of Yamanaka & Company served as resource person, calling on Miss Chie Hirano, Research Fellow in Chinese and Japanese Art at the Museum of Fine Arts, Boston, for additional information. Miss Aldrich, however, objected, insisting that only she, Miss MacFadden, her new curator, Elizabeth T. Casey, or Nakagawa himself handle or even glimpse the robes. Finally, after several months of concerted effort amid nervous secrecy, the exhibition opened and the catalogue, a cooperative effort mostly edited by Miss Casey, was published. An opening party was held on April 6, and Lucy made for her a most unusual contribution: a short speech. John D. Rockefeller, Jr., wired flowers and congratulated her on having done "a beautiful and generous thing in giving this collection and in housing it so appropriately."[35]

Nakagawa, who with Miss Casey had been instrumental in mounting the exhibition, came from Boston every Sunday to check on its progress, since Lucy herself had departed for London immediately after the opening. Many people had attended, he told her, and the Museum had invited Kojiro Tomita, who had succeeded Ernest Fenollosa's handpicked curator, Kakuzo Okakura, as curator of Asiatic art from the Museum of Fine Arts, Boston, to talk about the robes.

Tomita's lecture focused on the cultural aspects of the robes. Beginning with the definition of the word Nō – "accomplishment," or "art in acting" – he explained Nō as a "form of lyric drama," neither drama, nor opera, nor dance.[36] His lecture is worth quoting at length, since it is one of the first attempts in English by a Japanese art historian to explain this exotic and difficult form to Americans (see text, pp. 62-63).

"I wish you [had been] there to hear it," wrote Nakagawa to Miss Aldrich in London, adding that he would soon take down the robes, adding small cushions, or "futons," to protect the robes where folded.[37] It was apparently he who gave her the good advice to show the robes for only one month at a time (because windows in the galleries admitted natural light, very damaging to the fine silks), an admonition lifted a few years later when the windows were blocked in.

From this time on, changing exhibitions were hung in Miss Aldrich's gallery: Chinese, Persian, Indian, Indonesian, and Japanese tex-

Fig. 13
Kesa on display in the galleries, 1937. Museum of Art, Rhode Island School of Design.

tiles were exhibited for one-month periods. The depth and breadth of the collection are revealed by the large number of exhibitions, each composed of works from the collection that had never before been shown. In 1938 the Chinese costumes were displayed in all the Asian galleries, prompting the *Providence Journal* to enthuse about the collection of beautiful works of art that "gives Providence a distinction among curators of museums and connoisseurs of fine textiles throughout the country."[38]

The exhibitions continued through the war years, when Miss Aldrich's trips were curtailed, although letters from her London dealers kept her abreast of the blitz and its destruction. True to her generous spirit with those whom she knew as friends, she took in two English children, relatives of Endicott P. Saltonstall of Chestnut Hill, Massachusetts, for the duration.[39] Alarmed by several staff incursions into her storeroom, she insisted that the Museum rehire Elizabeth T. Casey – Miss Casey had left the Museum in 1942 – to take sole charge of the objects she had contributed.

Feeling less and less well, upset by the illness and death of Miss MacFadden in 1947, and bored in Providence, where she felt there was little for "a deaf person" to do,[40] she turned to Boston, and in 1947 she gave her Japanese porcelains to the Museum of Fine Arts. The sudden death of her sister Abby in 1948 devastated her, as it did the whole family, but it was this event that rekindled her interest in the Museum at Rhode Island School of Design and occasioned her last great contributions to it.

In 1934, Miss Aldrich had given the Museum her collection of European porcelains. Because the Museum had no special place to display them, she persuaded the Museum to turn a little-used gallery into a room for her porcelains, lined with paneling purchased in London at Stair and Andrew. The paneling, which had been modified to fit the space, came from an English country house, Chipstead Place, and was installed for the opening of the room in 1937. She found furniture from Madingley Hall, Cambridge, and eighteenth-century silk for curtains. By 1947 the gallery had become a busy passageway for visitors to the Museum going through to the Waterman galleries, and Lucy enlisted the help of John D. Rockefeller, Jr., in having a bridge built from the first floor of Pendleton House into the main building, so that most of the traffic would go that way. In this manner the Lucy Truman

Aldrich Porcelain Gallery became a quiet oasis for the contemplation of the lovely and valuable figurines.

The greatest change took place in the Asian galleries. Renaming her textile gallery, which she had earlier referred to as "the silk room," in honor of Abby Aldrich Rockefeller, she encouraged Abby's children to contribute to the refurbishment of the print gallery as a memorial to their mother. The young Philip Johnson was hired as architect for the room for Abby's prints and for two sculpture galleries on the east side of the top floor; Miss Aldrich hired William G. Perry of Boston to install an elaborate new lighting system for the textile gallery and for the room housing the Buddha. In the end, more than $17,778 had been given by the Rockefeller family for these projects, solely because of the patronage of Miss Lucy Truman Aldrich, and this was only one in the long series of benefactions to the Museum by this remarkable supporter. At the opening of the galleries in 1953, Miss Aldrich made another of her rare speeches, this time in memory of her sister, expressing her delight that the five new galleries and bridge were now in use. It would be the last of her public appearances at the Museum, but not her last gift. When she died in January 1955, her will contained the bequest of most of her textiles – textiles from Europe as well as Asia – and many of the remainder were given by her heirs, including a last *nuihaku*.

The gifts of Lucy Truman Aldrich to the Museum fulfilled her wistful desire to have her name perpetuated because she had no children, as she wrote to John D. Rockefeller, Jr.[41] However, the legacy of Lucy Truman Aldrich was of much broader impact, a gift to the entire Rhode Island community that ranks as a public act beside the gifts of Japanese art by the Fenollosa-Weld-Bigelow triumvirate to Boston, the gifts of Chinese and Japanese Art to Baltimore by William and Henry Walters, and to museums by other collectors of Orientalia all over the country. Her gift, like theirs, was more than just textiles or porcelains or prints. It was also a series of inspired acts that in themselves inspire. Countless additional donations to the Museum were made because of the renown of her donations, and thousands of visitors have been inspired by the sight of her textiles, by the prints she encouraged Abby Aldrich Rockefeller to donate, and by the many other gifts of her family. She deserves to be regarded

Fig. 14
Lucy Truman Aldrich,
about 1937. Museum of
Art, Rhode Island School
of Design.

as one of the primary benefactors of this
Museum, but also as a collector of noteworthy
importance, who had the vision and creativity
to see that the textiles that she loved and that
so few others were collecting would be of
artistic and historical significance far into the
future. This catalogue celebrates her accom-
plishments, but can never repay the Museum's
great debt.

1. Letter, Lucy Truman Aldrich (hereinafter
LTA) to Abby Aldrich Rockefeller (hereinafter
AAR), January [?], 1932; Rockefeller Foundation Archives,
Tarrytown, New York (hereinafter RFA). RG 3. 2AA.
Box 7. Folder 7.

2. Lloyd Lehrbas, China Press Staff Correspondent and a fellow captive who escaped after three hours,
interviewed Miss Aldrich in Tientsin for *The New York
Times*, May 10, 1923, 1:7,8. Lucy's letter to her sister
Abby about the experience was published in *Atlantic
Monthly*, 132:5 (June 1923), pp. 672-86. The kidnap-
ping became a major international incident and was
exhaustively covered in the press in the United States
and abroad.

3. AAR, scrapbook; RFA. John D. Rockefeller
Family—Relatives—Aldrich Family—Homes, No. 1005.

4. Photographs in Aldrich House, Rhode Island
Historical Society, Providence (hereinafter RIHS).

5. Scrapbooks at the Providence Art Club
provide details of activities over the years.

6. Sally S. DuPlaix, in Carol S. Cook, *Travel
and Exploration: A Catalogue of the Providence
Athenaeum Collection*. Providence: Providence
Athenaeum, 1988, "Foreword," p. ix.

7. Typescript; Museum of Art, Rhode Island
School of Design (hereinafter RISD), Registrar's office.

8. Scrapbooks; Providence Art Club.

9. Letter, LTA to AAR, February 28, 1947;
RFA. RG3. 2AA. Box 7. No. 92.

10. Louise Tharp, *Mrs. Jack; A Biography of
Isabella Stewart Gardner*. Boston: Little, Brown, 1965,
p. 87.

11. Louisine W. Havemeyer, *Sixteen to Sixty,
Memoirs of a Collector*. New York: privately printed,
1961, p. 16.

12. *Time*, 37:4 (January 27, 1936), pp. 28-29.

13. Will; Probate Records, Courthouse,
Warwick, Rhode Island; Will Book 24, pp. 378-81.

14. Letter, LTA to AAR, Miyako Hotel, Kyoto,
May 12, 1919; RFA. RG3. 2AA. Box 7. Letter C.

15. Ibid.

16. Letter, LTA to AAR, November 30, 1920;
RFA. RG3. 2AA. Box 7. No. 15A.

17. Letter, LTA to AAR, April 23, 1922; RFA.
RG3. 2AA. Box 7. No. 28.

18. Letter, Minnie A. MacFadden to AAR, June
11, 1923; RFA. RG3. 2AA. Box 7. No. 42.

19. Letter, LTA to AAR, June 15, 1923; RFA. RG3. 2AA. Box 7. No. 43.

20. Letter, LTA to AAR, April 15, 1923; RFA. RG3. 2AA. Box 7. No. 41.

21. Invoice, Yamanaka & Company, Kyoto, Japan, August 2, 1925; RIHS.

22. Haru Matsukata Reischauer, *Samurai and Silk; A Japanese and American Heritage.* Cambridge, Massachusetts: Harvard University Press, 1986, pp. 291-93.

23. *North Central Magazine,* 7:2 (December 19, 1928).

24. *Catalogue of an Exhibition of Ancient Japanese Brocades, Embroideries, and Fabrics.* Boston: Yamanaka and Company, Inc., 1935. The author wishes to thank Alan Kennedy for this information.

25. Clay Lancaster, *The Japanese Influence in America.* New York: Walton H. Rawls, 1963, pp. 152, 155.

26. Ibid., pp. 198-99.

27. The entire story is recounted in Charles Breasted, *Pioneer to the Past: The Story of James Henry Breasted, Archaeologist.* New York: Charles Scribner's Sons, 1943, pp. 376-97.

28. Letter, James H. Breasted to LTA, October 21, 1926; RIHS.

29. American Consular Service Invoice, Purchased Merchandise, November 13, 1929, seller Yamanaka & Company, Awataguchi, Kyoto, Japan; RIHS.

30. Letter, LTA to Dr. Rudolf Berliner, May 24, 1947; Museum of Art, RISD, Registrar's office, "Aldrich, Miss Lucy T. 1934-1947."

31. *Yomigaeru-bi; hana to tori to Rockefeller Collection ukiyoe ten.* Tokyo: Bun You Associates, 1990. Cynthea J. Bogel, Israel Goldman, and Alfred H. Marks, *Hiroshige: Birds and Flowers.* New York: George Braziller, 1988.

32. Letter, Virginia [Metcalf] to LTA, undated; RIHS.

33. See Alan Priest, *Japanese Costume.* New York: Metropolitan Museum, 1935, passim.

34. Letter, Kinsei Nakagawa to LTA, January 17, 1935, typescript; RIHS.

35. Letter, John D. Rockefeller, Jr., to LTA, April 5, 1937; RFA. RG3. 2H. Box 40. Folder 296—Purchases.

36. Typescript, Elizabeth T. Casey Papers; Museum of Art, RISD.

37. Letter, Kinsei Nakagawa to LTA, May 1, 1937, typescript; RIHS.

38. *Providence Sunday Journal,* March 6, 1938, IV: 3.

39. Letter, Helen Herbert to LTA, September 17, 1940; RIHS.

40. Letter, LTA to AAR, early July 1931; RFA. RG3. 2AA. Box 7. No. 69.

41. Letter, LTA to John D. Rockefeller, Jr., October 18, 1948, typescript; RIHS.

Where Poetry and Pattern Meet

Helen M. Nagata

AGAINST THE BARE, lustrous, square stage of polished cypress, movement and dance punctuated with sounds of flute, drums, and chanted verse define a supernatural world inhabited by specters, often famous characters from classical literature of the Heian (794-1185) or Kamakura (1185-1336) periods. In this world of gods, demons, and human spirits,[1] illusions of life and afterlife and of time and timelessness converge with great psychological tension. This is a realm of poignant memories and allusions created by highly symbolic staging. By the eighteenth and nineteenth centuries, when many of the robes in the Lucy Truman Aldrich Collection were made, Nō costume had long been not only an element of beauty and spectacle, but an eloquent prop, an iconographic code, and the embodiment of a soul. Robe type, color, pattern, combinations of dress, and style of draping all relayed to the educated audience significant information about a character's worldly place and spiritual nature. Within the context of this highly formalized costuming, however, there is a juncture in many robes where decorative effect merges with expressive, allusive possibilities.

Although eighteenth- and nineteenth-century Nō robes reflect the stylistic influences of fashions of the sixteenth or seventeenth centuries, of textiles worn by ancient or medieval military aristocracy, of religious garb, or even of the dress of rustic laborers, a large number strongly allude to the esthetics of courtly life and literature. Such references to Japan's classical tradition complement the central role classical poetry came to play in Nō. *Waka* poetry often shapes the most emotionally dramatic point in a play and forms the core around which a play turns. During the Heian period, superior skill in poetry was the ultimate sign of refinement and the special domain of legendary lovers and romantic heroes. Poems of 5-7-5-7-7 syllables were used to communicate feelings of love or longing, exhibit one's wit, sensitivity and literary prowess, or mark the significance of a special occasion. The great Nō playwright and esthetician Zeami Motokiyo (1363-1443), who enjoyed the patronage of Shogun Ashikaga Yoshimitsu (1358-1408) from a young age, was ensconced in the literary pursuits of the aristocratic elite. He is credited with making poetic esthetics central to Nō performance. Indeed, similarities between Zeami's ideals for Nō performance and contemporary ideals of court poetry have been observed in his call for the use of narrative settings famous for their literary or poetic associations; the development of *hana* (sometimes translated "fascination" or "soul"), which refers both to the appeal of a performance (or poem) and to the freshness of its effect; and *yūgen*, the beautiful grace or elegance associated with admirable noble women and men.[2] *Yūgen* was found in extraordinary courtiers such as Genji, or court ladies of superb refinement. It was a quality that distinguished fine language, music, and dancing. In Zeami's writings, it became paramount to good performance. Zeami encouraged actors to study poetry, and he used characters and poems from such classics as the *Tales of Ise* (tenth century), *Tale of Genji* (early eleventh century), or *Tales of the Heike* (thirteenth century) to create plays that would plumb the depths of a poem's original meaning even while situating that poem in a new dramatic context. It comes as no surprise that classical poetry, court culture, and Nō drama should converge in the imagery of a single Nō robe.

Metaphorical use of the robe goes back to Japan's earliest poetic anthologies. At the heart of the classical literary canon lies a tremendous body of poems gathered in such works as the *Manyōshū* of the eighth century (variously translated as *Collection of Myriad Leaves, The Ten Thousand Leaves,* or *Collection for Ten Thousand Ages*) or *Kokin wakashū*, ca. 905 (also called *Kokinshū,* or *Collection of Early and Modern Japanese Poetry*). In these collections, images of clothing carry tender feelings of love and longing. Sleeves drenched with tears wave in sad farewells; white sleeves must disengage from each other as day approaches; and belts or skirts remind one of a lover. In this poem of love in autumn from the *Manyōshū*, the quiet misery of a woman's longing is intensified by the wet chill of dew-soaked garments:

Asatode no kimiga ayui wo
  nurasu tsuyuhara
hayaku okiidetsutsu ware mo
  mosuso nurasana[3]

You start so early this morning,
  The dewy grass will wet your leg-ties;
I, too, out so early,
Will gladly dip the hem of my skirt.[4]

In a poem from the same anthology, a belt is both a cherished keepsake and a sad reminder of the present:

Hitoe nomi
Imo ga musubamu
Obi o sura
Mie musububeku
Agami wa narinu[5]

The belt that you, my woman,
wrapped once around my waist
I must wrap three times now,
so gaunt has yearning made me.[6]

Moreover, the making of a robe is beautifully adapted to expressions of love, as in the following poem:

Kimi ga tame tajikara tsukare
  oritaru kinu zo
haru saraba ikanaru iro ni
  suriteba yoken[7]

This is the cloth I wove for my lord
  With weary hands;
When the spring comes round,
In what colours shall I print it?[8]

The imagery of weaving is effectively applied to contemplations of nature as well. Ephemeral patterns of dewdrops and frost, like painstakingly woven silk fabrics, quickly unravel with a poignancy that captures the evanescence of happiness and beauty on this earth.

During the Heian period, a sensitivity to the colors and patterns of clothing was a virtuous refinement as important as the mastery of poetry, music, dance, or the connoisseurship of the fragrance of incense. When the "man of old" in *Tales of Ise* (featuring many poems traditionally associated with the poet and ideal courtier Ariwara no Narihira, 825-880) catches a glimpse of two beautiful sisters in Kasuga village, he tears a patterned strip from his robe to send to

them and writes:

Kasugano no
Wakamurasaki no
Surigoromo
Shinobu no midare
Kagiri shirarezu.

Like the random pattern of this robe,
Dyed with the young purple
From Kasuga Plain –
Even thus is the wild disorder
Of my yearning heart.[9]

The poet creates elegant puns using terms like *wakamurasaki*, which can mean either young women or a purple color, or *shinobu no midare*, which can refer to the chaotic pattern of his robe, as well as the excitement in his heart. In one terse poem, the poet unites the imagery of pattern and color with his attraction to the young women and the famous place called Kasuga. Conversely, inadequate sensitivity to textiles and matters of dress, even the slightest error in shades of color, could cause embarrassment.[10] Thus, in ancient times, robes were treasured for their beauty, their reflection of taste, and their close association with owners or makers, and noble men and women were admired for their sensitivity to these associations.

The symbolism of robe imagery in a Nō play often enhances the dramatic moment. In *Matsukaze* (*Pine Wind*) and *Aoi no Ue* (*Princess Hollyhock*), robes substitute for living persons and provoke impassioned actions. In *Matsukaze*, the ghosts of two fishergirls at Suma Bay eternally long for Ariwara no Yukihira (818-893), who had returned to the capital after completing three years of exile at Suma. Matsukaze and her sister Murasame (Autumn Rain) spend their days dipping brine buckets under the cold autumn moon. Murasame tells us, "Here at Suma Bay / The waves shatter at our feet, / And even the moonlight wets our sleeves / With its tears of loneliness."[11] The cloak and court hat which Yukihira had left as keepsakes of his love torment the sisters by calling forth fresh feelings of longing. In *Aoi no Ue*, a folded robe placed on the stage symbolizes the ailing Princess Aoi, who is the wife of Prince Genji and the object of Lady Rokujō's jealousy. Lady Rokujō's phantom of jealousy desires vengeance with such bitterness that it makes to strike at Lady Aoi several times before being fended off by the prayers of the saint of Yokawa.[12]

Elements of the robe are also powerful dramatic devices. When the old gardener in *Aya no Tsuzumi* (*The Damask Drum*) is stricken with love for a princess, he is led to believe through a message from her that she will show her face again if he beats a drum hanging on a laurel tree and the sound carries to her palace. As he prepares to beat the drum, the chorus intones,

> For if its sound be heard, soon shall he see
> Her face, the damask of her dress...
> Aye damask! He does not know
> That on a damask drum he beats,
> Beats with all the strength of his hands,
>   his aged hands,
> But hears no sound.
> "Am I grown deaf?" he cries, and listens,
>   listens:
> Rain on the windows, lapping of waves
>   on the pool –
> Both these he hears, and silent only
> The drum, strange damask drum.
> Oh, will it never sound?[13]

A single damask cloth represents a world of illusion. His desire and her heartless rebuff converge in a silent drumbeat that leads the old gardener to his death and his angry spirit to chastise the princess. In another play, *Kayoi Komachi* (*Komachi and the Hundred Nights*), an emotional, tense moment is created by the touching of sleeves. The ghost of Fukakusa no Shōshō (Captain Fukakusa), who had courted the famous and beautiful poetess Ono no Komachi, still resents her merciless treatment of him. Komachi, after agreeing to see Fukakusa if he slept one hundred nights outside her home, had cruelly mocked him when he was forced to miss the last night to attend to his father's death. Fukakusa no Shōshō cannot stand the thought of Komachi gaining instruction on the Buddhist path, leaving him to suffer alone. As he commands Komachi to desist, he comes up behind her and begins a bitter exchange:

> Shōshō: I'll take your sleeve
>   and hold you back!
>   (He puts his hand on
>   Komachi's
>   shoulder)
> Komachi: My sleeve in your grip,
> Shōshō: My own that pulls on yours.
>   (He draws back a little)

> Chorus: Both are drenched in a dew of
>   tears.[14]

The gesture is subtle, yet electrified with the passion and anger of both characters. The expressive function of the robe in Nō drama continues a tradition begun in classical poetic imagery and is both enriched and propelled by this long literary tradition.

A study of individual motifs worked into patterns of many robes in the Lucy Truman Aldrich Collection suggests a symbolism of yet another kind relating to the classical literary tradition. Nature motifs – plants and blossoms, elements of weather, birds and insects – associated with the seasons appear in robe patterns in seemingly endless variation. Such images not only conjure the essence of a season, but often allude to poetic motifs as well. A large number of poems in the *Manyōshū* and *Kokinshū* are grouped by seasons. The cry of a bird in autumn, winter, spring, or summer stirs the brooding heart of a poet. In the *Manyōshū* alone, 37 kinds of birds, 13 types of insects, and 157 different plants (including trees, bamboo, herbs, grasses, and flowers) appear in its poetic imagery.[15] The most poignant images are associated with autumn and spring, and images of autumn, such as the seven autumn grasses (*akikusa*),[16] crimson foliage, or chrysanthemums, have become some of the oldest, most widely used motifs in both the poetry and the pictorial arts of Japan. A *karaori* with a design of chrysanthemum and pampas grass seen through a lattice (cat. no. 9) points to a whole corpus of poems featuring these autumn plants. Softly swaying pampas grass brings to mind poems of longing, such as that from the *Kokinshū* by Ariwara no Muneyana (d. 898):

> *aki no no no*
> *kusa no tamoto ka*
>   *hanasusuki*
> *ho ni idete maneku*
> *sode to miyuran*

> are they the flowing
> sleeves of autumn grasses
>   in the ripening fields
> the waving tassels appear
> to be beckoning to us now[17]

Moreover, this pattern invites the viewer to play the part of a poet who peers into its rustic splendor. The popularity of autumn motifs for textile patterns, and even the use of their names to describe colors or color-and-pattern combinations, goes back to the Heian period.[18]

At the same time, poetic motifs of autumn and other seasons have a universal aspect that links the past with the present. Swallows darting through willow branches (cat. no. 31) instantly recall the fresh verdure and gentle breezes of spring, while young pines and snow-laden bamboo branches (cat. no. 11), two favorite winter motifs, are suggestive of celebrations of the New Year and quiet winter scenery. When the scholar-poet Ki no Tsurayuki (ca. 872-945) wrote in the preface to the *Kokinshū* that "Japanese poetry has its seed in the human heart (*kokoro*) and finds expression in myriad leaves of words (*koto no ha*),"[19] he stressed the timeless universality of emotions sung in Japan's classical poems and held out the idea of poetry as the supreme expression of emotion. The continuous reexpression of certain themes and motifs over the ages relates to a literary technique most associated with the celebrated poet Fujiwara Teika (1162-1241), whose poems figure greatly in the *Shin kokinshū* (*New Kokinshū*) of the early thirteenth century and who compiled authoritative versions of nearly the entire classical canon. Teika brought to prominence a technique known as *honka dori*, in which a phrase or image is taken from an older poem and reused in such a way as to bring new life to the older poem even while creating a "modern" poem identifiable with the present.

Almost as a visual counterpart to the literary technique of allusion called *honka dori*, the chrysanthemum appears in at least ten garments in this catalogue, each with a pattern unique in style, color, and pattern combination (see cat. nos. 3, 7-9, 12, 13, 17, 18, 21, 45). The literary associations of this motif lend a stately, conservative elegance, even as aspects of style and design give the robe fresh vibrancy. On one hand, use of the chrysanthemum motif is ancient. It appears in classical poems such as that by Ki no Tsurayuki:

> *aki no kiku*
> *niou kagiri wa*
> *kazashitemu*
> *hana yori saki to shiranu wa ga mi o*

> I will deck my head
> with autumn chrysanthemums
> at their lustrous best,
> for who can say whether my death

may come before they wither?[20]

Chrysanthemum imagery in poetry goes back to sometime after the eighth century, and it has come to be associated not only with autumn, but with Chinese legends of immortality, certain famous places, and the elegant gatherings, dances, and entertainments of the nobility. It became a popular motif in *yamato-e* painting (court painting of Japanese subjects), appearing especially in images of the four seasons (*shiki-e*), moon pictures (*tsuki-e*), famous-place pictures (*meisho-e*), and genre pictures (*fuzoku-ga*). As an auspicious symbol for long life and prosperity, the chrysanthemum image has accumulated multiple meanings through the ages.

On the other hand, the chrysanthemum as seen in the Museum's group of Nō robes is also revisualized through the influences of changes in fashion. For example, the flower roundels in an eighteenth-century *karaori* (cat. no. 5) or the scattered round fans (*uchiwa*) and triple lozenge shape called pine-bark diamonds (*matsukawa-bishi*) in the nineteenth-century *karaori* (cat. no. 15) are motifs that were popular during the Genroku era (1688-1704) in *kosode* (street-wear kimono) fashions. Both garments unite a sense of the splendor of the ancient classical era with that of the Genroku era, the golden age of the Edo period (1615-1868), when a blossoming urban culture fueled by new wealth led to a splendid burgeoning of the arts. The classical motif is reinvigorated with a hint of early Edo-period luxury. A nineteenth-century *hangire* (cat. no. 45) with a pattern of chrysanthemums and pine-tree medallions offers yet another example of a masterful blending of old and new. The chrysanthemum is just one of innumerable motifs that resonate with literary and cultural associations, yet have been given continued vitality through the ages by their countless appearances in designs for lacquerware, metalwork, ceramics, textiles, and painting.

There are many patterns that do not so much allude to any particular poetic motif as resonate with antiquity and court culture. A pattern type called *yūsokumon* is especially reminiscent of Japan's early court culture. Such patterns, which reflect the influence of precious Chinese weft-patterned textiles imported from the seventh century on, frequently incorporate Indian, Persian, and even Greco-Roman influences in their merging of auspicious plants, flowers, or birds into geometric or arabesque intersecting combinations. Variations of these patterns are used in many Nō robes, often serving as a geometric background design under larger motifs. The tortoise-shell-and-flower pattern on an eighteenth-century *nuihaku* (cat. no. 21), the auspicious motif of interlocking diamonds with floral centers used on the lower edges of a *chōken* (cat. no. 26) and the shoulders and hem of a *nuihaku* (cat. no. 22), and the pattern of overlapping circles known as interlocked seven jewels (*shippō-tsunagi*) stenciled in gold leaf on a *surihaku* (cat. no. 25) lend a rich texture and soft shimmer to the surface. Two majestic robes, a *happi* with a design of linked circles (cat. no. 37) and a *kariginu* with clouds and hawk-feather fans (cat. no. 33), have strong patterns of Chinese origin that suggest distant lands of legendary fame and magical tales.

In the mid-Edo period, an increasingly large array of motifs associated with ancient court life came to be featured in the Nō robe. Popular motifs of the *goshoguruma* or ox-drawn imperial carriages, scattered poem slips, and folding fans were soon joined by all manner of precious objects from the daily life of courtiers and court ladies of old. The motifs range from symbolic Buddhist jeweled wheels, gongs, and military paraphernalia (bow and arrows, armor), to architectural details (doors, painted folding screens, or thin bamboo rolled blinds) and objects of everyday pastimes (musical instruments, fans, game sets, writing implements, and eating utensils), to objects from outdoor settings (gardens, bridges, boats, *goshoguruma* wheels soaking in a river). Some motifs – the Buddhist jeweled wheel or *rimbō* (cat. no. 42), or the ox-carriage-wheel motif called Genji wheel (cat. no. 39), or medallions with swirling comma-shapes ringed with fire (cat. no. 38)[21] – are particularly useful for *atsuita* patterns that show military strength or the godly power of a male character. While *yūsokumon* patterns might recall the refined, rich textures of ancient treasured textiles, the motifs of secular, religious, and military objects of daily life celebrate the cultural setting of Japan's literary classics.

In a very different manner, some Nō-robe patterns invite the viewer into the classical setting. The tilted ground planes suggested by the arrow stands in the nineteenth-century *atsuita* (cat. no. 44) and by the rectilinear flower beds depicted in the eighteenth-century *nuihaku* (cat. no. 19) define a space to be shared by the viewer. In contrast, the lowered blinds (*sudare*) in the *nuihaku* with design of blinds and cherry

and mandarin-orange branches (cat. no. 23) invite the viewer to imagine the concealed person on the other side or poems shared between lovers separated by a single blind. In a manner similar to that of the *karaori* with chrysanthemums and pampas grass seen through a lattice fence (cat. no. 9), the viewer is drawn into an illusionary setting to play an imaginary role. Whether designs of this type can be interpreted as drawing the viewer away from the present into an ancient world or bringing the ancient world to life in the mind of the viewer, the result is the same – for the moment, at least, the classical world becomes a personal, psychological experience, and in that moment, the classical past lives again.

The element of *hana* in the performance of Nō is like a blossom that is beautiful not simply because of its sensuous qualities, but "because it would shed its petals."[22] The eternal opening of the flower in a performance is not unlike Teika's technique of *honka dori*: the past is ever embraced and brought to new life through performance. Within this dramatic context, the Nō costume visually echoes Zeami's emphasis on the eternal recreation of the esthetics of court literature and culture.

It is possible to move beyond the recognition and appreciation of individual motifs to respond to the expressive effects of overall patterns. Beyond an identification of a specific poetic allusion, there is the potential for an introspective cognizance of a mood or pure emotion, or even a metaphysical stance. Just as a pattern is composed of, yet essentially blurs the boundaries of individual motifs into a rhythmic, repetitive design, so do separate, symbolic motifs blend in meaning into a nonverbal resonance for the knowledgeable viewer. It is possible to divide these patterns into expressions of different emotional appeal, such as rustic elegance, refined chaos, infinite variation, or a quality that can be called "beyond variation."

A brilliant meshing of rusticity and refined elegance is apparent in the floral-and-fence (or basket) *karaori* patterns of cat. no. 9 (chrysanthemums, pampas grass, and lattice fence), cat. no. 4 (bamboo fence and peonies) or cat. no. 8 (chrysanthemums and bamboo fence). The juxtaposition of floral stands blooming beside bamboo or wooden fences invites the fantasy of a poet marveling at finding such exquisite beauty so far from the capital or feeling keenly for such lonely seclusion. These patterns might also suggest the secret trysts of the Heian lover who journeys through gardens or the silent agony of a court lady who contemplates the garden and suffers her lover's long absence.

The patterns of delicate chrysanthemum sprays floating on fans (cat. no. 7), of carefully painted fans juxtaposed against willow branches as though somehow helplessly caught there (cat. no. 14), or of bamboo grass struggling to survive in a wind-blown field (cat. no. 16) essentially juxtapose a scattering of delicate beauty against a larger, impersonal net of natural elements.

The designs seem to pictorialize a sense of both the sadness and transience of beauty in the world so esteemed by ancient court nobles. The scattered fans may serve as symbolic metaphors for frail souls at the mercy of the forces of nature. The blossoms and folding fans are all the more beautiful for their fragile and ephemeral nature. This esthetic, reflecting the influence of Buddhist concepts of time – of man's brief visit on earth as his spirit transmigrates through cosmic realms and countless lives – permeates much of Japan's classical literary and poetic tradition. The discovery of nobles in the forbidding wilds and harsh terrain of the countryside, in exile, after suffering misfortune, or after renouncing the world, is made more poignant by the stark contrast of the noble's displacement and separation from loved ones. The lonely soul left drifting in the wilds is a recurring theme in tales of romance and war alike. A particularly moving example is created in *Semimaru* (*The Blind Prince*), one of the few plays set in this world rather than the afterworld. In this work, Princess Sakagami has wandered to Mount Osaka, where she comes to a straw-thatched hut and is moved by the beautiful, sharply nostalgic sounds of a *biwa* lute. Her blind brother, Prince Semimaru, is just as surprised as she to be reunited in such a place. Brother and sister weep as they consider their fates. The chorus sings:

> To think it was only yesterday you lived
> In jeweled pavilions and golden halls;
> You walked on polished floors and wore
> bright robes.
> In less time than it takes to wave your
> sleeves,
> Today a hovel is your sleeping place.
> Bamboo posts and bamboo fence,
> crudely fashioned
> Eaves and door: straw your window,
> straw the roof,

> And over your bed, the quilts are mats of
> straw:
> Pretend they are your silken sheets of old.[23]

Their joy of meeting is tempered with sad contemplation of the past, and their happiness in being together quickly turns to sorrow as they part once more.

A variation of the scattered effect can be seen in the layering of bamboo grass and pampas grass over a background of large blocks of alternating colors in cat. no. 16, which also creates an effect of chaos. The pattern is carefully planned in motif and color combinations, yet appears subtly dynamic in its seemingly random disorder of constantly shifting colors and overlapping shapes. Even the use of gold in the bamboo grass and plume patterns is restrained and balanced by the even intensity of the colors, but shines with a breathtaking luster. The *nuihaku* with chrysanthemum and paulownia (cat. no. 21) offers a different type of elegant chaos in its rich layering of patterns. The textile creates a multiplicity of shimmering, tactile effects and an illusion of three-dimensionality while remaining undeniably flat. Like the poet in *Tales of Ise* who finds in the "random pattern" of his robe a metaphor for the excited chaos in his heart, the viewer might also be tempted to see such patterns of refined disorder as visual metaphors for the heart's agitation.

Three designs – standing chrysanthemums on a blue ground (cat. no. 3), weeping cherry branches on blue, brown, and red blocks of color (cat. no. 6), and chrysanthemum sprays on a red ground (cat. no. 12) – balance a sense of endless variation with that of endless repetition. Each robe has at first glance a fairly repetitive two-dimensional pattern evenly spread over the entire length and width of the garment. Each robe features a profusion of blossoms that are the same size and shape. The flatness of the surface is accentuated by the overlapping of motifs laid against a solid background color (as in cat. nos. 3 and 12) or in the case of cat. no. 6, squares of color unified by a geometric pattern of a type of key-fret design taken from architectural detail. On closer inspection, however, the viewer is hard put to find a single pair of blossoms or arrangement of motifs exactly repeated anywhere on the robe. While usually working with limited color groupings, the weaver has managed to create endless variations in color combinations. The seemingly scattered array of colored blossoms and the slight changes in shape and arrangement of motifs keep the patterns from looking stamped or mechanical. Moreover, floral sprays or blossoms turn in different directions – sideways or backwards – or hide underneath adjacent floral or leaf shapes. A rich depth is suggested by the illusion of shifting space where brighter colors contrast against darker. While these patterns appear carefully planned and orderly, they also seem deliciously fluid and whimsical. Such designs seem to play on the theme of stasis and movement, or renewal and death, and offer a visual counterpart to Buddhist ideas of the continual birth and rebirth of man, and of the cyclical nature of beauty, happiness, or prosperity in this world. The pattern effect has a sense of eternal repetition and variation that may be likened to the endless "rediscovery" of classical poetry in the literary tradition.

Whereas the designs described above first appear static, only to become more dynamic the longer one contemplates the variation in colors and turning shapes, a second group of designs (cat. nos. 24, 29, and 35) seems to move in the opposite direction. In this group, elements of nature – swirling water, air (or water and light), and peonies and grass with dew – normally in constant flux are geometricized and stylized into repetitious motifs stayed by a magical force. The exquisite lush undulation and soft rhythm of water in cat. no. 24 is also frozen and given an icy, austere beauty by the overall use of stenciled silver and solid horizontal bands of color. The *mitsu tomoe* pattern (cat. no. 35) forever locks the large, swirling symbols in a dizzying grid of triangles turning like pinwheels; yet, the design is extremely flat, bold and abstracted enough to appear to have no association with movement or a natural motif at all. In the pattern of peonies and dew (cat. no. 29), however, the delicate, evanescent beauty of dew lingering on a field of grasses and the full, gorgeous blossoms of each individual peony raise the idea of a transient moment to a realm of majestic, shining stasis. Without appearing at all organic or true-to-life, the image nonetheless captures the delicacy and gentle acquiescence of plant forms to the greater forces of wind and temperature. In each robe, a clear restraint in color, variety of shapes, and the illusion of space moderates naturalism and creates a new, resplendent vision of a realm beyond distinctions of time, space, or color. Each design creates an illusion of an unchanging order that is all the more striking for its use of natural motifs.

Moving away from colorful, variegated form, such patterns suggest an achromatic tranquility of quiet resolution.

The very quest to find poetic expression in a pattern could be viewed as a paradox of sorts. Yet, the distinction between "expressive" art and "decorative" craft appears to collapse in an analysis of Nō-robe designs. Standardization of type and stylization of motif are significant features of the expressive power of a Nō robe. By reusing classical and poetic motifs in "new" patterns and designs, Nō robes of the eighteenth and nineteenth centuries have the dignity and elegance of ancient eras, yet the refreshing spirit of recent times. The relationship between the esthetics of Nō drama and classical poetry is not surprising given the close relationship between classical poetry and Nō. It is remarkable, however, that Nō robes should have patterns so visually attuned to literary esthetic ideals. The sculptural effect, tactile richness, gorgeous coloring, and shimmering golds and silvers of Nō costume have a spectacular physical reality that contrasts marvelously with the metaphysical, ghostly nature of the spirit characters. The degree of complexity and variation produced by the collaborative expertise of those who designed, dyed, wove, and sewed such robes is astonishing. Moreover, these robes were then carefully donned and, depending on the type of robe, sometimes folded over and tucked under *obi* (sashes), or perhaps overlapped and partially hidden from view. All these elements of pattern, design, and production, which instantly command attention and can be independently moving, are vital components of the reverence and celebratory response accorded the Nō performance.

1. In early, traditional programs of five plays, the usual sequence opens with a ceremonial "god play," followed by a "warrior (or man) play" of a samurai spirit, a "woman play" of a departed court lady, a "realistic (or frenzy) play" about a human rather than a ghostly life, and ends with a climactic "demon play" that often describes a battle between man and demon. For more information on the five categories of plays, see Makoto Ueda's introduction to *The Old Pine Tree and Other Noh Plays*. Lincoln: University of Nebraska Press, 1962, pp. vii-xxiv.

2. Janet Goff, *Noh Drama and the Tale of Genji: The Art of Allusion in Fifteen Classical Plays*. Princeton: Princeton University Press, 1991, p. 36.

3. Nippon Gakujutsu Shinkōkai, trans., *The Manyōshū: One Thousand Poems*. New York and London: Columbia University Press, 1965, p. 338. The poetic pattern here of 5-7-7-5-7-7 syllables may represent an earlier style called *sedōka*, which is believed to have preceded the shorter *tanka* form.

4. Ibid., p. 55.

5. Masatoshi Kinoshita, *Manyōshū zenchū*, vol. 4. Tokyo: Yukikaku, 1983, p. 384.

6. Ian Hideo Levy, trans., *The Ten Thousand Leaves*. Princeton: Princeton University Press, 1981, p. 326.

7. Nippon Gakujutsu Shinkōkai, op. cit., p. 338.

8. Nippon Gakujutsu Shinkōkai, op. cit., p. 54.

9. Helen Craig McCullough, trans., *Tales of Ise: Lyrical Episodes from Tenth-Century Japan*. Stanford: Stanford University Press, 1968, p. 69.

10. Ivan Morris, *The World of the Shining Prince: Court Life in Ancient Japan*. Great Britain: Oxford University Press, 1964 (reprinted in the United States by Alfred A. Knopf, Inc., 1964, and Peregrine Books, 1969; reprinted Penguin Books, 1979), p. 206. Morris translates a passage from the diary of Lady Murasaki, the author of *Tale of Genji*, which describes the unfortunate moment when a court lady in attendance showed a slight error in taste: "When she approached His Majesty to put something in order, the High Court Nobles and Senior Courtiers who were standing nearby noticed the mistake and stared at her... It was not really such a serious lapse of taste; only the colour of one of her robes was a shade too pale at the opening."

11. Royall Tyler, trans., *Matsukaze*, in Donald Keene, ed., *Twenty Plays of the Nō Theater*. New York and London: Columbia University Press, 1970, p. 22.

12. Arthur Waley, trans., *The Nō Plays of Japan*. New York: Grove Press, Inc., 1911, pp. 179-89.

13. Ibid., p. 174.

14. Eileen Kato, trans., *Komachi and the Hundred Nights* (*Kayoi Komachi*), in Donald Keene, op. cit., p. 59.

15. Nippon Gakujutsu Shinkōkai, op. cit., pp. lxiii-lxvii.

16. Designs of the autumn grasses, also called *aki no nanakusa* (seven grasses of autumn), might feature one or more of the following plants: pampas grass (*susuki*), fringed pinks (*nadeshiko*), bush clover (*hagi*), patrinia (*ominaeshi*), Chinese bellflower (*kikyō*), arrowroot (*kuzu*), and gentian (*rindō*).

17. Laurel Rasplica Rodd with Mary Catherine Henkenius, trans., in *Kokinshū: A Collection of Poems Ancient and Modern*. Princeton: Princeton University Press, 1984, p. 117.

18. Shigeki Kawakami, "Aki o yosoou: ishō ni miru aki no ishō" ("Clad in Autumn: Autumn Designs on Robes"), in *Bunkazai* (October 1990), p. 20.

19. Edward Kamens, "The Past in the Present: Fujiwara Teika and the Traditions of Japanese Poetry," in *Word in Flower: The Visualization of Classical Literature in Seventeenth-Century Japan*. New Haven: Yale University Art Gallery, 1989, p. 16.

20. Helen C. McCullough, trans., *Kokin Wakashū*. Stanford: Stanford University Press, 1985, p. 68.

21. The origin of this motif is not clear, but it is considered symbolic of swirling water (or possibly designed after the shape of ancient *magatama*, the comma-shaped jade beads found in ancient tombs of the third century) or related to a symbol for temples. It is popularly used on drums and, as an auspicious symbol to protect from fire, on circular roof tiles.

22. Masakazu Yamazaki, "Artistic Theories," in J. Thomas Rimer and Masakazu Yamazaki, *On the Art of the Nō Drama: The Major Treatises of Zeami*. Princeton: Princeton University Press, 1984, p. xxxiv.

23. Susan Matisoff, *The Legend of Semimaru: Blind Musician of Japan*. New York: Columbia University Press, 1978, pp. 188-89.

Nō Costumes from Conception to Use

Monica Bethe

No TWO NŌ COSTUMES are exactly alike. Even costumes that are ostensibly copies of older robes generally show variation in pattern and color scheme. This is as it should be, for Nō is a one-time art. The performance is now, never to be repeated by the same people in the same place.

At the same time, tradition lies at the heart of the art of Nō performance and the weaving and tailoring of its costumes. Formulaic patterns are the building blocks of the lyric, symbolic texts, of the restrained, suggestive dance movements, of the punctuating drumbeats that set the rhythms of the play, and of the melodies of the chant. Established rules determine everything from the rendering of a line to the composition of a play. It is the interplay of these patterns– as drummer responds to the chant and dancer echoes with alliterating stamps– that breathes life into the set formulas. Fourteenth- and fifteenth-century texts, prescribed structure, and lifetimes of practice passed down through generations as a living tradition lie behind the performance of a Nō play. Similarly, at the core of the conception of Nō costumes lie sixteenth-century clothing design, the structure of the draw loom (which sets the parameters of the physically possible), and timeworn motifs. These are the frameworks that find new expression in each performance and in each costume.

The Nō drama developed out of folk performances of wandering acting guilds known as *sarugaku* players. Four of these guilds attached to the Nara temple of Kōfukuji are the forerunners of the modern Nō schools.[1] Through the innovative approach and superb acting of Kan'ami Kiyotsugu (1333-1384), the Kanze troupe came to the notice of the young shogun, Ashikaga Yoshimitsu (1358-1408). On seeing Kiyotsugu's son act, the shogun immediately took over his education. Thus Zeami

Motokiyo (1363-1443) received a first-class training in literature and esthetics that he applied to refining *sarugaku* into a noble art aimed at an aristocratic audience.

He centered his plays around a single character, drawn generally from legends or the classics, and presented the inner core of that figure's life in poetic narrative. In his dream Nō (*mugen nō*) time often flows backwards, as memory piles on memory and ghosts relive the intense experiences that keep them bound to this world. Zeami focused all elements of performance on the evocation of mood: congratulatory (*shūgen*), or forceful, or graceful (*yūgen*). He stressed spiritual elegance, the highest levels of acting being expressed by such metaphors as the "sun shining at midnight in Sulla [Korea]" or "snow in a silver bowl."[2] One indication of the overriding influence Zeami had on Nō is that the texts of a large portion of Nō plays in the modern repertory were written or revised by him.

In his treatises Zeami comments on costume, suggesting that inappropriate dress can destroy a performance. For roles of court ladies, he says in the *Fūshi kaden* (*Secret Writings on the Style and the Flower of Acting,* 1418) that one must be guided by actual court styles so as not to offend anyone in the audience, but for madwomen the costume can afford to be gaudy, and for Chinese roles the garb can be unusual to give a sense of foreignness.[3] In the *Sarugaku dangi* (*Lectures on Sarugaku*, notes taken down by Hata no Motoyoshi, 1430?) he warns that for the ritual play *Okina*, most solemn of the whole repertory, the costume should avoid ostentation.[4]

Even today, the sophisticated Nō audience is trained to read the actor's interpretation of a role in his costume. Since the garment types and draping for each role are set by tradition, the actor's choice is in the color and pattern. He selects that which best evokes the mood of the play, matching the season and the status of the role portrayed. In addition he looks for novelty.

Novelty (*mezurashisa*), Zeami states in his discussion of the secrets of the flower of great acting (*hana,* "flower") in the *Fūshi kaden* (chapter 7), is the key to a successful performance. "The flower," he says, "blossoms when a feeling of novelty awakens in the hearts of the spectators."[5] Costume helps create an impression of novelty; thus Zeami in the *Sarugaku dangi* discusses the potential effects of various costumes for a certain play.

In *Ishikawa* [*Stone River*], for his first appearance, the actor should dress simply. If the play is performed in the summer, he might wear an unlined gown embroidered with colored thread, or a *soba-tsugi* [sleeveless vest]. Alternatively, a lightly colored *mizugoromo* [traveling cloak) might work. An actor from the Ōmi troupe might wear a white cap. For us [Kanze troupe] this would be quite novel.[6]

The novelty that Zeami praises, however, stays within the established form. Like the flowers blooming in season, it adds freshness, life, zest, but does not alter the basic vocabulary.

The novelty of a costume is the same. Each costume had to be traditional–orthodox in color, style and motif–and yet special, distinctive, a standout. This accounts for the limited spectrum of patterns, colors, and weaving techniques across the centuries, as well as for the infinite variety of robes. It accounts also for what I would like to term "sister" robes. These garments appear to be either variants created by adjusting one element in the weaving or somewhat adjusted copies of other robes. Before turning to some examples, I will briefly outline the process by which a robe comes into being.

The drawing of the draft sketch was the first step in the long process from design to finished robe. Today the draft sketch is done on graph paper, two warp and two weft threads represented by each square (fig. 15). The sketch indicates warp by warp the pattern to be woven for one pattern block (*koma*), which until the late Edo period tended to be half the width of the cloth and some eight to ten inches high.[7] At different stages in the making of the robe, the draft sketch went to three different people: the heddle slingers, the draw boy (replaced today by a card puncher), and the weaver.

The draft sketch specified the loom set-up, and this laborious process took place in stages in a series of specialty houses in Nishijin, the weavers' district of Kyoto and the center of Nō costume production at the time.[8] The harness set-up was strung in one house, the heddles slung with lead strings in another.

In the meantime, a dyer had bound and dyed the warp and the necessary weft colors. The threads were wound onto large frame

Fig. 15
Draft sketch for supplementary weft patterns. Each square indicates two warp and two weft threads. Along the edge runs a color separation chart.

Fig. 16
Adachigahara. An old woman wearing a mesh traveling cloak (*yore mizugoromo*) winds thread onto a large frame spool.

spools, as portrayed on stage in the Nō play *Adachigahara* (*Adachi Fields*; fig. 16), before they were measured out for warping at another specialty house. The warp would then be wound onto a warp beam. If the warp had been *ikat* dyed to form blocks (*dangawari*), this involved not only maintaining an even tension across the entire width of some five thousand warp threads, but also making adjustments in the placement of individual threads so as to line up the color shifts as evenly as possible.[9]

Finally, at the weaving studio, the warp threads were tied individually to the lead threads, pulled through the heddles, and secured at the breast beam. The loom used for weaving patterned silks with large motifs and long floats such as *karaori* (cat. nos. 1-17) and

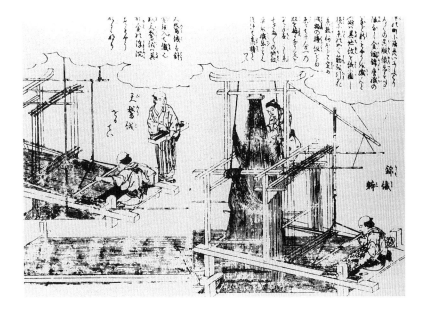

Fig. 17
Sorabiki-bata or Japanese draw loom from *Miyako meisho-zu* (*Famous Scenes of the Capital*). Edo period, woodblock on paper.

atsuita (cat. nos. 38-44) was the standing draw loom (*sorabiki-bata*; fig. 17). All the warp threads were passed through two separate heddle systems. One system produced the ground weave, a twill, plain weave, or satin weave, and was controlled by heddles in frames, one warp thread per heddle, slung according to a prescribed order of frames all the way across the fabric width. The other heddle system was used to produce a supplementary float pattern that resembles embroidery in the finished fabric. These supplementary pattern heddles were long, weighted strings with "eyes" at the height of the warp. Five or six adjacent warp threads were passed through each pattern heddle, which could then be operated individually by being pulled or drawn up. In the Edo period (1615-1868) a draw boy would sit atop the draw

loom to operate these pattern heddles, working in rhythm with the weaver, who sat at the warp beam weaving in the weft and operating the ground weave with foot pedals attached to the heddle frames.

Cooperative weaving of this sort is the subject of the Nō play *Kureha* (*Wu Weavers*).[10] *Wu* (*Kure* in Japanese) was an ancient province in western China from which weaving, according to the eighth-century *Nihon shokki* (*Chronicles of Japan*, book ten), was brought to Japan at the time of Emperor Ōjin (270-310).[11] The central characters in the play are Kurehatori, or "One who weaves on a Wu loom," and Ayahatori, or "One who weaves the *aya* [figured twill]." Together, they weave cloths worthy of the Emperor. Kurehatori sits at the loom, Ayahatori "picks up and pulls the threads."[12] The dancer stands at a large prop loom strung with many-colored warp stripes (fig. 18), while the song of the chorus reverberates with the clatter of loom sounds: "Weaver of the sky, rarely met traveler, beating, beating out the treasured figured twill."[13]

The draw boy had to follow the pattern on the draft sketch. He managed to pick up hundreds of haphazardly spaced individual heddles in quick succession by preparing a pattern frame (*mon-age*). The heddles were hung vertically from the top of the loom. Through these he passed horizontal strings going over all heddles that the draft sketch indicated as idle and under all heddles that would be pulled up to allow the weaver to place in the pattern weft. String by string, he worked up the pattern unit until it was all strung (fig. 19). During the weaving, all he had to do was to pull toward himself each of these horizontal pattern strings in order from bottom to top. If the pattern reversed, as it did at the shoulder of the garment to avoid flowers with blossoms down and stems up, the draw boy doubled back and worked from top to bottom. Today essentially no working draw looms remain in Japan, having been replaced in the late nineteenth century by French looms using a Jacquard system.[14] Instead of stringing a heddle frame, a man or woman now sits at a machine like a player piano and reads off the draft pattern while punching holes into cards. In recent years, even this worker is beginning to be replaced, for computerization has again revolutionized the weaving industry.

Once the warp threads were secured with even tension onto the breast beam, the loom

Fig. 18
Kureha (*Wu Weavers*). The dancer mimes weaving, standing behind a large prop loom strung with many-colored silk threads.

was dressed and ready for weaving. The weaver sat with the draft sketch hung nearby to guide him in producing the pattern. Although the sketch usually indicated colors, the weaver actually had to make many color choices on his own, as the specific balance usually changed each time a new block was woven.[15] In the *karaori* with design of lattice fence, chrysanthemums, and pampas grass (cat. no. 9), the comparatively large pattern unit appears three times over the length of the front and back of each side of the garment, and once on each side of each sleeve. No two renderings are the same, but an overall sense of color control is apparent. For instance, the chrysanthemum leaves of each pattern unit are rendered consistently in a single color, varied unit by unit, so as to suggest staggered blocks despite the single ground color. The same is true of the coloring of the long grasses. In contrast the chrysanthemum flowers appear in some ten different shades, with several in each block and no two blocks presenting the same color distribution. Herein lies the weaver's art. Tradition and experience guide his judgment as he actualizes a single sample sketch of a pattern in sixteen different ways while keeping an overall color scheme in mind.

The weaver perhaps progressed from the bottom right main panel up to the shoulder and down to the back hem, then to the other main panel, the sleeves and the overlap panels, weaving all elements of the pattern as he went along. The *atsuita* with clouds and arrows on a red and green ground (cat. no. 44) will serve as an example. This robe has three distinct layers of weaving structure corresponding to its three layers of design. The ground (*ji*), which forms the basic fabric, is a 1/2 twill woven on a six-harness loom in alternating blocks (*dangawari*) of red and green. To achieve this with clear color resolution, it was necessary to *ikat* dye the warp threads before warping the loom, creating a large-scale rectangular pattern of red and green on the dressed loom. The ground weft was then matched to the color of the warp, establishing a clear dividing line that sharpened the blurred transition created by the *ikat*-dyed threads.

The next level in the weaving structure is a background pattern (*jimon*) of gold triangles forming a scale pattern (*uroko*) done with a supplementary weft of thin strips of paper to which gold leaf has been glued.[16] After weaving in two ground threads, the weaver would pull a single gold-leafed strip through the shed with

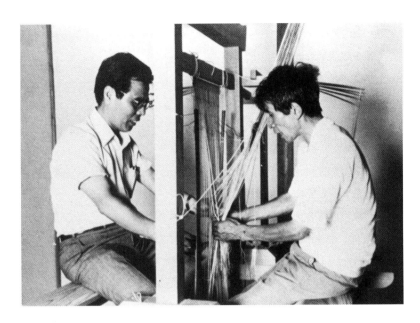

a long hooked stick (fig. 20). When these gold-leafed strips pass from motif to motif and traverse the width of the cloth, they are referred to as "continuous" supplementary wefts. Occasionally, these supplementary wefts have been clipped at the edges of each motif. In these robes, the gold-leafed paper strips are "discontinuous," since they occur only in discrete areas. The background pattern may sometimes be a combination of continuous and discontinuous wefts, depending upon the design being woven. Where the gold-leafed strips appear on the front, they are tied in a 2/1 twill that goes over two and under one warp, repeating every six warps with warps two, four, and six remaining inactive. This forms a "coarser" twill than the ground twill, where all warps are active. On the wrong side of the cloth the gold-leafed paper strips ride over all the warps not used in

Fig. 19
Setting up the pattern unit for the draw strings on the draw frame (*monage*). Photograph courtesy of the Yamaguchi Nō Costume Research Center.

Fig. 20
When weaving in the gold, a long wooden hook is used to pull the pre-cut strips of gold-leafed paper into place.

Fig. 21
The back of a *karaori* showing the continuous gold-leafed paper-strip wefts. Black areas are where the gold appears on the front of the cloth. Discontinuous supplementary wefts appear in discrete areas.

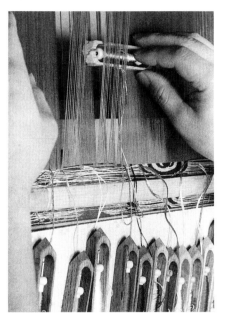

Fig. 22
Weaving in discontinuous supplementary wefts to form the floating pattern.

colored silk threads or metallic-leafed paper strips only in the short widths required by the pattern, so they double back and forth in discrete areas to form a float on the surface of the fabric (fig. 22). Since these pattern threads do not pass from motif to motif across the width of the fabric, but remain in discrete areas, they are referred to as "discontinuous." The right side of the cloth faced down on the loom. In this way, it was possible to produce large pictorial designs with long pattern floats on a sturdy, strong fabric. The effect resembles embroidery and differs from other Japanese textiles patterned on the loom (e.g. *kinran, mon-ori;* see p. 50) in the scale of the pattern repeat as well as in the variety of colors used.[18]

The three layers of pattern fit together so as to enhance each other. Although the ground (layer one) forms distinct blocks in checkerboard fashion, the background pattern (layer two) covers this with an undifferentiated overall pattern that helps to blur the delineation into blocks and unify the garment. In contrast the float motifs (layer three) have been lined up to form repeated bands of clouds and arrows horizontally across the front.

The three layers of pattern maintain an independence while also interacting and interlacing. Since each layer was operated separately on the loom, it was possible to make adjustments in one without altering the others. An example is the way the back sleeves have been woven without the cloud pattern, altering the balance found elsewhere. Another is the occasional reversal of the pattern creating a mirror view on the left back and right front panel of the main body of the robe. The pattern is also reversed top to bottom as it goes over the shoulder line so that the arrows point up on both the front and the back of the garment. The mirror image reversal, commonly found in Nō costumes, requires separate threading of the draw pattern, reading the draft sketch flipped over.

When the weaving was finished, the cloth was cut from the loom and sent to the tailor. Following specific standard measurements, he would cut the long strip of cloth at predetermined places in the pattern and assemble the strips to form a garment. Minor shifts in pattern alignment could make for striking changes in effect. A good example is the *atsuita* with clouds and arrows owned by the Tokyo National Museum (fig. 23). As a piece of weaving, this robe is almost identical with its sister in Provi-

the pattern, so they appear as long floats (fig. 21).

Bulging out from the ground fabric is the top level of the weaving structure, the floating pattern (*uamon*), with two large pictorial float patterns, one of clouds enveloping circles with wheels in them and the other of arrows standing upright in paper screens. The float patterns are often woven with soft, glossy, silk-floss wefts of many colors known as "weft floats" in English and "picture wefts" (*enuki*) in Japanese.[17] Unlike the ground weave and the gold-leaf background pattern, which were woven in twill and operated with foot pedals by the weaver, the float patterns were controlled by the draw strings operated by the draw boy, or later by punch cards. Using small bobbins of colored weft, the weaver inserted dence. The green and red ground is the same. The gold triangles are the same. The arrows in screens are the same; the clouds have the same shape, but contain circles with three comma-shapes (*tomoe*) instead of wheels, and in the blocks from the waist down, extra small cloud motifs appear. This slight variation is hardly noticeable, and the robes would look the same were it not for the distribution of the float pattern over the blocks and the tailoring. Instead of lining up the patterns in a band, the weaver has staggered the motifs according to the color of the ground. All the green blocks have clouds, the red ones arrows. The result is a lighter, more vibrant robe, with greater elegance but less vigor than cat. no. 44.

A slight addition in the floating pattern, an addition that was not used throughout the robe, is all that distinguishes the loom set-up of these two sister robes. The rest is a matter of shifting elements against each other. The simplicity of this mechanism suggests that both these robes may have been produced on the same loom one after the other, or at least in the same workshop.

Another striking example of such sister robes is the *karaori* with fans on an orange-red ground, cat. no. 14, and a similar *karaori* in the Ikeda collection housed at the Hayashibara Art Museum, Okayama Prefecture (fig. 24). At first glance one would think that these were the same robe. The total correspondence of ground color, pattern rendering, and technical finesse mark them as coming, if not from a single warping, at least from the same workshop at the same time. They both make effective use of the three-dimensional possibilities of supplementary-weft weaving. The background pattern of weeping willow leaves, instead of being tied down and flattened in a twill, as is typical of background patterns (*jimon*, layer two), is given flesh and bulk by being woven with short weft-float threads. In contrast the fan papers, which schematically are floating patterns (*uamon*), or level-three design motifs, are made to appear like stiff, flat paper by being held down with the warp threads in a "coarse" twill. Only the pictures on the fan papers appear to rise up out of the flat papers with bulky colored picture-weft threads, as is usual with floating patterns.

The Providence and Hayashibara Art Museum robes differ in two respects: the addition of flying birds in the Hayashibara robe and the tailoring. Both garments have mirror-image patterns on the left and right sides of the main

Fig. 23
Atsuita with design of standing arrows and clouds over a scale pattern on a ground of alternating blocks of green and red. Late Edo period, early nineteenth century. Tokyo National Museum.

Fig. 24
Karaori with design of weeping willows and scattered fans on a red ground. Late Edo period, early nineteenth century. Hayashibara Art Museum.

body of the garment, but while the Providence garment panels alternate left right left right as one reads across from sleeve to sleeve, the Hayashibara garment panels are arranged right right left left, making for a clearer division between left and right side of the body (*katamigawari;* see p. 51). In neither case is the manipulation of pattern outstanding, for the overall impression is one of uniformity. One might speculate that the Providence robe may also have originally belonged to the Ikeda family in Okayama, since other garments in the Providence collection were once the property of the Ikeda household, as evidenced by their labeled paper wrappers. The question then would be why have two such similar garments? A number of answers come to mind. If one really likes a pattern, it is good to have an extra garment in reserve, particularly if it is to be worn in amateur performances.[19] As these robes are elegant but not ostentatious, they could be used for any number of young women's roles

Fig. 25
The two Soga brothers dance for their mother before departing to avenge the murder of their father.

and would be a popular choice for an actor whose performance should not be overpowered by his costume. Another possibility is that they might have been made to appear in a paired role. A number of Nō plays have two dancers performing in unison, such as *Futari Shizuka* (*Two Shizukas*), in which the ghost of Shizuka Gozen, an elegant courtesan and mistress of the famous general Minamoto Yoshitsune, takes spiritual possession of a shrine maiden. Once the shrine maiden has donned the robe that formerly belonged to the ghost, she rises and dances, her movements manipulated and echoed by the ghost in identical garb. Although in present-day practice, the shrine maiden and ghost generally wear embroidered *nuihaku,* it would be possible to substitute *karaori.* Another play with identical costumes for a paired lead role is *Kosode Soga* (*The Soga Brothers;* fig. 25), where the Soga brothers Gorō and Jūrō perform a dance together, rejoicing that their mother has forgiven Gorō for leaving the priesthood and has blessed them both before they go off to avenge their father's death.

The ease with which one can produce "new" garments without the laborious effort of redrafting the pattern and redressing the loom would suggest a high probability of there being many sister costumes in which only one element is changed, or in which the interplay between layers has been shuffled for a different effect, or in which color shifts or tailoring adjustments have changed the appearence of the garments. Actually there are fewer than there might be, and most of them date from the late Edo period. What one finds more commonly is robes with close resemblance, which seem to have used the same draft sketch with minor adjustments. When two such robes were owned by different people, one may imagine the wholesaler adjusting patterns for competitive daimyo seeking to imitate what they felt had been effective, but searching for an element of originality. When two such robes existed within the holdings of a single household, as is the case in the next example, it may be that one was a copy of an older, damaged robe.

Two robes in the Ikeda family collection at the Hayashibara Art Museum (figs. 26, 27) are remarkably similar to the *karaori* with design of lattice and chrysanthemums with pampas grass, cat. no. 9. Five or six other robes in the Hayashibara Art Museum appear to be variations on the same theme. In addition, similar thematic and technical aspects can be seen in robes in the Tokyo National Museum, the Tokugawa collection in Nagoya, and in the Kongō family collection.

The most striking characteristic of the Providence *karaori* (cat. no. 9) shared by the two Hayashibara robes is the inversion of the standard foreground and background. The background pattern woven in "coarse twill" (layer two) consists of vertical and horizontal lines forming a lattice pattern done in gold-leafed-paper strips, but it spans the garment in unbroken lines, lying on top of the picture motif of large sprigs of flowers (layer three). It is as if one peers into a garden through a lattice fence.

Judging from the quality of the colors, looseness of the weft thread twist, and the fact that the picture motifs do not spill over the boundaries set by the ground blocks of alternating brown and tan, the robe from the Hayashibara Art Museum (fig. 26) is the oldest. Fig. 27 has a simplified background with an overall red ground. This switch in ground color to red puts the newer robe into the category of a robe "with color" (*iroiri;* see p. 48), considered appropriate for young women's wear. The older robe, being "without color" (*ironashi*), would be used for roles of middle-aged or old women.

A careful study of the picture-weft pattern suggests that both of the peony motifs are based on the same draft sketch. They appear to be essentially the same size with the same flowers in the same place. The *karaori* cat. no. 9 gives a very similar impression to the Hayashibara robe in fig. 27, for it also has a red ground and similarly spaced gold lattice. Even the flower motifs that seem to peep from behind the gold fence appear to have a similar weight and color distribution, but instead of being peonies, they are chrysanthemums. The season has switched from spring to autumn. Cat. no. 9, though conceptually similar to fig. 27, would have to have been redrafted. One may imagine a daimyo or actor going to a wholesaler and requesting "something along the lines of …, but …." The wholesaler would then pull out a number of pattern books and color sample books, and the two would confer about specifics. The details of the decision would be passed on to the draftsman.

We have already seen how tailoring can alter the effect of a pattern. In cat. no. 9 the pattern reads from left sleeve to right: A-B-A-B. Adjustments in length and size of sleeve were possible (for historical changes in measurements, see p. 49). The short body of a number of the Providence robes indicates they were made for child roles. The flare at the bottom of the main panels of some *karaori* dates the robes to the nineteenth century, when draping styles became more accentuated.

Once the robe passed into the hands of a patron or acting troupe, it was added to a stock of garments from which the actor could select the most appropriate combination for the role he was about to perform. It is likely that the occasion of the first wearing of a newly made robe was chosen with care. The impact would be great, the novelty value high. Thus, for instance, the *atsuita* with standing arrows and clouds (cat. no. 44) might have been donned first by a young, promising actor in the play *Ebira* (*Quiver*) to portray the warrior Kajiwara Kagesue, who entered battle with a peace token of a plum branch among his arrows. Since the right sleeve of the outer robe would be slipped off, rolled up, and tucked into the back belt (fig. 30), the *atsuita* sleeve could be seen displaying its rows of upright arrows, as if they were an ironic counterstatement to the plum branch placed in the quiver slung over the actor's shoulder.

The green and red ground as well as the pattern motifs would also make this garment suitable for other warrior plays. In addition, the symbolic value of the two motifs, clouds

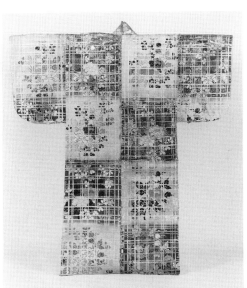

Fig. 26
Karaori with design of lattice over peonies on a ground of alternating blocks (*dangawari*) of blue and tan. Edo period. Hayashibara Art Museum.

Fig. 27
Karaori with design of lattice over peonies on a red ground. Edo period. Hayashibara Art Museum.

and standing arrows, recalls the imagery of the play *Kamo* (*The Thunder God of Kamo*). In the first half of the play, a stage prop with upright arrow stands at center front, a symbol of an ancient miracle when the thunder god, in the form of an arrow, impregnated a woman while she was washing clothes in the Kamo river. Later the thunder god descends from his billowing clouds to replenish the earth with life-giving rain. The dynamic arrangement of a band of clouds across the upper front and upper central back of the robe suggests the power of the thunder god, though once he is fully clad, the broad-sleeved *kariginu* cloak worn over the *atsuita* would all but conceal it. One might say also that the staggered distribution of motifs on its sister robe in the Tokyo National Museum would be more appropriate to warrior roles, where not only the power of a warrior, but also the sensibility of a courtier must be expressed.

It must be remembered, however, that the poetic esthetic of Nō demands that visual

Fig. 28
When dressing for the role of a warrior, the *atsuita* is donned as the first layer of visible costume. The robe is carefully fitted to the body and snugly secured.

Fig. 29
Putting on the divided skirts (*ōguchi*). The large wooden fork placed at the center back will hold up the hump of the back pleat.

Fig. 30
The right sleeve of the *chōken* is slipped off, rolled up and tucked in the belt at the back, exposing the right sleeve of the *atsuita*.

symbolism in costume motifs never descend to being explanatory, as the symbolism in Kabuki very often is. Motifs that fit the content of the play too well become trite and evoke an intellectual rather than an emotional response. In his choice of costume, an actor shies away from explicit commentary and places more importance on overall color balance and the impressionistic effect of pattern. One costume, even if first ordered for a specific role, can generally be worn in any number of plays and combined in various ways with other robes.

For roles of young warriors of the Heike family, as in the Nō plays *Ebira*, *Kiyotsune*, or *Tadanori*, the *atsuita* is worn over a white padded undergarment (fig. 28). Divided skirts, either *hangire* (cat. nos. 45, 46) or *ōguchi* (fig. 40), depending on the actor's choice, are tied in place over it (fig. 29). An outer cloak, either a *happi* (cat. nos. 34-37) or a *chōken* (cat. nos. 26-28), is next draped to suggest armor. The right sleeve of the outer cloak may be slipped off, folded, rolled up, and tucked into the belt at the back (fig. 30) to free the right hand to use a sword, or alternatively both sleeves of the outer cloak may be hiked up and stitched in place at the shoulders. In either case the cloak is secured with a long embroidered sash (*koshi-obi*; cat. no. 47), and the folds are carefully arranged (fig. 31). A sword fitted to the waist, warrior's lacquer cap, wig, and mask complete the outfit (fig.32).

The same *atsuita* that forms an underrobe for male roles is worn as an outer cloak for the role of the mountain crone in the play *Yamamba* (*The Mountain Crone*; fig. 33). The draping style (*tsuboori* over divided skirts) is one used with *karaori* for court ladies, creating the enigma of a male robe draped in a female style. This is intentional, for the mountain crone is at once a frightful hag haunting mountain depths and an enlightened being descending to mingle with humans and invisibly help them.

The types of garments worn for each play are set by tradition and define the role portrayed, yet the same robes are rarely combined in precisely the same way twice. The color scheme defines a mood. The imagery evokes a season and possibly refers to the literary heritage of Nō drama. In addition, since there is little or no scenery on stage, visual interest centers on the characters and is provided by the color and pattern of the costumes. The occasional stage prop, generally fashioned by draping cloth over a bamboo frame, appears as an extension of the costumes.

Although the world of Nō may appear limited from the outside, encased in rules set by tradition, the variation in performance details is infinite. From a small vocabulary of movement and musical patterns, from a prescribed number of traditional colors and motifs rise myriad variations. The spectator becomes engrossed in the novelty of discovering ever-new interpretations. Just as the layering of robes creates the costume for a role, so costume, too, is but one layer of performance. As the sleeves of the robes sway with the movement of the actor or momentarily rest on the crown of a heavenly maiden, the colors, textures, and designs come alive.

Even off the stage, Nō costumes beg the eye to travel back and forth along the garment, focusing on ever-widening worlds that emerge from the images seen and reseen, always in new context. Like Nō performance, the costumes are an invitation into dream worlds where time flows with the mind and where imagery reinterprets life onto a new plane.

Fig. 31
The *koshi-obi* (waist sash) secures the *chōken* at the waist, the decorated ends falling in front of the divided skirts. The *chōken* cords are tied elegantly to the belt, and a sword is attached.

Fig. 32
A lacquer warrior's hat (*eboshi*), wig of flowing black hair, white hair band (*katsura-obi*), and mask (*chūjo*) complete the costume.

Fig. 33
In *Yamamba*, the mountain crone's ambiguous identity is reflected in her costume: male *hangire* (divided skirts) and male *atsuita* draped in a feminine style (*tsuboori*), also used for sprites.

1. The fourteenth-century troupes that remain as "schools" of Nō, each with their own performance traditions, are Kanze, Hōshō, Kongō, and Komparu. The Kita school branched off from the Kongō school in the Edo period.

2. Akira Omote and Shuichi Katō, eds., "*Kyūi*" ("Nine Levels"), in *Zeami Zenchiku* (*The Writings of Zeami and Zenchiku*), vol. 24 of *Nihon shisō taikei* (*Anthology of Japanese Thought*). Tokyo: Iwanami Shōten, 1979 (fifth edition), p. 174.

3. Omote and Katō, eds., *Fūshi kaden*, op. cit., pp. 21, 23. A translation of the *Fūshi kaden* appears with the title *Style and the Flower* in J. Thomas Rimer and Masakazu Yamazaki, *On the Art of the Nō Drama: The Major Treatises of Zeami*. Princeton: Princeton University Press, 1984, pp. 13-15.

4. Omote and Katō, eds., *Sarugaku dangi*, op. cit., pp. 292-93.

5. Omote and Katō, eds., *Fūshi kaden*, op. cit., p. 56.

6. Omote and Katō, eds., *Sarugaku dangi*, op. cit., p. 286.

7. Late Edo-period costumes often have design blocks covering the entire width of the cloth and are thus doubly complex in their loom set-up.

8. For a detailed discussion of present-day Nishijin specialization, see Ronald Haak, "Nishijin Weavers: A Study of the Functions of Tradition in Modern Japanese Society," Ph.D. dissertation, University of Illinois at Urbana-Champaign, 1973; University Microfilms: Ann Arbor. Gary Leupp discussed Edo-period Nishijin in a lecture at the Japan Foundation, Kyoto, March 1991.

9. A standard warp count for *karaori* or *atsuita* was about twenty-eight hundred doubled.

10. Kentarō Sanari, *Yōkyoku taikei*, vol. 2. Tokyo: Meiji Shoin, 1931, pp. 975-88. A translation of *Kureha* appears in Royall Tyler, *Japanese Noh Dramas*. London: Penguin Classics, to be published 1992.

11. See W. G. Aston's translation, *Nihongi, Chronicles of Japan from the Earliest Times to A.D. 697*. Tokyo: Charles E. Tuttle, 1972, p. 271.

12. Some have interpreted the word *Ayahatori* as "spinning" or "winding threads," but the word *aya* ("figured twill") and the cooperative effort implied suggest a draw loom. Clearly at that time the draw loom must have been very primitive, possibly a forerunner of the backstrap draw loom still used in some provinces in China today. The history of the draw loom in Japan is shrouded in mystery. Textiles from the eighth century include fine examples of both warp and weft brocades; however, no implements used to make these remain. According to Toshirō Koma, no standing draw looms were in use until the sixteenth century, when the Japanese began the attempt to produce textiles in imitation of Chinese imported cloth; Toshirō Koma, "*Sengoku no oritetachi*" ("Weavers During the Civil Wars"), *Taiyō, some to ori no shiriizu: Kosode, nō shōzoku* (Summer 1977), pp. 121-24. Akira Yamaguchi, however, suggests that the *sorabiki-bata* was used at least from the eighth century on ("*Sorabiki-bata:* Draw Loom," in *The World of Noh Costumes*. Kyoto: Yamaguchi Nō Costume Research Center, 1989, p. 50).

13. The Japanese text (see Sanari, op. cit., p. 987) is filled with "t" alliteration ("*tanabata no tamatama aeru tabito, takara no aya o oritate, oritate*"). *Tanabata* refers to the star Vega (The Weaving Girl), who meets her star lover Altair (The Cowherd) once a year on the seventh night of the seventh month of the old Japanese lunar calendar. This day (*tanabata*) would fall in July or August each year.

14. In 1967 the members of the Nishijin guild built a draw loom (*sorabiki*) and tried to operate it. Later Akira Yamaguchi, as a part of his research into Edo-period Nō costumes, copied this and learned how to operate it from the one man then living who knew. He has woven a few experimental Nō robes on this loom. See Yamaguchi, op. cit., p. 50.

15. The actual extent to which color was prescribed and controlled by the designer probably varied greatly.

16. Gold-leafed paper is made of thinly hammered twenty-four carat gold pasted onto hand-made Japanese *washi* paper treated with rice paste and lacquer as adhesives. In the Edo period, these sheets were then hand-cut into very thin, threadlike strips. Today they are cut by machine, producing a more even but less interesting effect.

17. *Uamon* refers to the top pattern layer (float pattern) in design conception. In Momoyama- and early Edo-period costumes, this is almost invariably woven with weft floats of silk floss. Part of the sophistication of late Edo-period costumes is textural play incorporating into the *uamon* design gold-leafed paper or colored silk floss tied into the structure of the fabric with the coarse twill of the background pattern, but woven with discontinuous wefts in *uamon* style.

18. Pre-sixteenth-century Japanese weft-patterned textiles have anywhere from four to ten repeats of a pattern as read across the width of the fabric. Early *karaori* and *atsuita* fabrics have the width divided in half, left repeating right, and the pattern height ranges from twenty-five to forty centimeters. By the late eighteenth century, many garments, like this *atsuita*, appear with a single pattern unit spanning the entire width of the fabric. The height varies. In cat. no. 44 a full unit spans two blocks of the ground-weave pattern and is composed of two separate design elements: clouds and arrows in screens.

19. In a private conversation with the author in January 1992, Akira Yamaguchi of the Nō Costume Research Center stated that orders of multiple costumes were documented in the Edo period.

A History of Nō Costume

Iwao Nagasaki

(Translated and adapted by Monica Bethe)

Nō costumes attained their superb refinement and distinctive character over the six hundred years between the fourteenth century, when Nō emerged as a stage art, and the present day. Today each costume type has a designated shape and style, but these are not necessarily identical with those used in the fourteenth century. At the outset of Nō, everyday garments worn by the samurai class were the basis for the majority of the costumes, actual street wear appearing frequently on stage. Some of the costumes were retailored for greater stage effect, creating new styles of garments unique to the Nō stage. The oldest extant garments date from the late sixteenth century, when they paralleled street clothing. Techniques continued to parallel street wear until the seventeenth century, when woven decoration for street wear gave way to dyed designs, either tie-dye or resist. Nō costumes, however, continued to use fabrics with woven decoration as well as embroidery and gold- or silver-leaf stenciling, both popular in the late sixteenth century. In the early Edo period, *karaori* carried on sixteenth-century styles, while *nuihaku* followed the changing designs of street wear more closely. By the middle of the Edo period, cloth was woven specifically for stage costumes with increasingly complex techniques aimed at dramatic effectiveness and designed to evoke an atmosphere of elegance, known as *yūgen*, particularly associated with the Nō stage. Nō costumes had now also attained their distinctive style and form as garments made expressly for the stage. Designs became more integrated, with ground and background elements working to enhance motifs and create a sense of depth. Subsequent costumes maintained the established forms with only slight variation and slow evolution. In the late Edo period, stylization and technical virtuosity, rather than innovative design, came to the forefront.

Nō Costumes of the Muromachi Period (1336-1573)

Nō drama developed out of folk skits known as *sarugaku nō* and was refined into a stage art suitable to an educated and aristocratic audience by two master actors, Kan'ami Kiyotsugu (1333-1384) and his son, the actor-playwright-theorist Zeami Motokiyo (1363-1443). We have scant concrete evidence of the costumes they used since garments designated specifically as Nō costumes no longer remain from their lifetime, but literary sources suggest that costumes used on the stage differed little from garments used as street wear. For example, Zeami in his first theoretical treatise on the art of acting, the *Fūshi kaden* (*Secret Writings on the Style and the Flower of Acting,* 1418), states that when dressing for roles of high-ranking women such as ladies-in-waiting, rather than risk creating an improper impression, the actor should assiduously study the styles of draping actually in use at court.[1] Similarly, in his comments to amateurs recorded in the *Sarugaku dangi* (an account of Zeami's reflections on *sarugaku nō* as recorded by his second son, Hata no Motoyoshi, 1430), he warns that for the main role in the ritual play of *Okina*, the costume should not be too gaudy, but rather calm and serene, imported silk and gold weft-patterned textiles (*kinran*) being totally out of place.[2] This suggests that in accordance with the spiritual aims of his art, Zeami did not approve of ostentatious costumes that sought

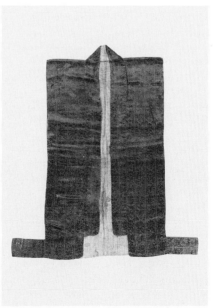

Fig. 34
Sleeveless garment (*soba-tsugi*) weft-patterned in a design of birds and flowers with narrow paper strips to which silver leaf has been glued (*ginran*). Muromachi-Momoyama periods, sixteenth century. Kasuga Shrine, Gifu Prefecture. Important Cultural Property.

superficial admiration, but rather desired realistic costumes suited to the roles played.

On the other hand, another entry in the *Sarugaku dangi* relates Zeami's great respect for certain actors of the similar and competing performing art, *dengaku nō*. Undoubtedly, *sarugaku nō* costumes were influenced by the comparatively more brilliant costumes of *dengaku nō*. Moreover, appreciative members of the audience began to reward actors that they felt deserved special recognition for their superior art by doffing their own brilliant and expensive garments of Chinese gold or silver weft-patterned textiles (*kinran* and *ginran*; fig. 34) and throwing them on the stage. The fabrics of these stripped garments inevitably became the models for Nō costumes, the first step in establishing what was to be their distinctive

Fig. 35
Figured satin (*donsu*).
Muromachi period, fourteenth to fifteenth century.
Tokyo National Museum.

Fig. 36
Hunting cloak (*kariginu*) of *ōdon* cloth with silk warp, cotton ground wefts, and silk and metallic patterning wefts in a design of beasts and flowers. Muromachi-Momoyama periods, sixteenth century. Kasuga Shrine, Gifu Prefecture. Important Cultural Property.

character – rich, gorgeous, weft-patterned fabrics and fabrics embroidered with pictorial motifs.

Imperial and military court garments were also presented as donations to Nō actors. Various records relate that in 1464, a crowd of viewers including the shogun attended a subscription performance of Nō on the dry river bed in Kyoto. Over the course of three days they took off and donated 240 *ryo* worth of "small-sleeved" *kosode* (street-wear kimono),[3] probably tailored from Chinese weft-patterned textiles, including those with gold supplementary wefts (*kinran*) and "Chinese weave" (*karaori*) with pictorial patterns woven with supplementary weft floats appearing somewhat like embroidery, figured satin (*donsu*; fig. 35), and *ōdon* (satin weave with silk warp and cotton weft for the ground and silk or gold patterning wefts; fig. 36).[4]

The ravaging Ōnin civil wars (1467-1477) put a stop to the trend towards ever more gorgeous and elaborate Nō costumes, but only temporarily. Twenty years later, revitalized Kyoto workshops were using new techniques learned during their time of refuge in the port city of Sakai (South Osaka) and were producing more and more magnificent textiles.

At this time Nō costumes began their divergence from the tailoring styles of mainstream clothing, a process which would take at least a century. The writings of the fifteenth-century Nō actor Komparō Zempō (1454-1530?) indicate that classification by type of costume had already begun.[5] He mentions terms for Nō costumes that include street garments of the military class, such as broad-sleeved cloaks (*hirosode*) belonging to matched suits like the *hitatare* (fig. 37) and *suō* (fig. 38), as well as garments derived from the wardrobe of the court nobility, like the cloaks *chōken* (cat. nos. 26-28) and *kariginu* (cat. nos. 31-33). In addition, for the first time the names of some costumes found only on the Nō stage appear, such as the traveling cloak *mizugoromo* (fig. 39), the dancing cloak *maiginu* (cat. no. 29), the dynamic broad-sleeved jacket *happi* (cat. nos. 34-37), and the *happi* vest *sobatsugi* (also called *sodenashi* or "sleeveless"; fig. 34). Among the *kosode*-style garments, Zempō mentions "*karaori-mono*" ("thing of Chinese weave"), a garment tailored from *karaori* cloth. Robes of fabrics with red in the ground or pattern (*iroiri*) he designates as suitable for roles of young women, while for roles of older women, those without red (*ironashi*, or "without color") would be worn. He divides women's roles between those using *karaori-mono* and those where a plain-weave *kosode* with glossy weft and unglossed warp (*nerinuki*) would be worn. In *Bugei rokurin* (*The Six Wheels of the Art of Dance*) Zempō mentions, along with other details on costuming, not only the pantaloons worn by the samurai, *ōguchi* (fig. 40), and those of the nobility, *sashinuki* (fig. 41), but also a special pantaloon style peculiar to the Nō, the *hangire* (cat. nos. 45, 46). These many references to costume names indicate that the basic types of Nō costumes known today were being set in the late fifteenth and early sixteenth centuries.

Nō Costumes of the Momoyama Period (1568-1615)

The esthetic characteristics of densely weft-patterned or embroidered pictorial designs found in Nō costume were set in the Momoyama period (1568-1615), one of the most brilliant periods in Japanese textile history, when Nō costumes, particularly *kosode*-style garments, increased in splendor. For roles of upper-class women, which in Zeami's time had been portrayed as realistically as possible, the elaborately woven Chinese-style weft-patterned *karaori* now became the standard robe. In the secret writings of the Momoyama-period actor, Shimotsuma Shōshin (1551-1616), *Shōshin nōdenshō*, and in his collection of comments on various plays, *Dōbushō* (1596), another *kosode*-style robe, the embroidered and gold- or silver-leaf-patterned *nuihaku* (cat. nos. 18-23; fig. 42), is mentioned along with *karaori* as a standard costume for women's roles. Apparently, in Shimotsuma's time the use of each type was not yet clearly delineated, and it is thought that in most instances the actor was free to choose one or the other.[6]

The late sixteenth century is the first period for which there are a sufficient number of actual examples of Nō costumes to form a reliable picture of what they were like. At this time Nō costumes had not yet fully separated from the mainstream of Japanese clothing, and many still shared style, materials, techniques, and/or designs with street wear. For example, *kosode*-style Nō costumes like the *karaori*, *nuihaku*, and gold- or silver-leaf stenciled *surihaku* (cat. nos. 24, 25) shared tailoring styles with street-wear *kosode* in their wide central panels (*mi-haba*); narrow sleeve width (*sode-*

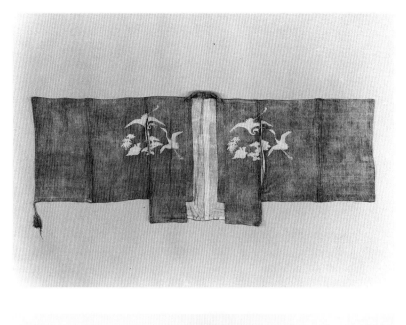

haba); short distance from center back to sleeve opening (*yuki*); narrow neck opening at shoulders (*erikata-aki*); short distance from shoulder to top of overlap (*okumi-sagari*); short distance from lower edge of collar to lower edge of overlap (*tatezuma*); approximately equal width of front and back central panels (*mae-mi-haba* and *ushiro-mi-haba*); and narrow sleeve openings (*sode-guchi*; figs. 44, 45).

Fabrics also still corresponded to those commonly used for street-wear *kosode*, such as the glossed-weft plain-weave *nerinuki* silk used for *nuihaku* and *surihaku*. In fabrics with woven designs, little fundamental difference can be seen between the weft-patterned *karaori* and figured twill fabrics used for Nō costumes and those used in other *kosode*. The same applies to broad-sleeved garments (*hirosode*), like the *hitatare* and *suō* suits.

Techniques of decoration typically used

Fig. 37
Lined matched hemp suit (*hitatare*) with paste-resist design of cranes, turtles, pines, and bamboo on a light-blue ground. Sixteenth century. Kasuga Shrine, Gifu Prefecture. Important Cultural Property.

Fig. 38
Unlined matched hemp suit (*suō*) with paste-resist design of flowers and decorative papers on a dark-blue ground. Sixteenth century. Kasuga Shrine, Gifu Prefecture. Important Cultural Property.

Fig. 39
Unlined traveling cloak (*mizugoromo*). *Mizugoromo* can be made of plain-color plain-weave silk (*shike*), mesh (*yore*), or striped ramie (*shima*). This eighteenth-century example at the Tokyo National Museum is light-green mesh.

Fig. 40
Broad divided skirts with ribbed back panels (*ōguchi*). Although generally plain colored, some, called *mon-iri*, or "patterned" *ōguchi*, are decorated. This one has a design of chrysanthemums in rushing water on a red ground. Edo period, eighteenth century. Tokyo National Museum.

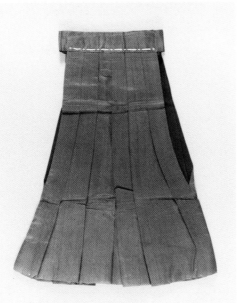

Fig. 41
Courtier's pantaloons (*sashinuki*), bound at the ankle. Purple silk. Edo period, eighteenth century. Tokyo National Museum.

on Momoyama-period costumes include embroidery, gold- and silver-leaf stenciling, *ikat* dyeing, and weft patterning. Embroidery was done with thick, soft, untwisted silk thread (*kamaito*), and the design was rendered primarily in *watashi-nui* (see Glossary), a type of satin stitch (*hira-nui*; see Glossary) in which the threads travel back and forth primarily horizontally and only on the face of the cloth, with only tiny anchor stitches on the back of the cloth. The result produces a soft, pliant finished product. Supplementing the *watashi-nui* are a stem stitch used for outlining (*matoi-nui*; see Glossary) and a filler stitch using uneven stitch lengths and varied directions to produce realistic effects (*sashi-nui*; see Glossary). In select areas, for such motifs as reeds and heads of pampas grass, sometimes threads of several colored strands were twisted together (*mokuito*). For gold- and silver-leaf design work (*surihaku*; fig. 46), gold or silver foil was applied to the woven cloth, using an adhesive painted onto the cloth through a decorative pattern cut into stencil paper.

The terms *surihaku* and *nuihaku* refer both to decorative techniques and to *kosode*-style garments made with these techniques. In the same way, *karaori* referred both to the weaving technique of the fabric and, later on, to *kosode*-style garments sewn out of *karaori* fabric. These, too, were popular street wear in the Momoyama period, though they subsequently went out of fashion, remaining only as Nō costumes.

The textile known as *karaori* is a weft-patterned cloth (*mon-ori*) usually woven with a 2/1 twill ground and polychrome supplementary weft floats. While the weft pattern in *kinran* textiles is basically gold (occasionally other colors are added as accents) and is always tied into the structure of the fabric with warp stitches at regular intervals (either in a twill or a plain weave), in *karaori* the weft pattern is of colored silk floats rising above the fabric (possibly with an occasional gold accent). In later centuries weavers sometimes inserted an intermediary background pattern done in gold- or silver-leafed paper cut into very narrow strips and tied into the warp with a 2/1 twill over six warps skipping every other warp to produce a "coarse" twill (in contrast to the 2/1 twill over three warps used for the tight ground twill; see pp. 39–40). Early *karaori* not only lack the gold or silver in the design, but also have very long supplementary pattern weft floats. In later years, intermediate warp stitches (*toji*; see Glossary) were placed somewhere in the middle of the float to reduce the possibility of snarling or breaking the threads when the costume was worn. In Momoyama-period costumes soft, full, long floats without warp stitches (fig. 47), resembling the *watashi-nui* of embroidery, were preferred, unless the floats were so long as to cause serious practical problems.

Momoyama-period Nō costumes also share decorative techniques with everyday clothing of the time.[7] Freedom and diversity characterized the selection and combination of motifs. *Nuihaku* and *karaori* display motifs of flowers (chrysanthemum, paulownia, willow, wisteria, plum, and cherry blossom), animals (butterflies, the mythical phoenix, and birds), and geometrical designs (hexagons, pine-bark lozenges, a variation of linked diamonds, and circles). These appear to be randomly combined to form patterns, without a strong sense of interrelation or contrast. With very few exceptions,[8] no hint of specific literary content is discernible, in contrast to the motifs on Nō costumes of later dates. Floral motifs tend in the Momoyama period to include flowers of all four seasons in one design, rather than to evoke a specific season through the choice of appropriate flora, like autumn grasses and chrysanthemums, as was common in the Heian period (794-1185). Similarly, animal and geometric motifs are combined freely according to what pleases the eye, with no other obvious rational correlation.

Momoyama-period motifs, whether rendered in embroidery or weft patterning, were densely packed into blocks that were arranged on the garments according to one or another set layout. Shoulder and hem areas of the garment might be filled with pattern, but the midriff left clear (*katasuso*; figs. 42, 43, 49); blocks of differing motifs might be arranged to form a checkerboard pattern (*dangawari*; fig. 48); or patterns on the right and left side of the garment might differ (*katamigawari*; fig. 47). In Momoyama-period garments, the motifs stay enclosed within the fields and never cross over the established boundaries. Furthermore, within the fields, the design construction is two-dimensional. Even though the individual motifs overflow with a sense of life, their arrangement lacks perspective and a conscious use of space, as if the concern in rendering them has been simply to fill up similar spaces (fig. 48).

Lastly, the depiction of the motifs follows

Fig. 42
Embroidered Nō robe (*nuihaku*) with design of flowering plants at shoulders and hem (*katasuso*) on a white ground. Momoyama period, sixteenth century. Tokyo National Museum. Important Cultural Property.

Fig. 43
Embroidered *kosode* with design of cherry and paulownia at shoulder and hem (*katasuso*) on a white ground. Momoyama period, sixteenth century. Ura Shrine, Kyoto. Important Cultural Property.

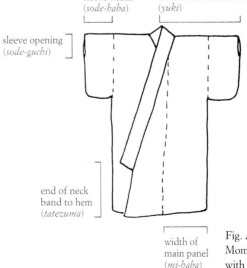

Fig. 44
Momoyama-period *kosode* with broad main-body panels and narrow sleeve panels.

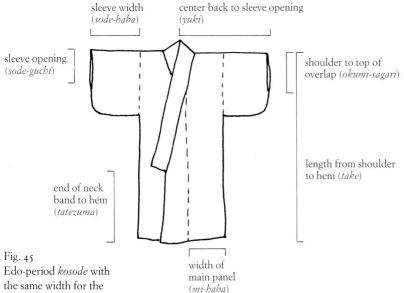

sleeve width (*sode-haba*)

center back to sleeve opening (*yuki*)

sleeve opening (*sode-guchi*)

shoulder to top of overlap (*okumi-sagari*)

length from shoulder to hem (*take*)

end of neck band to hem (*tatezuma*)

width of main panel (*mi-haba*)

Fig. 45
Edo-period *kosode* with the same width for the main-body panels and the sleeve panels.

Fig. 46
Nō robe (detail) with stenciled gold-leaf design (*surihaku*) of decorative papers and grapes on a purple ground. Momoyama period, sixteenth century. Tokyo National Museum. Important Cultural Property.

two characteristics shared with Momoyama-period painting, screen decoration, and dyed textiles: magnification and standardized rendering of types. Many examples display a love of enlarged, close-up depictions. Floral motifs focus on either the section from the stem up, or just the flower (fig. 49). Realistic rendering of worm-eaten leaves cradling a drop of fresh dew gives concrete expression to the magnified view. At the same time, there is a standard rendering of similar objects, no matter what technique is used. A tree trunk, for example, is depicted using the same set image, whether it be a willow tree or a weeping cherry. Likewise, for plum blossoms, chrysanthemums, or paulownia flowers, each has a set form as viewed from one angle. Furthermore, the same forms

appear on all types of garments, whether woven into *karaori*, stenciled onto *surihaku*, or embroidered onto *nuihaku* (figs. 50, 51). Stylization can also be seen in details of embroidery that catch the special characteristics of a plant in an impressionistic rather than a realistic manner: flowers and leaves may appear in varied colors with irregular color divisions (figs. 49, 50).

All these characteristics of form, technique, and design appear in everyday clothing of the Momoyama period as well as in Nō costumes, the distinction being rather one of brilliance in technique and design as the Nō costumes gradually moved toward becoming stage apparel. At the end of the Momoyama period, during the Keichō era (1596-1615), costumes began to diverge from the mainstream with a standardization of measurement for each type of costume. In the Edo period (1615-1868) costumes came to be designed specifically for the Nō stage, their patterns, designs, and techniques developing along different lines from street wear.

Nō Costumes of the Edo Period (1615-1868)

In 1603 Tokugawa Ieyasu was anointed shogun and took over the task of ruling a newly unified Japan. A part of the ceremony proclaiming his new title was a performance of Nō. Following this precedent, Nō became a ritual art performed for important ceremonies of the shogunal government. As a result, Edo-period Nō drama placed increasing importance on the observance of formalities. Technique, style, and adherence to tradition were valued over creative ingenuity. Performances were meant to be dignified, formal affairs. The Tokugawa government both protected and vigilantly supervised Nō.[9] With the purpose of diminishing the financial resources of the local rulers (daimyo), the government encouraged them to maintain Nō troupes and spend lavishly on Nō costumes. In selecting and ordering Nō costumes, the daimyo class was not restricted by sumptuary regulations such as those that controlled the dress of the commoners and the costumes for Kabuki, the theater of the merchant class. Under these circumstances, Nō costumes inevitably developed along different lines from street wear and at the time of the Genroku era (1688-1704) became an independent genre specifically designed for the stage.

By the late seventeenth century, *kosode* for street wear tended to be decorated with magnificent pictorial patterns using new dye techniques such as hand-drawn paste resist (*yūzen*). Nō costumes, on the other hand, continued to use the decorative techniques of the Momoyama period: weft patterning, embroidery, and gold- and/or silver-leaf stenciling. The end of the seventeenth century and the early eighteenth century saw increasingly elaborate techniques in every area of Edo textile production. Weaving, centered around the Nishijin area in northwest Kyoto, responded to the demands of the Nō world and gave birth to even more stunning costumes. Since elaborate weaving was no longer used for the mainstream of clothing, technical advances and evolution of design developed independently of fashion and tended to hark back to Momoyama-period esthetics. Because embroidery and gold- and silver-leaf stenciling were surface decoration techniques also used on street wear of the time, they developed along with the mainstream. As a result, Nō costumes using these techniques, like the *nuihaku* and the *surihaku*, show a closer correspondence in styles and techniques to street wear than do costumes with woven patterns.

Because of the antiquarian styles of Nō costumes, however, it is not necessarily easy to grasp the details of the changes that took place in techniques and patterns during the Edo period, even though many examples remain from that time. Written records or other indisputable evidence of origin exist for only a small number of robes, and of the robes that are documented, most date from the late Edo period. In addition, very few written records remain concerning the changes in shape, technique, and design that took place in Nō costumes. Given this state of affairs, the only adequate way to establish a reasonable formal progression is to organize the existing garments and make analogies based on the few records available. Concentrating on *karaori* as examples of garments with woven patterns and *nuihaku* as examples of garments with surface decoration, one may trace their development from the early Edo period, when patterns and styles were beginning to be codified; through the mid-Edo period (eighteenth century), when Nō costumes had attained the standardized forms and uses they retain today and when technical advances in production led to more integrated and complex patterning; to the late Edo period (late eighteenth century and first half of the nineteenth century), when technical virtuosity came to the fore.

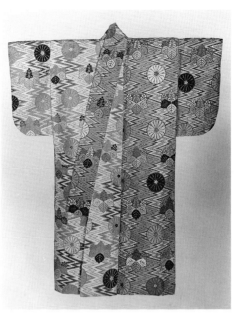

Fig. 47
Weft-patterned Nō robe (*karaori*) using long supplementary weft floats; design of chrysanthemum and paulownia flowers over mountain-path or lightning vertical zigzags on split body (*katami-gawari*) ground with left side red and right side moss green. Momoyama period, sixteenth century. Mōri Museum, Yamaguchi Prefecture. Important Cultural Property.

Fig. 48
Embroidered Nō robe (*nuihaku*) with design of flowering plants, poem papers, and plank bridges on a ground of alternating blocks (*dangawari*) of red and white. Momoyama period, sixteenth century. Tokyo National Museum. Important Cultural Property. For detail, see fig. 50.

Fig. 49
Detail of embroidered *kosode* (*nuihaku*) with design of paulownias, phoenixes, reeds, cherry blossoms, and snow-covered bamboo at shoulder and hem (*katasuso*) on a white ground. Momoyama period, sixteenth century. Tokyo National Museum.

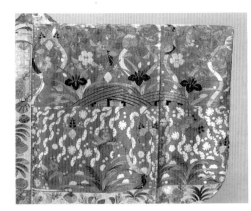

Fig. 50
Detail of embroidered
Nō robe (*nuihaku*) with
design of flowering plants,
decorative papers, and
plank bridges on a ground
of alternating blocks (*dangawari*) of red and white.
Momoyama period, six-
teenth century. Tokyo
National Museum.
Important Cultural
Property. See fig. 48.

Fig. 51
Detail of weft-patterned
Nō robe (*atsuita*) with
design of snow-laden
willows, paulownias, chrysanthemums, wisterias,
and plum blossoms on a
green ground. Momoyama
period, early seventeenth
century. Tokyo National
Museum.

Fig. 52
Karaori with design of
scattered double-petaled
chrysanthemums and fac-
ing cranes in diamonds on
a white ground. Edo
period, seventeenth cen-
tury. Itsukushima Shrine,
Hiroshima Prefecture.

Karaori of the Early Edo Period

The Nō actor Tokuta Tozaemon, who
was patronized by the daimyo of Kishū, provides
us with detailed information on the condition
of Nō costumes at the beginning of the
eighteenth century in his personal writings

entitled *Rinchū hishō gaihen* (*Secret Writings of
Rinchū*). According to that record, during the
infancy of Tozaemon until the early Genroku
period (the end of the seventeenth century),
karaori were not patterned with gold thread.
Popular weft-patterned textile designs of the
day were crane rounds on a tortoise-shell hexagon background pattern and red ground, or
paulownia motifs on a background pattern
representing lightning. Both these impressed
him as being "light."[10]

An examination of the few robes preserved
from the seventeenth century suggests the
accuracy of his statements and provides a clue
as to how to interpret his meaning of "light."
The *karaori* with scattered double-petaled
chrysanthemums and facing cranes in diamonds
at Itsukushima Shrine, Hiroshima Prefecture
(fig. 52), comes close to his description in its
techniques and motif construction, though the
ground color differs. The Tokyo National
Museum owns a seventeenth-century *atsuita*
(which shares its basic weave structure with
karaori fabrics) with tortoise-shell hexagon
background pattern that confirms Tozaemon's
claim as to its popularity (fig. 53).

These design compositions carried on
Momoyama-period trends seen in some of the
atsuita dated to the Momoyama period in the
Tokyo National Museum. One has a tortoise-
shell-hexagon background pattern on a red
ground over which are scattered crane diamonds
(fig. 54), and another has scattered crests over a
background pattern of nested diamonds on a
red ground (fig. 55). Fig. 47, thought to be a
work of the Momoyama period, has the lightning
pattern Tozaemon mentions. A comparison
of these sixteenth- and seventeenth-century
garments with similar patterns shows that the
scattered medallionlike floating-pattern motifs
on the seventeenth century robes are larger and
spaced farther apart.

The popularity of the red ground can be
seen in a group of *karaori* that formed a part of
the dowry sent with Chiyohime, the daughter
of the third shogun, Yoshimitsu, when her
marriage with Owari Tokugawa Mitsutomo was
arranged in 1639. All the *karaori* presented on
this occasion, which are now preserved in the
Tokugawa Reimeikai Foundation, Tokyo, and
are presumably of the early seventeenth century,
have red grounds.

None of the above *karaori* or *atsuita* use
gold thread, just as described by Tozaemon.
A *karaori* with a design of sprigs of chrysan-

themums over cobblestone triangles (*uroko*, "scales"; fig. 56) at Itsukushima Shrine stands as a rare exception, for it is woven with a small amount of gold thread, even though its construction with narrow sleeves and wide main panels (see p. 49) suggests that it dates from the very early Edo period.[11] Another indication that gold was occasionally used in *karaori* during the early Edo period comes from Tozaemon's own comments in his *Rinchū kenmonshū* (an account of events witnessed by Tozaemon). Here he records that on the occasion of the Nō entertainment at the dry river bed in Uji, Wakayama, in 1678, the actor Shibue Saburōuemon Dōshū wore a *karaori* with a ground of alternating blocks (*dangawari*) on which appeared a "seven jewel" (*shippō*) pattern in gold and a weft-float design of white chrysanthemums.[12] The design evoked by this description is rather old-fashioned, and it is not until the beginning of the eighteenth century that we find *karaori* beginning to include gold thread to any large extent. The weaving in of gold-leafed paper strips required tying the strips down with warp "stitches" spaced at short intervals so as to weave the gold tightly into the structure of the fabric. The result was a heavier, stiffer cloth. In comparison, early Edo-period *karaori*, which did not use gold, certainly must have given an impression of "lightness," just as Tozaemon describes.

A number of characteristics apply in general to these *karaori* from the early Edo period. The color schemes tend to be dark and dignified. Background patterns are, to a large extent, derived from patterns on Heian-period imperial court garments (*yūsoku*), such as hexagons, triangles, and diamonds. Finally, the background pattern and floating motif have equal weight; neither supports or emphasizes the other, in contrast to the clear apportionment of supportive and dominant roles seen in the designs of *karaori* regarded as products of the mid-Edo period.

Karaori of the Mid-Edo Period

A glance at extant robes from the mid-Edo period makes clear that, compared to early Edo-period *karaori*, mid-Edo-period *karaori* display a wide variety of patterns and brilliant colors (cat. nos. 1–10). Plants, with an emphasis on autumn flowers and grasses, are overwhelmingly profuse, followed by butterflies and birds, and finally objects like fans, shells, decorative

Fig. 53
Atsuita with design of flowers, tortoise-shell hexagons, and wisteria roundels on a dark-green ground. Edo period, seventeenth century. Tokyo National Museum.

Fig. 54
Atsuita with design of crane diamonds over a background pattern of flower-filled tortoise-shell hexagons on a red ground. Momoyama period, sixteenth century. Tokyo National Museum.

papers, ox carriages used by courtiers (*goshoguruma*), and screens.

In the mid-Edo period the background pattern acts to enliven or strengthen the effect of the floating motif and becomes subordinate to it. The number and use of colors as well as the size and form of the patterns were carefully planned. Also, when the ground was *ikat* dyed to form alternating blocks (*dangawari*), the aim was to produce a three-dimensional effect. At this time the use of alternating blocks still followed the traditional design composition of the Momoyama period, and the float-pattern motifs were almost always contained within the borders of the blocks.

Mid-Edo period *karaori* are of three types, reflecting a chronological progression

Fig. 55
Atsuita with design of
scattered crests over a
background pattern of
nested diamonds on a red
ground. Momoyama
period, sixteenth century.
Tokyo National Museum.

Fig. 56
Karaori with design of
sprigs of chrysanthemum
over a background pattern
of cobblestone triangles
(*uroko*), highlighted with
gold, on a dark-brown
ground. Early Edo period,
seventeenth century.
Itsukushima Shrine,
Hiroshima Prefecture.

corresponding to technological developments,
although, of course, the simpler ones continued
to be made throughout the period. The earliest
and most straightforward are those in which
the background pattern and the float motif
change with each block (cat. no. 2). The second
group has an evenly distributed background
pattern, but the float motif changes with the
blocks. In the third group both the background
pattern and the float motifs spill over the borders
of the block, being arranged freely with no
consideration for the colored blocks of the
ground (cat. nos. 6, 16). The trend towards
more and more magnificent costumes prevailed,
despite a short period at the beginning of the
eighteenth century when the government
warned against this.[13]

At the same time that the design and
woven structure worked towards more elaborate
detailing, the categorization and nomenclature
of costumes also became more sophisticated.
For example, the simple division of Nō *kosode*
into *atsuita* for male roles and *karaori* for female
roles was now expanded to include the hybrid
atsuita-karaori (fig. 57), to be worn by elegant
courtier-warriors. Reference to the *atsuita-
karaori* appears in a diary written by the *waki*
player under the patronage of the Kishū
Tokugawa household, Fujita Iemon Toyotaka.
The diary is said to have been written between
about 1710 and 1758, and one may suppose
from this that the *atsuita-karaori* garment also
appeared sometime during the early eighteenth
century.[14] The description in the diary, however,
brings to mind a garment rather similar to a
regular *atsuita* with "masculine" patterns and
quite different from the garment with both
"masculine" and "feminine" patterns that is
called an *atsuita-karaori* today. According to
the same diary, by this time *mizugoromo* cloaks
(fig. 39) were differentiated into plain weave
(*shike*) and mesh (*yore*) fabrics.

The appearance of the *atsuita-karaori* and
of new fabrics for the *mizugoromo* indicates a
strong trend towards incorporating additional
techniques, fabrics, and designs in mid-Edo-
period Nō costumes. Other examples can be
found in Tozaemon's *Rinchū hishō gaihen*
mentioned earlier, in which he notes *hangire*
(weft-patterned divided skirts; cat. nos. 45, 46)
with an innovative standing-wave pattern and
purple *ōguchi* (divided skirts; fig. 40) designed
specifically to suit the taste of the Kishū daimyo
Tokugawa Mitsusada.

Karaori of the Late Edo Period

A number of robes from the nineteenth
century bear inscriptions that provide a good
basis for dating other, similar costumes. Those
at Itsukushima Shrine on the sacred island of
Miyajima, south of the city of Hiroshima, will
serve as an example.[15] The collection of Nō
costumes at this shrine gives a good insight into
the development of Nō costumes in general,
because Nō drama had been incorporated into
the sacred performances of the shrine and was
performed there at set dates every year on a
striking stage that jutted out into the tide waters,
the stage having been built by the Mōri daimyo
family in the sixteenth century. For these
performances the shrine amassed costumes,

beginning in the sixteenth century with what may have been hand-me-downs from the daimyo and his family and continuing to the end of the Edo period. Only the late Edo-period robes bear donation inscriptions, like that on the lining of the *karaori* (fig. 58) with a design of autumn flowers and basket-weave background pattern. It reads, "Made the Third Lunar Month of the Year of the Monkey, Bunka 9 [1812]." The Bunka era lasted from 1804 to 1818. The "Year of the Monkey" refers to the Chinese and Japanese zodiac by which time is divided into cycles of twelve units, each represented by a specific animal. Another *karaori* at Itsukushima Shrine with dandelions and violets over a net pattern is inscribed, "Good Luck Day in the Third Lunar Month, The Year of the Cock, Bunka 10 [1813]." On the *karaori* with design of facing cranes in diamonds over a tortoise-shell hexagon background pattern (fig. 59), the inscription reads, "Good Luck Day in the Third Lunar Month, Year of the Dog, Bunka 12 [1815]."

The patterns on these *karaori* of the late Edo period, while continuing the forms of *karaori* of the mid-Edo period, have become increasingly elaborate. Many have relatively small patterns crowded together with little space between motifs, giving an impression of intricacy and complexity (cat. nos. 11, 12). Many others have large patterns composed of individual motifs rendered in a stylized form that may seem boring (cat. no. 13). Near the end of the Edo period especially, one finds pieces that clearly may be thought of as copies of older styles. At first glance these look like pieces from the beginning of the seventeenth century, but their expression is hard, fixed, and without the expansiveness characteristic of early Edo-period costumes. In addition, quite a number of pieces thought to be of the late Edo period have weft float threads treated in the same manner as gold-leafed paper threads, tightly bound into the fabric with regularly spaced warp "stitches" (cat. no. 14). Since the length of the picture weft floats is shorter than that of the mid-Edo period, the designs often give an impression of flatness (cat. no. 16).

Atsuita

The changes in *atsuita* follow in broad outline those described for *karaori*. A few further points specifically characterize *atsuita* designs, many of which have scattered motifs. A number

Fig. 57
Atsuita-karaori with design of paper-mulberry leaves over a woven-fence background pattern on a ground of alternating blocks (*dangawari*) of green and white. Edo period, eighteenth century. Tokyo National Museum.

Fig. 58
Karaori with design of autumn flowers over a basket-weave background pattern on a ground of alternating blocks (*dangawari*) of brown and light blue. Edo period, 1812. Itsukushima Shrine, Hiroshima Prefecture.

of examples among early Edo-period *atsuita* continue the orthodox trend of using designs derived from Heian-period imperial court textiles (*yūsoku*). Typical are undulating vertical lines, hexagons, and large roundels. In contrast, mid-Edo-period *atsuita* show a greater variety of scattered patterns. In late Edo-period *atsuita* the design construction shows a tendency to become diffuse and the rendering of the patterns stiff (cat. no. 42); many give an impression of tedious stylization.

Nuihaku of the Early Edo Period

Unlike *karaori* and other garments patterned on the loom, *nuihaku* Nō costumes followed the trends in everyday clothing more closely. During the opening years of the Edo period, the most common techniques for surface decoration on *kosode* combined *ikat* dyeing, stenciling, and embroidery. *Surihaku* garments

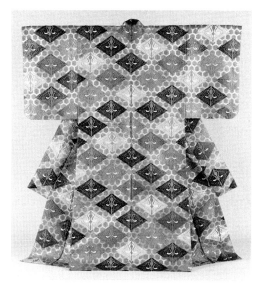

Fig. 59
Karaori with design of facing cranes over tortoise-shell hexagons on a brown ground. Edo period, 1815. Itsukushima Shrine, Hiroshima Prefecture.

with stenciled gold- or silver-leaf and *nuihaku* garments with additional embroidery were worn by many on the streets. Quite a few *nuihaku* that are now regarded as Nō costumes may not have originally been designed for the stage. A typical example of such early Edo-period *nuihaku* is a robe with scattered cherries and roundels in the Hayashibara Art Museum (fig. 60). Reminiscent of Momoyama-period *kosode*, the sleeves of this *nuihaku* are narrower than the main body panels (see p. 49), but both design and techniques share characteristics with *nuihaku* of the early Edo period. For example, the cherries and ivy are rendered in minute detail rather than with the strong, comparatively large and bold expression typical of floral motifs of Momoyama-period pieces, and the mountain shapes have been abstracted to evoke an overall pictorial sense of space, very

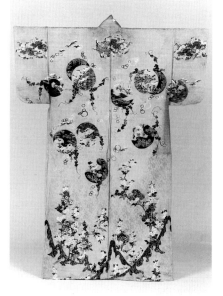

Fig. 60
Nuihaku with design of scattered cherries and roundels on a red ground. Edo period, seventeenth century. Hayashibara Art Museum.

different from Momoyama-period *nuihaku* based on filled fields or block construction. Finally, the dark shade of red used in the ground color is analogous to that used for *karaori* of the early Edo period and deeper than the red found on most Momoyama-period robes.

Few *nuihaku* from the mid-seventeenth century remain that can be irrefutably confirmed as Nō costumes. Given their similarity to street wear, however, one may conjecture from remaining examples of embroidered seventeenth-century *kosode* that the mid-seventeenth-century *nuihaku* had larger-scale patterns and rougher sewing techniques than those of the earlier period, and that the empty spaces were filled with small stenciled patterns in the manner of a ground pattern.

Nuihaku of the Mid-Edo Period

By the eighteenth century (mid-Edo period), *nuihaku* were produced with a wide variety of finely executed motifs (cat. no. 22). Although the combination of gold- or silver-leaf stenciling with embroidery had gone out of style for streetwear, *nuihaku* being produced now primarily for the Nō stage, many Nō *nuihaku* continued to follow the styles of street *kosode* in both expression and composition, avoiding, however, patterns that were too bold or strikingly stylized. For street wear, embroidery now embellished dyed decoration (*yūzen*) or other designs with increasingly refined techniques. These new stitches and approaches to design carried over to the embroidery done on Nō *nuihaku*. Most predominant was satin stitch (*hira-nui*; see Glossary) with loose floats and needle points well-aligned. Couching (*koma-nui*; see Glossary) and the realistic filler using long and short stitches (*sashi-nui*; cat. no. 22) appeared as embellishment in select spots. On *nuihaku*, empty spaces were filled in with various gold- or silver-leaf stenciled patterns.

Produced expressly for the Nō stage, mid-Edo-period costumes surpassed themselves in brilliance (fig. 61). Representative of their increased magnificence are the *dōhaku*, or *nuihaku* with solid gold or silver ground. These were reserved for roles of noblewomen.

Nuihaku of the Late Edo Period

Dated inscriptions on robes at Itsukushima Shrine also provide facts about late Edo-period *nuihaku*. The *nuihaku* with brown ground and design of pine forests (fig. 62) has an inscription reading, "Made in the Third Month of the Year of the Monkey, Bunka 9 [1812]." The unit designs are all small and scattered over the entire robe in clumps. The embroidery has short stitches pulled tight; the fullness found in mid-Edo-period costumes is lost. The increasing tightness and formality of design are even more apparent in two other *nuihaku* with scattered rounds at Itsukushima Shrine bearing inscriptions in ink of "Good Luck Day in the Third Month of the Year of the Tiger, Kansei 6 [1794]" and "Bunsei 9 [1826]," which continue these trends.[16]

Conclusion

The evolution of Nō costumes spanned some four hundred years from the fourteenth to the early eighteenth century. Actual garments remain only from the late sixteenth century on, when they paralleled street clothing. In the early Edo period, *karaori* carried on sixteenth-century styles, while *nuihaku* followed the changing designs of street wear more closely. By the mid-Edo period, Nō costumes had attained their distinctive style and form as garments made expressly for the stage. Designs became more integrated, with ground and background elements working to enhance motifs and create a sense of depth. Subsequent costumes maintained the established forms with only slight variation and slow evolution. In the late Edo period, stylization and technical virtuosity, rather than innovative design, came to the forefront.

Fig. 61
Nuihaku with poppies embroidered over a gold pattern of floating boats on a yellow ground. Edo period, eighteenth century. Tokyo National Museum.

Fig. 62
Nuihaku with pine forests on a brown ground. Edo period, 1812. Itsukushima Shrine, Hiroshima Prefecture.

Nō Costumes in
the Lucy Truman Aldrich Collection

The Japanese textile collection in the Museum of Art, Rhode Island School of Design, comprises several hundred pieces. These include over one hundred *kesa*, or priests' robes, forty-seven Nō costumes, thirty-eight *kosode*-style garments, four costumes for the court dance (*bugaku*), two *jimbaori* vests, one Kabuki costume, one Ainu robe, and one altar cloth (*uchishiki*). All the Nō costumes, most of the *kesa*, and many of the others were donated by Lucy Truman Aldrich.

The Nō costumes form the core of the collection due to their high quality. Because

most were produced between the early eighteenth and the early nineteenth centuries, they display the special characteristics of Edo-period Nō costumes. The designs and decorative techniques used follow mainstream developments seen in Nō costumes of the mid- to late Edo period, still many of the costumes in the collection deserve special mention for their high technical and/or design standards. Moreover, the condition of the pieces is extremely good, with only a very few showing traces of fading, color change, stains, or other damage. Good handling has been a major factor in their preservation, because for many years Miss Aldrich allowed no one but herself and a very few select members of the Museum staff to handle the costumes. For the same reason these fine robes have remained essentially unknown to the public until now.

A number of the robes have paper wrappers with ink inscriptions and labels such as "Estate of Lord Maeda" or "Estate of Lord Ikeda," indicating that they were once the property of old daimyo families. Since many of the Nō costumes that Miss Aldrich collected were bought through the firm of Yamanaka & Company, it is highly probable that the firm was responsible for these inscriptions and labels. During the Meiji (1868-1912) and Taishō (1912-1926) periods daimyo families and other famous houses sold off paintings, sculptures, and other artifacts at large auctions, where a number were purchased by Yamanaka & Company. The attributions, then, can be taken to be relatively reliable. The robes that have paper wrappers with inscriptions are all extremely fine pieces, and the data appears to suggest a verification of the original owners. Further investigation should provide more information.

An exception may be the paper wrapper around the *nuihaku* with red glossed-weft ground (*nerinuki*) and design of clouds and long-tailed birds (cat. no. 20), which is of thicker paper than the paper wrappers for the other robes and has inscribed on it a number and a description of the costume including technique and design. Two labels with ink inscriptions are attached to the paper, reading "Estate of Lord Maeda part of number 381" and "valuable *nuihaku* number 13," as well as two tabs written in red and reading "*nuihaku* 17." These suggest that the paper wrapper dates from the time when the robe was the property of the Maeda family and that when it was sold, or after it had come into the hands of the antique dealer, additional labels were attached. The piece itself is a *nuihaku* with gold leaf and embroidery cleverly used to fine effect. It demonstrates a high level of perfection in line with its attribution.

The classification of the Nō costumes in the collection shows a preponderance of *kosode*-style garments – seventeen *karaori*, six *nuihaku*, two *surihaku*, and seven *atsuita*. Broad-sleeved *ōsode* include three *kariginu*, four *happi*, three *chōken*, and one *maiginu*. In addition there are two *hangire*, one *koshi-obi*, and one *katsura-obi*, so that the greater portion of the types of Nō costumes are represented, making the collection good research material.

The *karaori* dating from the early eighteenth century are excellent pieces with elegant style

(cat. nos. 1-3); their nearly perfect condition brings out the brilliant color esthetic. Also of note is the *nuihaku* with a design of rounds of chrysanthemums and patrinia flowers over a basket-weave pattern on a black satin ground (cat. no. 18), thought to have been made at the beginning of the eighteenth century. Although the black ground has deteriorated considerably due to the iron mordant used to set the tannin dye, the design of chrysanthemums and patrinia flowers done in colored silk and the basket-weave pattern of stenciled gold-leaf strips is resplendently colorful. The salient feature is the empty space at the left hip area on the back of the garment that gives weight to the right side of the design layout. This type of design construction and the motif of flower roundels were very popular in street-wear *kosode* from the end of the seventeenth century to the beginning of the eighteenth century. This piece is a rare example in which the Nō costume directly reflects *kosode* design. The *nuihaku* of the Aldrich collection date from the eighteenth century, with one exception (cat. no. 23), and exhibit excellent craftsmanship.

One *kariginu* stands out for its pictorial design (cat. no. 31), which covers the entire costume. This large-scale conception is rare, since designs on *kariginu* are generally based on scattered repetitions of a single pattern.

For more details about Miss Aldrich, how she acquired the costumes, and how they came to be donated to this museum, see the essay by Susan Anderson Hay (pp. 10-27).

1. Akira Omote and Shūichi Katō, eds., "*Fūshi kaden*," in *Zeami Zenchiku (The Writings of Zeami and Zenchiku)*, vol. 24 of *Nihon shisō taikei (Anthology of Japanese Thought)*. Tokyo: Iwanami Shōten, 1974, p. 21.

2. Omote and Katō, eds., "*Sarugaku dangi*" ("*Lectures on Sarugaku*"), op. cit., pp. 292-93.

3. Ise Sadayori, *Sōgo Ōzōshi (Writings of Sōgō)*, 1528, in *Gunshoruijū (Collection of Important Writings)*, vol. 22. Tokyo: Zoku-Gunshoruijū Kansei Kai, 1959, p. 582.

4. Although no *kosode* are among them, there are examples of Momoyama-period *kariginu* (fig. 36), *happi*, and *sobatsugi* (fig. 34) of *kinran, ginran, ōdon*, and other weft-patterned weaves at Kasuga Shrine in Gifu Prefecture and at Tenkawa Benzaiten Shrine and Katte Shrine in Nara Prefecture. It is probable that during the Muromachi period the upper classes used imported cloths of fine quality for their *kosode*.

5. Zempō Zōtan, *Hogo uranosho* (*Performance Commentary*), in Akira Omote and Masayoshi Ito, eds., *Komparu kotensho shūsei* (*Collection of Ancient Writings of the Komparu Family*). Tokyo: Wanya Shoten, 1969, pp. 350-62.

6. Shimotsuma Shōshin, *Dōbusho* (*Comments on Nō Plays*), 1596, in Hōsei University Nō Research Center, ed., *Nōgaku shiryō shūsei* (*Collection of Writings on Nō*), vol. 1. Tokyo: Wanya Shoten, 1973, p. 69. The costuming of the play *Bashō* (*The Spirit of the Plantain Tree*) reads as follows: "1. Taiyū [main actor]: white gown. For outer garment: *karaori nuihaku*. Either, undecided." The *karaori* mentioned here refers to the material. It verifies that for outer garments in women's roles, not only the *karaori*, but also *nuihaku* were used, and also that just before the beginning of the Edo period, costuming had a large element of flexibility.

7. This applies primarily to *kosode*-style garments. Broad-sleeved cloaks (*ōsode*) were to a large extent made from imported cloths like *kinran*.

8. A notable exception is a Momoyama-period *nuihaku* in the Tokyo National Museum with a design of bridge planks and irises known as *yatsuhashi*, which refers to an episode in the Heian-period poetic stories, *Tales of Ise*.

9. Seishi Imanaga, "Edo Period Noh Costumes," in *Special Exhibition of Noh and Kyōgen Costumes*. Tokyo: Tokyo National Museum, 1987.

10. Ken Kirihata, "Okayama Art Museum Nō Costumes," in *Okayama Bijutsukan-zo, Ikeda ke denrai nō shōzoku* (*Nō Costumes of the Ikeda Family at the Okayama Art Museum*). Kyoto: Kyoto Shōin, 1986, p. 75.

11. The inclusion of gold thread in a *karaori* of this period is rare, but it is not unimaginable, since gold thread was being used in embroidery of *kosode* of the time, although the techniques and types of gold thread used were different.

12. Ken Kirihata, op. cit., p. 77.

13. One such sumptuary edict from February 1704 reads, "Recently one sees extremely magnificient robes among the Nō costumes, but from now on, with the exception of costumes already in existence, simple, more modest pieces are recommended." (Takayanagi Shinzō, Ishii Rōsuke, ed., *Ōfuregaki kampo shūsei*. Iwanami Library, 1934).

14. Ken Kirihata, op. cit., p. 77.

15. Yoshiko Harada, *Itsukushima jinja no nō shōzoku* (*The Nō Costumes of Itsukushima Shrine*). Kyoto: Kyoto Shōin, 1981, p. 262.

16. Ibid.

On the Occasion of an Exhibition of the Lucy Truman Aldrich Collection of Japanese Costume, 1937

Kojiro Tomita

THE FOLLOWING is excerpted from a lecture by Kojiro Tomita, Curator of Asiatic Art, Museum of Fine Arts, Boston, presented on the occasion of an exhibition of Japanese costume from the Lucy Truman Aldrich Collection at the Museum of Art, Rhode Island School of Design, Providence, on April 29, 1937 (text in the curatorial files of the Museum of Art, Rhode Island School of Design).

...The word *Nō* in Japanese ... may be translated as "accomplishment" or "art in acting," and refers to a form of lyric drama which has been performed in Japan since the latter part of the fourteenth century. A Nō performance consists in the main of singing, posturing, and dancing on the part of the players, with a chorus which remains seated throughout the play, and an orchestra. The passages are partly sung, partly chanted, and partly spoken. Even the spoken part is slightly intoned. Usually a Nō play is based on a legend or an historical event. Very often the religious element predominates, and in general the Nō play embodies some human emotion or a deep spiritual quality. The libretto is written partly in prose and partly in verse. There are about fifteen hundred such librettos known, although only about two hundred are considered standard and included in the repertoire.

... The stage is a raised platform about 18 feet square, open on three sides and provided with a roof supported on four pillars.... a survival from the time when the Nō was performed out of doors.... Projecting diagonally from the back, left-hand corner of the stage... is a narrow, covered gallery on which the actors make their entrances; and at the opposite corner is a small doorway through which the chorus and orchestra come on.... [On] the back wall of the stage... is painted a... pine tree, – this and the bamboos painted on the short wall at the right being the only decoration of the kind sanctioned by tradition.... The peculiar equipment under the stage is noteworthy, that is, a number of large, empty earthern jars suspended from three sticks by means of wire. There are five under the stage proper, two under the orchestra, and three under the gallery. These jars are placed so that the sound of the stamping of feet on the floor and of the music may reverberate. Surrounding the stage on three sides sit the quietly dressed spectators and on the stage itself, along the back and right-hand margin respectively, sit the orchestra of flute and drum players and the chorus with their leader – all in perfect keeping with the serious atmosphere of the occasion. Into these almost austere surroundings come the gorgeously dressed actors... some wearing the skilfully carved wooden masks that may be demanded by their parts, and each carrying a fan decorated with colors and gold.... with every movement or attitude of his body the otherwise gently diffused light is so caught and intensified in the folds of his brilliant dress as to produce rich color-effects which contrast vividly with the other more somber appointments of the play.

In every play there are at least two characters, the *shité* or principal character, and the *waki*, or second; but there are also other minor characters who appear according to the nature of the play. They are the *shitetsuré*, who is subsidiary to the *shité*, the *wakitsuré*, who appears in like relation to the *waki*; and often there are a number of minor personages, including occasionally a child.

The *waki*, perhaps a traveling priest, comes to the stage, explaining as he walks who he is, that is, the role he is taking, and that he is journeying from a certain place to another; then, moving about on the stage, he sings [intones] a passage which notes the scenery which he is passing. In a few minutes he reaches his destination, and ... takes a seat at one corner of the stage. He is followed by the *shité*, the hero or the principal character – a farmer or a fisherman, for example [but in reality a warrior, or a spirit, or a woman of Heian times] – who chants a passage describing the scenery where the play is taking place; or possibly, as he appears on the stage, he may be addressing the *waki* and discussing the scenery with him. In this way the audience is made to visualize the background or stage setting which does not exist in reality. After finishing this conversation, the *shité*, quietly withdraws. The *waki* sings again, perhaps describing the passage of time between the first and second appearances of the hero. When the hero reappears, he has already assumed his true nature and performs the chief role, dancing and narrating his past life in a singing tone. Occasionally the hero and the second engage in a dialogue, and the chorus from time to time sings to interpret the circumstance… while the orchestra throughout emphasizes the singing or chanting. When the hero finishes the dance, with appropriate words he leaves the stage and the other actors follow.

I must make it clear that in the Nō plays only male actors take part. Wherever a female role is required, an actor appears wearing the mask of a woman and dressed appropriately. Masks are a very important part of a performance. Each school of Nō players has its own selection of masks for various plays, and in all there are about 120 varieties of masks, all carved in wood and painted in gesso… No amount of description will give an adequate picture of a Nō performance. It must be seen with one's own eyes…

Happily, the costumes… are so important in themselves as to find admirers like Miss Aldrich who generously allows others to share her own enjoyment of them. Allow me to congratulate the Museum and its friends upon having this splendid collection.

The Catalogue

Nō costumes are classified according to tailoring, patterning techniques, design pattern, and use. Tailoring differences suggest a division into three main groups: garments with broad sleeves open at the cuff (*hirosode*, "broad sleeve," or *ōsode*, "large sleeve"), garments with arm-length box sleeves sewn up at the cuff to leave only a small opening for the wrist (*kosode*, "small sleeve"), and garments worn as pants. In addition there are various accessories, such as waist sashes (*koshi-obi*) and hair bands (*katsura-obi*).

Among the broad-sleeved garments, most of which are descendants of Heian- (794-1185) and Kamakura-period (1185-1336) robes worn by the nobility and military aristocracy, further classification generally depends on tailoring, for each has a definite and characteristic shape with set proportions. In addition, each broad-sleeved type of garment has one or more typical weave structures and one or more typical design layouts. Broad-sleeved garments are worn as the outermost layer, as cloaks or jackets. They include *kariginu, happi, mizugoromo, chōken, maiginu, hitatare,* and *suō.*

Small-sleeved garments, *kosode,* are all of one cut (with slight historical variation), similar to that of today's kimono. *Kosode* were worn as underrobes by the nobility during the Heian period, but emerged during the middle ages to become the basic robe of all classes and both sexes in the Edo period (1615-1868). As they came out from under layers of broad-sleeved robes, these plain white garments grew more and more decorative. *Kosode* are classified by decorative technique. The basic techniques for decorating Nō robes stem from Muromachi- (1336-1573) and Momoyama-period (1568-1615) styles. Pictorial weft-patterned silk robes include the *atsuita, atsuita-karaori,* and *karaori,* which are distinguished from each other by design patterns and use. Softer and more pliable than these are *haku* (white undergarments of lightweight silk); *surihaku* (*haku* decorated with stenciled gold- or silver-leaf patterns); and *nuihaku* with embroidery in addition to stenciled metallic-leaf patterns. The *noshime* is a plain-weave *kosode*-style garment with stripes or checks.

Traditional Japanese pants tend to be full, since they are worn over the basic *kosode*-style garment. Front pleats and a bulge over the backside are typical. The plain-colored "wide mouth" *ōguchi* used in the Nō drama are a direct descendant of the medieval military aristocracy's "pants," while the boldly decorated *hangire* of similar construction were devised specifically for the Nō stage. The pleated *sashinuki* gathered in at the ankles are worn over the *ōguchi* in typical Heian courtier style.

Karaori

A weft-patterned, box-sleeved, *kosode*-style garment with feminine designs, the *karaori* is used mainly as a costume for women's roles, but may also be used by sprites and as an underrobe for young courtier-warriors.

The weave structure consists of a supplementary discontinuous patterning weft (*uamon*) with long floats of soft, glossy silk that has had its natural covering of "gum" removed, woven into a 2/1 twill ground (*ji*) of "unglossed" or natural silk warp and weft. The repeat is large (approximately one-half or the whole width of the cloth squared), and the colors vary with each repeat. An additional pattern layer (*jimon*) may appear between the ground and the supplementary patterning weft floats; the *jimon* is typically of thin strips of gold- or silver-leafed paper tied down by every other warp thread in a 2/1 twill. Although the 2/1 twill worked on a three-harness loom is standard, many weavers today, and some in the Edo period, used more harnesses.

The ground is either a single color or follows typical Muromachi-period design schemes, the most common being alternating blocks (*dangawari*) forming a large checkerboard pattern and created by *ikat*-dyeing the warp into bands of color. The supplementary weft pattern may fit within the individual ground blocks, overlap the borders of the blocks, or ignore them completely. Floral motifs predominate. These are combined with birds, other animals, and objects like fans, shells, poem papers, carts, baskets, and fences. Many of the motifs have their origins in Heian-period decorative designs and thereby evoke a distinctly Japanese sensibility.

A basic garment for women's roles, the *karaori* may be worn either as an inner or as an outer robe, either straight or tucked up. In the first half of a Nō play, when there is little energetic movement and the main character (*shite*) appears as a woman of the locality, the *karaori* is generally draped in *kinagashi* style, pulled snug around the hips and legs, but allowed to form a wide V at the neckline. The front lapels are crossed over closer to the neck when the *karaori* functions as an underrobe. Women when working or traveling and old women wear a *mizugoromo* (cloak) over the *karaori*.

Women deranged from emotional strain and women engaged in physical labor, like rowing, slip off the right sleeve of the *karaori*, allowing it to hang down at the back (*nugisage* style). This exposes the *haku* undergarment. Court ladies in semiformal attire, princesses, and sprites wear broad divided skirts (*ōguchi*) and often have a *karaori* draped over them, tucked up at the waist, as a kind of jacket (*tsuboori* style). A similar tucked-up draping of the *karaori* may be worn directly over a *kosode*-style robe to suggest a court lady's outdoor wear. A courtier-warrior may wear a *karaori* under a *chōken* (cloak) to emphasize his elegant refinement.

I

KARAORI
Edo period, early eighteenth century
Paulownia arabesques and butterflies on a yellow
ground
35.479

On a bright yellow ground, now faded, the discontinuous supplementary-weft design of paulownia arabesques is woven with shades of brown, red, blue, green, purple, and white silk. The butterflies are executed in the same colors with the addition of gold-leafed paper strips. Although the length of the floats is relatively short, the supplementary weft does not give the feeling of being tightly bound, but rather of being soft and pliable. Gold is used only for one part of the body of the butterflies, lending an effective accent to the color scheme.

The design is composed of units of arabesques of paulownia facing in four directions combined with six butterflies. These are repeated from top to bottom, but, perhaps because of the deft color choice for the various parts of the pattern, the design appears to be complex rather than simple. The style of both paulownias and butterflies is commonly found in Nō costumes and *kosode* (street-wear kimono) of the

eighteenth century. This robe is sewn to somewhat small proportions and has a green lining, which is not often seen; it may have been retailored at a later date.

WEAVE STRUCTURE: 1Z2 twill ground, floating pattern of supplementary continuous and discontinuous gold-leafed paper patterning wefts tied in 2Z1 twill over 6 warps, 2, 4, and 6 remain inactive, and supplementary discontinuous silk patterning weft floats.
GROUND: MAIN WARP: Silk, unglossed; slight Z twist, 2 or 1 end; yellow, now faded; 144 per in.
MAIN WEFT: Silk, unglossed; no twist, X ends; yellow, now faded; 84 per in.
FLOATING PATTERN: SUPPLEMENTARY WEFT 1: Gold-leafed paper lamellae; 40 per in.
SUPPLEMENTARY WEFT 2: Silk, glossed; no twist, 3 ends; white, beige, brown, red-brown, orange-red, light orange-red, yellow-green, green, dark blue, blue, light blue, light light blue, purple, light purple, pink; 40 per in.
MEASUREMENTS: CENTER BACK LENGTH: 52 1/4", 132.7 cm.
CENTER BACK TO SLEEVE EDGE: 26", 66.1 cm.

2

KARAORI
Edo period, early eighteenth century
Wisteria with a cypress-fence background pattern
on a ground of alternating blocks of orange-red,
brown, white, and green
35.472

The blocks (*dangawari*) of the ground are formed by
ikat dyeing the warp threads and matching the main
weft threads with red, brown, white, and green.
A background cypress-fence pattern is woven in
continuous and discontinuous supplementary gold-
leafed paper patterning wefts, and a floating pattern
of trailing wisteria woven with discontinuous
supplementary patterning wefts of polychrome silk
and gold-leafed paper strips forms the top layer.

This three-layered construction is thought to
have become popular after the beginning of the
eighteenth century. While the designs of the latter
half of the eighteenth century have the background
and float patterns spilling over the boundaries of the
blocks to form an overall composition, those of the
first half of the eighteenth century rarely have patterns
that cross over the boundaries of the blocks. In this
karaori, the float designs of wisteria are all placed in
the same position relative to each block and are
neatly contained within the blocks.

That the silk of the floating pattern is woven
entirely as weft floats also suggests that this work

belongs to the first half of the eighteenth century.
By the second half of the eighteenth century, the
tendency was to create textural variety by tying some
of the colored discontinuous supplementary threads
of the floating pattern into the fabric using a coarse
twill set up like that of the gold background pattern.
In this robe the float threads have not been tied into
the twill in this manner and retain a loose flow.

WEAVE STRUCTURE: 1Z2 twill ground, *ikat* dyed;
background pattern of supplementary continuous and
discontinuous gold-leafed paper patterning wefts tied in
2Z1 twill over 6 warps, 2, 4, and 6 remain inactive; floating
pattern of supplementary discontinuous gold-leafed paper
patterning wefts tied in 2Z1 twill over 6 warps, 2, 4, and 6
remain inactive, and supplementary discontinuous silk
patterning weft floats.

GROUND: MAIN WARP: Silk, unglossed; no twist,
2 ends; originally ivory, *ikat*-dyed brown, orange-red,
green; 152 per in.
MAIN WEFT: Silk, unglossed; no twist, X ends; ivory,
brown, orange-red, green; 80 per in.

BACKGROUND PATTERN: SUPPLEMENTARY
WEFT 1: Gold-leafed paper lamellae; 40 per in.

FLOATING PATTERN: SUPPLEMENTARY WEFT 1:
Gold-leafed paper lamellae; 40 per in.
SUPPLEMENTARY WEFT 2: Silk, glossed; no twist,
X ends; white, beige, orange-red, light orange-red, yellow-
green, green, dark blue, blue, light blue, purple, pink; 40
per in.

MEASUREMENTS: CENTER BACK LENGTH:
55", 139.7 cm.
CENTER BACK TO SLEEVE EDGE: 24 3/4", 62.9 cm.

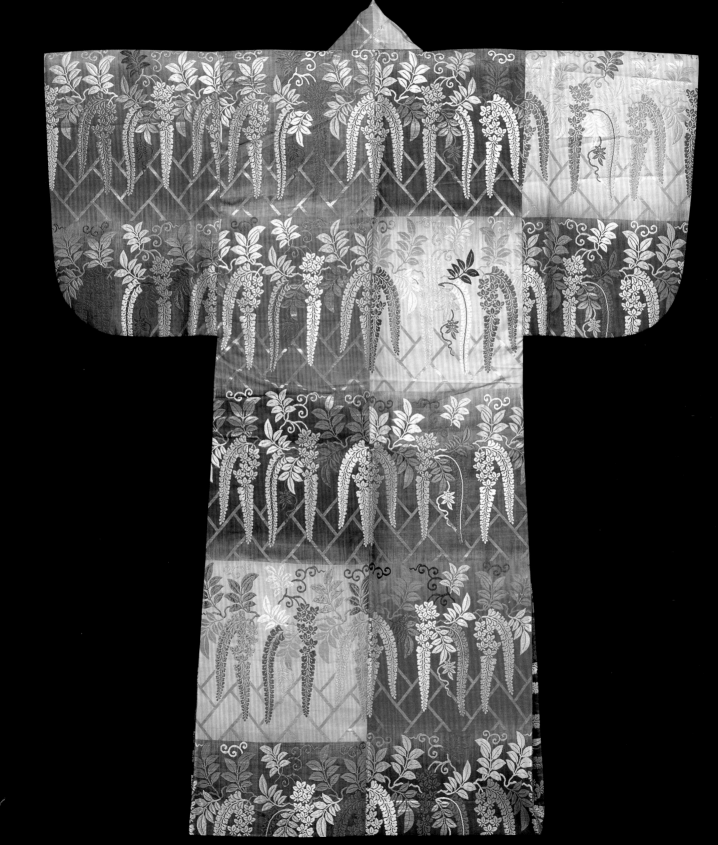

3

KARAORI
Edo period, first half of the eighteenth century
Standing chrysanthemums on a light-blue ground
35.486

The standing-chrysanthemum design is woven with
weft floats of white, yellow, yellow-green, green,
purple, shades of red-orange, and blue on a light-blue
ground. The patterning weft threads lie loosely in
long floats over the ground, making the design full
and soft. The pattern unit – two types of chrysanthemum sprigs lined up – is reversed alternately as
one proceeds from top to bottom of the robe. The
chrysanthemum flowers are depicted not just from
the front, but also from the side and back, as well as
in the bud. The buds are delicately bent, and the
depiction of the leaves is also extremely naturalistic.

While the buds and leaves are green, the flowers
have shades of orange-red as a base, with other colors
used to balance these off nicely. Since the green of
the stems and leaves blends into the light-blue ground,
the chrysanthemum flowers appear all the more to
float above them.

The looseness of the weave and absence of
gold in the design composed entirely of colored
supplementary wefts are reminiscent of *karaori* made
in the seventeenth century. The design, however,

being neither sparse nor scattered, but spread over
the garment evenly, suggests a date in the first half of
the eighteenth century.

WEAVE STRUCTURE: 1Z2 twill ground; floating
pattern of supplementary discontinuous silk patterning
weft floats.
GROUND: MAIN WARP: Silk, unglossed; Z twist, 1 or
2 ends; light blue; 144 per in.
MAIN WEFT: Silk, unglossed; no twist, X ends; light
blue; 72 per in.
FLOATING PATTERN: SUPPLEMENTARY WEFT 1:
Silk, glossed; no twist, X ends; white, dark brown, orange-
red, gold, yellow, yellow-green, green, dark blue, blue, light
blue, purple, pink; 39 per in.
MEASUREMENTS: CENTER BACK LENGTH:
44 3/4", 113.7 cm.
CENTER BACK TO SLEEVE EDGE: 23 1/4", 59.1 cm.

been worked out at the time the draft sketch was drawn (see pp. 37-40), before the weaving began. The large-scale pattern formation and the *koshigawari* construction indicate that the piece required considerable coordinated planning.

The color choices also create a very balanced effect. For example, the colors in the float patterns have been correlated to the colors in the ground blocks, so that on the blue ground there is frequent use of red or red-related colors, while conversely on the red and brown blocks blue-related colors appear comparatively often. Still, among the various unit patterns there is no single color scheme.

The bamboo fence and peonies appearing as the float design are rendered very naturalistically, and one feels little of the stiffness characteristic of weaving patterns. In particular the peonies are rendered pictorially, cleverly shown as if the viewer were looking down at the flowers, leaves, and buds from above, giving a painterly effect. The technical virtuosity and good condition of this piece make it one of the outstanding *karaori* owned by the Museum.

In the minds of the Japanese, peonies are associated with China and a Chinese sense of feminine beauty, in contrast to Japanese femininity symbolized by the cherry blossom. Thus for roles of Chinese beauties, like the renowned beauty Yang Kuei-fei (Yōkihi), mistress of the Tang emperor Hsuan Tsung in the Nō play *Yōkihi*, robes like this one with peonies in their pattern are often chosen, although there is no set rule concerning this.

4

KARAORI
Edo period, eighteenth century
Peonies and bamboo fences with a background pattern of interlocked seven jewels on a ground of alternating blocks of orange-red, blue, and brown
35.481

The alternating block (*dangawari*) pattern of the ground is created by *ikat* dyeing the warp threads and matching the ground wefts accordingly with the orange-red, blue, and brown. Incorporated in the design is a blue band that spans the waist area both front and back, making a waist-change (*koshigawari*) pattern. The design has a background pattern of interlocked seven jewels (*shippō*) in gold-leafed paper wefts. Over this is a floating pattern of a bamboo fence with peony flowers woven in silk and gold supplementary wefts. Both background pattern and float pattern spill over the borders of the blocks in this mid-Edo period *karaori*, unlike Momoyama and early Edo-period *karaori*, in which the motifs are contained within the blocks (cat. no. 2).

The general conception, based on a repetition of unit patterns, conforms to *karaori* construction, but the back view of the main body and sleeves and the front view of the main body, sleeves, front overlap panels, and collar have been sewn to form a single large continuous design, which would have to have

WEAVE STRUCTURE: 1Z2 twill ground, *ikat* dyed; background pattern of supplementary continuous gold-leafed paper patterning wefts tied in 2Z1 twill over 6 warps, 2, 4, and 6 remain inactive; floating pattern of supplementary continuous gold-leafed paper patterning wefts tied in 2Z1 twill over 6 warps, 2, 4, and 6 remain inactive, and supplementary discontinuous silk patterning weft floats tied at intervals (*toji*).

GROUND: MAIN WARP: Silk, unglossed; Z twist, X ends; *ikat* dyed brown, orange-red, blue; 160 per in. MAIN WEFT: Silk, unglossed; no twist, X ends; brown, orange-red, blue; 76 per in.

BACKGROUND PATTERN: SUPPLEMENTARY WEFT 1: Gold-leafed paper lamellae; 38 per in.

FLOATING PATTERN: SUPPLEMENTARY WEFT 1: Gold-leafed paper lamellae; 38 per in.

SUPPLEMENTARY WEFT 2: Silk, unglossed; no twist, X ends; white, brown, orange-red, light orange-red, yellow-green, green, dark blue, blue, light blue, light light-blue, purple, pink; 36 per in.

MEASUREMENTS: CENTER BACK LENGTH: 57", 144.8 cm.
CENTER BACK TO SLEEVE EDGE: 27 1/2", 69.9 cm.

5

KARAORI
Edo period, eighteenth century
Flower roundels and scattered cherry blossoms with a background pattern of broken lattice on a brown ground
35.488

On a dark-brown ground, a background pattern of broken lattice is woven in gold-leafed paper wefts. Over this in polychrome silk patterning weft floats and gold-leafed paper wefts tied in "coarse" twill is a floating pattern of flower roundels containing peonies, irises, balloon flowers, and scattered cherry blossoms. The flower roundels form units of peony/iris and peony/balloon flower alternating left and right from shoulder to hem. The cherry blossoms lie scattered, filling up the open space between roundels.

Flower roundels were a popular pattern for *kosode* (street-wear kimono) of the late seventeenth and early eighteenth centuries and are seen frequently not only on extant garments, but also in sample books for *kosode* design (*hinagatabon*) and in ukiyo-e paintings and prints. The conservatism of Nō costumes makes it likely that a certain time lapse occurred before the fashionable patterns for *kosode* were incorporated into Nō costume styles (see p. 53). Furthermore, the time lapse was greater for robes with woven decoration, like the *karaori*, than for those with surface decoration, like the *nuihaku*, which shared many decorative techniques with *kosode*,

because for the *karaori*, the pattern would have had to have been recast into a format suited to weaving.

Be that as it may, the pattern seen in this robe gives a feeling of flow and youthful vitality. The float threads are soft and full; the gold has a subdued luster; and the color scheme of the flowers is refined. The robe is elegant and beautiful, appropriate for the role of a young woman in a Nō play set in spring or summer.

WEAVE STRUCTURE: 1Z2 twill ground; background pattern of supplementary continuous gold-leafed paper patterning wefts tied in 2Z1 twill over 6 warps, 2, 4, and 6 remain inactive; floating pattern of supplementary discontinuous gold-leafed paper patterning wefts tied in 2Z1 twill over 6 warps, 2, 4, and 6 remain inactive, and supplementary discontinuous silk patterning weft floats.

GROUND: MAIN WARP: Silk, unglossed; Z twist, 2 or 1 end; brown; 152 per in.
MAIN WEFT: Silk, unglossed; no twist, X ends; brown; 84 per in.

BACKGROUND PATTERN: SUPPLEMENTARY WEFT 1: Gold-leafed paper lamellae; 43 per in.

FLOATING PATTERN: SUPPLEMENTARY WEFT 1: Gold-leafed paper lamellae; 43 per in.
SUPPLEMENTARY WEFT 2: Silk, glossed; no twist, X ends; white, red-brown, light red-brown, orange-red, light orange-red, yellow, yellow-green, green, dark blue, blue, light blue, light light-blue, purple, pink; 43 per in.

MEASUREMENTS: CENTER BACK LENGTH: 58 ¼", 148 cm.
CENTER BACK TO SLEEVE EDGE: 25 ¾", 65.5 cm.

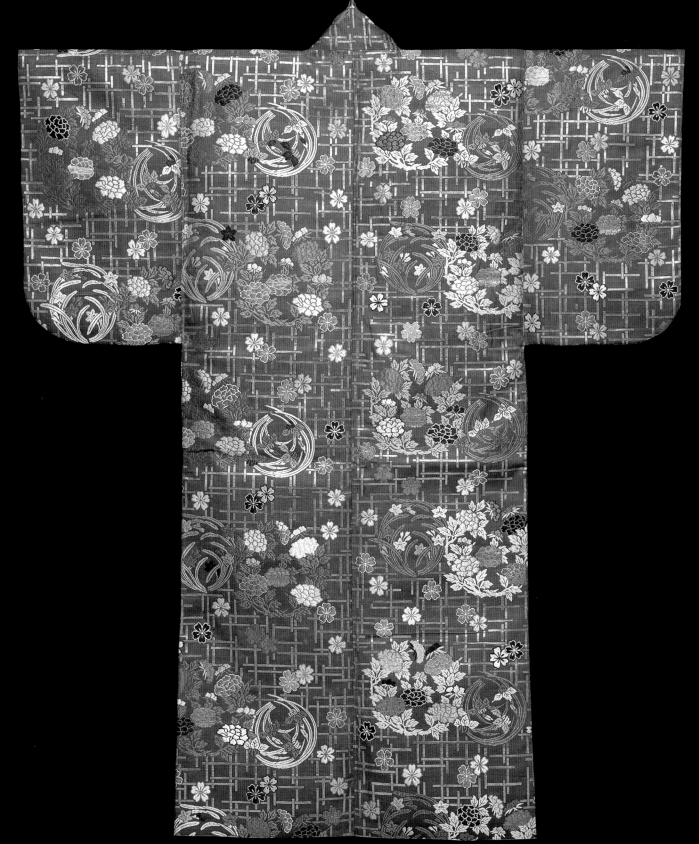

6

KARAORI
Edo period, second half of the eighteenth century
Weeping cherry branches with a key-fret lozenge
background pattern on a ground of alternating
blocks of light blue, brown, and orange-red
35.489

This *karaori* is characterized by its layered design
construction. The ground consists of large, alternating,
ikat-dyed blocks (*dangawari*) of light blue, brown,
and orange-red. An overall background pattern of
key-fret lozenges (*sayagata*) is woven in with supplementary gold-leafed paper patterning wefts, and over
this is a floating pattern of branches of weeping
cherries woven with discontinuous supplementary
patterning wefts of colored silk floss. The bold color
scheme of the alternating blocks is held together by
the uniform gold background pattern; the floating
pattern adds delicate color variation, creating a
three-dimensional impression, for while the cherry
branches are a single shade of green, the flowers,
woven in many hues, seem to float above them.
Although no two similarly placed cherry flowers are
rendered in the same colors, varied shades of the
same color and related colors have been placed close
to each other, creating a sense of repose within
magnificence. The cherry branch float design spills
over the borders of the blocks, a characteristic of

designs of the latter half of the eighteenth century.
    The cherry motif makes this robe suitable for
a Nō play set in the spring, such as *Yuya*, in which the
mistress of the lord Taira no Munemori dances for
him under the cherry blossoms at the temple of
Kiyomizu in Kyoto. The use of red places the robe in
the category of those "with color" (*iroiri*), appropriate for roles of young women.

WEAVE STRUCTURE: 1Z2 twill ground, *ikat* dyed;
background pattern of supplementary continuous gold-
leafed paper patterning wefts tied in 2Z1 twill over 6 warps,
2, 4, and 6 remain inactive; floating pattern of supplementary
discontinuous silk patterning weft floats tied at intervals
(*toji*).

GROUND: MAIN WARP: Silk, unglossed; no twist,
2 ends; *ikat* dyed brown, orange-red, light blue; 152 per in.
MAIN WEFT: Silk, unglossed; no twist, X ends; brown,
orange-red, light blue; 80 per in.

BACKGROUND PATTERN: SUPPLEMENTARY
WEFT 1: Gold-leafed paper lamellae; 40 per in.

FLOATING PATTERN: SUPPLEMENTARY WEFT 1:
Silk, glossed; no twist, X ends; white, light red-brown,
orange-red, light orange-red, yellow, yellow-green, green,
dark blue, blue, light blue, light light-blue, purple, pink;
40 per in.

MEASUREMENTS: CENTER BACK LENGTH:
52", 132.1 cm.
CENTER BACK TO SLEEVE EDGE: 24 3/4", 63 cm.

Karaori with design of chrysanthemums and running water on a red ground. Edo period, eighteenth century. Tokyo National Museum.

7

KARAORI
Edo period, second half of the eighteenth century
Chrysanthemum sprigs and fans with a background pattern of running water on an orange-red ground
35.484

A design of flowing water is woven in gold on an orange-red ground. Over this is scattered a design of fans with sprigs of chrysanthemums laid over them, woven with polychrome silk and gold-leafed paper patterning wefts. Between two types of chrysanthemum-laden fan-patterns lies a half-open fan. The three motifs together form a long, large pattern unit. In the context of other *karaori* made after the late mid-Edo period, many of which have designs dense with multiple repeats of small pattern units, this large-scale repeat stands out. The design is refreshing, and the weft floats, since they are uniformly short, avoid a feeling of tightness.

The motif of running water combined with chrysanthemums originated in a Chinese legend, "*Kikusui*," "Chrysanthemum Water." The water of this river is sweet, since it gathers from the dew trickling off the chrysanthemums on the mountain wayside. It is said that if one drinks this water one will never grow old. The Nō plays of *Kiku Jidō* (*Chrysanthemum Lad*) and *Makura Jidō* (*Pillow Lad*) center around attempts to obtain this elixir of long life. As a decorative motif for textiles, lacquer ware, and pottery, one finds many examples of chrysanthemum flowers floating in running water, and occasionally, as here, whole chrysanthemum sprigs are shown. This pattern is noteworthy also because of the accompanying fans. The motif of scattered fans by themselves is common and can be seen in the *karaori* with fans over weeping willows (cat. no. 14) and the *chōken* with fans (cat. no. 26) as well.

The Tokyo National Museum has a garment with orange-red ground, very similar gold running-water pattern, and scattered chrysanthemums accompanied by numerous leaves (at left). Other similar examples abound, many with naturalistic chrysanthemum flowers shown not only frontally, but also from the side and as buds.

WEAVE STRUCTURE: 1Z2 twill ground; background pattern of supplementary discontinuous gold-leafed paper patterning wefts tied in 2Z1 twill over 6 warps, 2, 4, and 6 remain inactive; floating pattern of supplementary discontinuous gold-leafed paper and silk patterning wefts tied in 2Z1 twill over 6 warps, 2, 4, and 6 remain inactive, and supplementary discontinuous silk patterning weft floats.

GROUND: MAIN WARP: Silk, unglossed; Z twist, 2 ends; orange-red; 152 per in.

MAIN WEFT: Silk, unglossed; no twist, X ends; orange-red; 84 per in.

BACKGROUND PATTERN: SUPPLEMENTARY WEFT 1: Gold-leafed paper lamellae; 40 per in.

FLOATING PATTERN: SUPPLEMENTARY WEFT 1: Gold-leafed paper lamellae; 40 per in.

SUPPLEMENTARY WEFT 2: Silk, unglossed; no twist, X ends; white, brown, orange-red, yellow, yellow-green, green, dark blue, blue, light blue, light light-blue, pink; 40 per in.

SUPPLEMENTARY WEFT 3: Silk, glossed; no twist, X ends; white, brown, orange-red, light orange-red, yellow, yellow-green, green, dark blue, light blue, light light-blue, purple, pink; 40 per in.

MEASUREMENTS: CENTER BACK LENGTH: 57 ½", 146.1 cm.
CENTER BACK TO SLEEVE EDGE: 25 ½", 64.8 cm.

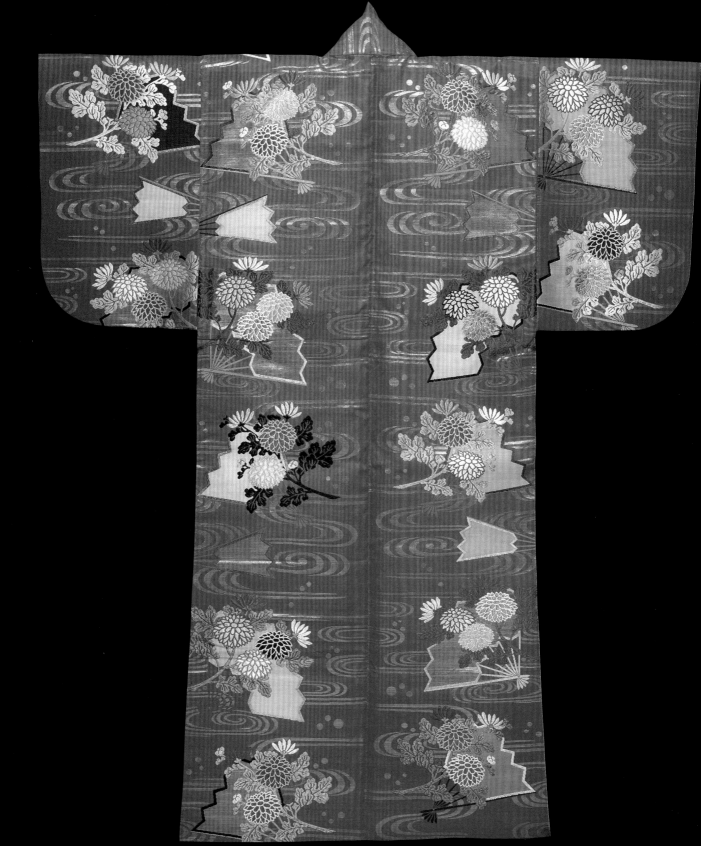

of each motif, despite the stylization and somewhat stiff portrayal, comes to life as a result of the placement of the patterns, so that the garment as a whole gives a pictorial effect.

This robe was probably produced late in the eighteenth century or early in the nineteenth, since there is very little blank space between motifs and the glitter of the gold is strong.

WEAVE STRUCTURE: 1Z2 twill ground; background pattern of supplementary continuous gold-leafed paper patterning wefts tied in 2Z1 twill over 6 warps, 2, 4, and 6 remain inactive; floating pattern of discontinuous gold-leafed paper patterning wefts tied in 2Z1 twill over 6 warps, 2, 4, and 6 remain inactive, and supplementary discontinuous silk patterning weft floats.

GROUND: MAIN WARP: Silk, unglossed; no twist, 2 ends; ivory; 144 per in.

MAIN WEFT: Silk, unglossed; no twist, X ends; ivory; 80 per in.

BACKGROUND PATTERN: SUPPLEMENTARY WEFT 1: Gold-leafed paper lamellae; 37 per in.

FLOATING PATTERN: SUPPLEMENTARY WEFT 1: Gold-leafed paper lamellae. 40 per in.

SUPPLEMENTARY WEFT 2: Silk, glossed; no twist, 3 ends; white, ivory, red-brown, light red-brown, orange-red, light orange-red, yellow-green, green, dark blue, blue, light blue, light light-blue, purple, pink; 40 per in.

MEASUREMENTS: CENTER BACK LENGTH: 58″, 147.4 cm.
CENTER BACK TO SLEEVE EDGE: 28″, 71.2 cm.

8

KARAORI
Edo period, late eighteenth century to early nineteenth century
Chrysanthemums with a background pattern of bamboo fences on an ivory ground
35.474

On an ivory ground a rough bamboo fence (*magaki*), woven with continuous gold-leafed paper patterning wefts, crisscrosses the garment as a background pattern. Standing chrysanthemums form a floating pattern rendered bountifully in light and dark shades of orange-red, blue, green, white, purple, and brown, as well as spots of gold-leafed paper for some flowers. A mature color control lends this robe a special grace.

The chrysanthemums are rendered so that on a single stem one sees buds together with blossoms in front, side, and back views. Three flower stems together with the fence form a single pattern unit the width of a panel, and the unit is mirror reversed for each repeat, producing a zigzag in the fence in each of the four main panels of the robe. On the left and right main panels of the back of the garment, the pattern unit is slightly adjusted so that the fence also forms a zigzag over both panels. The painterly style

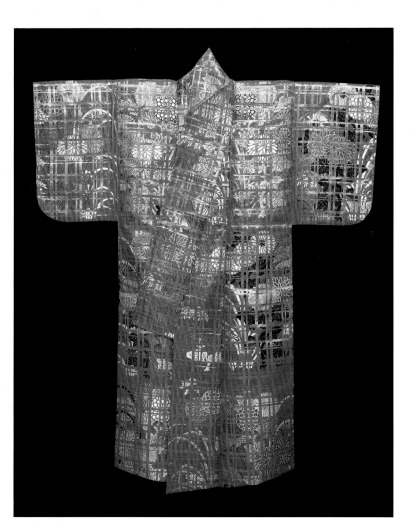

senting the design as if one were viewing a garden through the slats of a fence makes a strong impression on the viewer and is one of the great attractions of this robe. By veiling the chrysanthemums and pampas grasses with the lattice, the somewhat stylized rendering appears natural, and at the same time an autumnal atmosphere is expressed.

Although it is tailored to somewhat small proportions, the state of preservation is good and the robe beautiful. (For comparative robes, see p. 43.) The use of red in the robe categorizes it as *iroiri* ("with color"). This robe would be appropriate for any number of Nō plays that are about young women and take place in the autumn. A good example is *Nonomiya* (*The Shrine in the Fields*), a play based on the eleventh-century novel *The Tale of Genji*. In the play, the ghost of Lady Rokujō relates how her neglectful lover, the Shining Prince Genji, on hearing that she had retired to a forlorn shrine in the fields, pushed his way through dried undergrowth to visit her for the last time.

WEAVE STRUCTURE: 1Z2 twill ground; background pattern of supplementary continuous and discontinuous gold-leafed paper patterning wefts tied in 2Z1 twill over 6 warps, 2, 4, and 6 remain inactive; floating pattern of supplementary discontinuous silk patterning weft floats.

GROUND: MAIN WARP: Silk, unglossed; Z twist, 2 ends; orange-red; 140 per in.

MAIN WEFT: Silk, unglossed; no twist, X ends; orange-red; 80 per in.

BACKGROUND PATTERN: SUPPLEMENTARY WEFT 1: Gold-leafed paper lamellae; 38 per in.

FLOATING PATTERN: SUPPLEMENTARY WEFT 1: Silk, glossed; no twist, X ends; white, brown, brown-red, orange-red, light orange-red, yellow, yellow-green, green, dark blue, blue, light blue, light light-blue, purple, pink; 40 per in.

MEASUREMENTS: CENTER BACK LENGTH: 54 ½", 138.4 cm.

CENTER BACK TO SLEEVE EDGE: 25 ¼", 128.3 cm.

9

KARAORI
Edo period, late eighteenth century to early nineteenth century
Pampas grass and chrysanthemums with lattice fence on an orange-red ground
35.478

This robe has thick and thin lattice in gold-leafed paper lamellae covering sprays of chrysanthemums and pampas grass woven in polychrome silk weft floats on a red ground. It demonstrates well the characteristics of *karaori* made after the late mid-Edo period, for the rendering of both the chrysanthemums and the pampas grasses is somewhat stiff and formalized, and the design motifs are crowded together, leaving little blank space. The outstanding characteristic of this robe, however, is that the lattice appears not as a background pattern, but rather overlies the chrysanthemums and pampas grasses. Commonly, when a naturalistic motif such as autumn grasses is combined with a geometric motif like lattice, the latter becomes the background pattern and the former a floating pattern on the surface, but in this piece the reverse is true. The unique idea of repre-

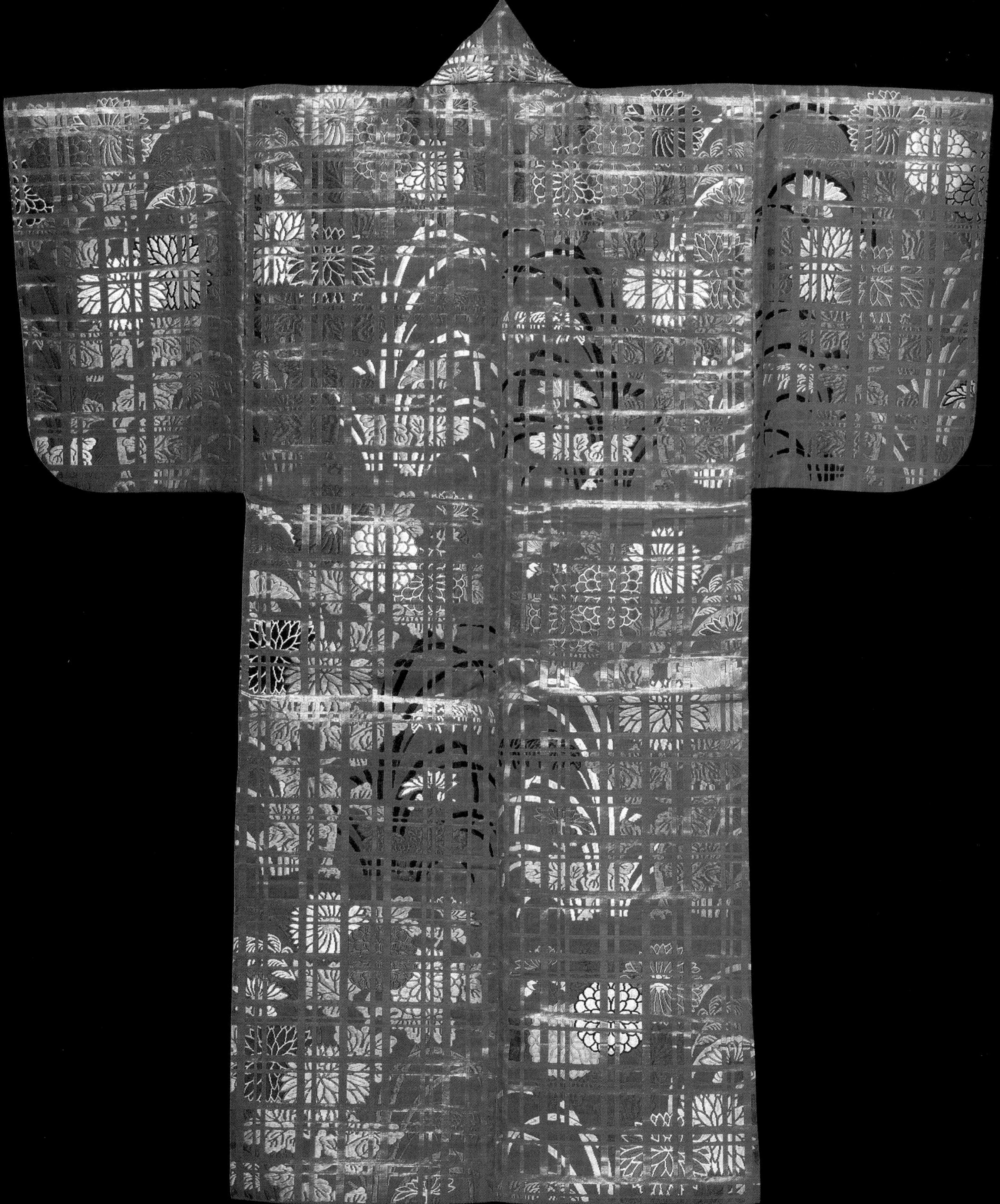

10

KARAORI
Edo period, late eighteenth century to early
nineteenth century
Egrets and reeds with a background pattern of
running water on an orange-red ground
35.485

Running water is rendered in gold-leafed paper wefts
on an orange-red ground, and the egrets and reeds in
polychrome silk thread. The sense of relative weight
and three-dimensionality is deftly expressed by
textural control of the floating pattern done with
discontinuous supplementary wefts. The reeds
growing out of the running water are composed of
weft floats, while the egrets lightly flying above them
have been worked into the "coarse" ground twill.

The design is extremely pictorial. The pattern
unit is of reeds in running water with two egrets
about to take flight and two egrets about to land, an
image that derives from painting, where it appears
frequently. The lines of the running water are variously
thick or thin and have a rhythmical feel to their
movement.

Garments like this with red in the ground or
pattern are known as *iroiri* ("with color"), and are
worn for young women's roles.

WEAVE STRUCTURE: 1Z2 twill ground; background
pattern of supplementary discontinuous gold-leafed paper
patterning wefts tied in 2Z1 twill over 6 warps, 2, 4, and 6
remain inactive; floating pattern of supplementary discontinuous silk patterning wefts tied in 2Z1 twill over 6 warps,
2, 4, and 6 remain inactive, and supplementary discontinuous silk patterning weft floats.
GROUND: MAIN WARP: Silk, unglossed; Z twist, 2
ends; orange-red; 152 per in.
MAIN WEFT: Silk, unglossed; no twist, X ends; orange-red; 84 per in.
BACKGROUND PATTERN: SUPPLEMENTARY
WEFT 1: Gold-leafed paper lamellae; 40 per in.
FLOATING PATTERN: SUPPLEMENTARY WEFT 1:
Silk, glossed; no twist, X ends; white, brown, yellow; 40 per
in.
SUPPLEMENTARY WEFT 2: Silk, glossed; no twist,
X ends; white, yellow, yellow-green, green, dark blue, blue,
light blue, light light-blue, purple, pink; 40 per in.
MEASUREMENTS: CENTER BACK LENGTH:
56 ½", 143.5 cm.
CENTER BACK TO SLEEVE EDGE: 25 ½", 64.8 cm.

I I

KARAORI
Edo period, early nineteenth century
Young pines and snow-laden bamboo on an orange-
red ground
35.483

On an orange-red ground young pines and snow-
laden bamboo are rendered in silk floats of green,
yellow-green, purple, light purple, blues, orange-red,
yellow, and white with a few gold-leafed paper patterning wefts. The floats are extremely short and the
tension of the threads strong.

In design, this *karaori* is composed of a repetition of short units that have the width of the material
as their longer side, making them wider than they are
tall. The young pines and snow-laden bamboo appear
to have been scattered over the whole robe without
leaving any empty areas. The lack of breathing space
between the motifs and the lack of free flow in the
design expression are characteristics shared by other
nineteenth-century *karaori*.

The Metropolitan Museum of Art, New York,
owns another *karaori* with exactly the same colors
and design, likewise sewn to a small size, suggesting
that the New York and Providence examples are
products of the same workshop at about the same
period.

The orange-red ground and small size of the

garment suggest that it was used for a role played by
a child actor. The motifs set the play in winter, for
the evergreen pine is poetically associated with
winter and long life. Moreover, pine, bamboo, and
plum are traditionally grouped together as congratulatory symbols and are integral to New Year
celebrations.

WEAVE STRUCTURE: 1Z2 twill ground; floating
pattern of supplementary discontinuous gold-leafed paper
patterning wefts tied in 2Z1 twill over 6 warps, 2, 4, and 6
remain inactive, and supplementary discontinuous silk
patterning weft floats tied at intervals (*toji*).
GROUND: MAIN WARP: Silk, unglossed; Z twist,
2 ends; orange-red; 160 per in.
MAIN WEFT: Silk, unglossed; no twist, X ends; orange-
red; 84 per in.
FLOATING PATTERN: SUPPLEMENTARY WEFT 1:
Gold-leafed paper lamellae; 36 per in.
SUPPLEMENTARY WEFT 2: Silk, glossed; no twist,
X ends; white, brown, orange-red, yellow, yellow-green,
green, blue, light blue, purple, light purple; 38 per in.
MEASUREMENTS: CENTER BACK LENGTH:
47 ¾", 121.3 cm.
CENTER BACK TO SLEEVE EDGE: 24 ¼", 61.6 cm.

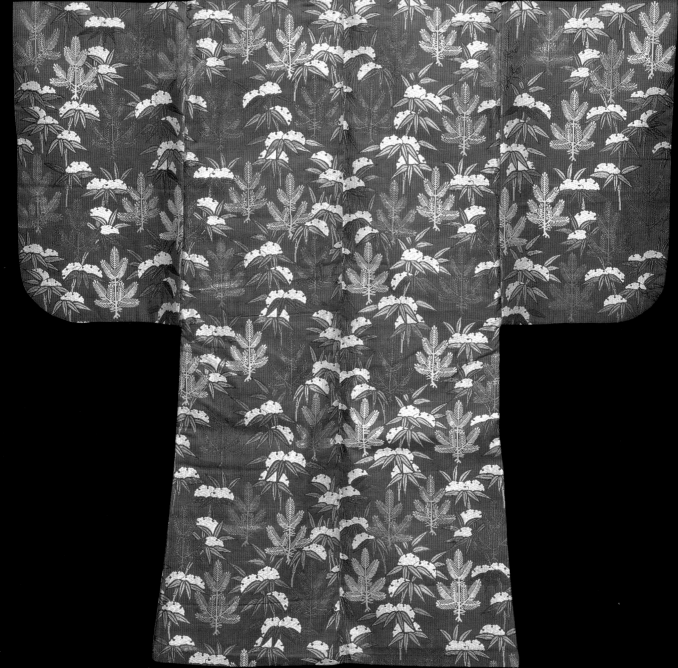

12

KARAORI
Edo period, early nineteenth century
Chrysanthemum sprays on a red ground
35.487

The chrysanthemum sprays, woven in gold-leafed paper lamellae and polychrome silk patterning wefts, appear as if they had been scattered on the red ground. The design composition has pattern units of delicately intermeshed chrysanthemums repeated above and below, leaving essentially no blank space. Although this design format of filling in all the empty spaces with motifs is seen frequently in *karaori* made since the second half of the eighteenth century, this pattern is so dense that it appears to choke, indicating that the robe was made in the nineteenth century.

The colors used for the flowers, leaves, and buds show detailed variation, but not necessarily to the advantage of the work as a piece of art, since the pattern is so crowded that the colors interfere with each other, leaving an impression of over-complexity and oppressiveness.

WEAVE STRUCTURE: 1Z2 twill ground; floating pattern of supplementary discontinuous gold-leafed paper patterning wefts that double back at the edges of each motif and are tied in 2Z1 twill over 6 warps, 2, 4, and 6 remain inactive,

and supplementary discontinuous silk patterning weft floats tied at intervals (*toji*).

GROUND: MAIN WARP: Silk, unglossed; Z twist, 2 ends; orange-red; 148 per in.
MAIN WEFT: Silk, unglossed; no twist, X ends; orange-red; 80 per in.

FLOATING PATTERN: SUPPLEMENTARY WEFT 1: Gold-leafed paper lamellae; 40 per in.
SUPPLEMENTARY WEFT 2: Silk, glossed; no twist, X ends; white, orange-red, light orange-red, gold, yellow, yellow-green, dark green, green, dark blue, blue, light blue, light light-blue, purple, pink; 40 per in.

MEASUREMENTS: CENTER BACK LENGTH: 59 ¾", 151.8 cm.
CENTER BACK TO SLEEVE EDGE: 27 ⅛", 69 cm.

13

KARAORI
Edo period, first half of the nineteenth century
Chrysanthemums and morning glories on a ground
of alternating blocks of pale blue and ivory
35.482

Over *ikat*-dyed alternating blocks (*dangawari*) of
pale blue and ivory are woven large, dense patterns
of chrysanthemums and morning glories in gold-leafed
paper and polychrome silk patterning wefts. The
design disregards the block boundaries, and little
blank space is left between motif elements, characteristics of late Edo-period *karaori*. As in cat. no. 8,
the chrysanthemum flowers combine front and back
views, but the expression is entirely formalized and
the sense of reality thin. The morning glories appear
flat, despite an attempt to render them naturalistically.
The above all suggest that the robe was made during
the first half of the nineteenth century.

WEAVE STRUCTURE: 1Z2 twill ground, *ikat* dyed;
floating pattern of supplementary discontinuous gold-leafed
paper patterning wefts tied in 2Z1 twill over 6 warps, 2, 4,
and 6 remain inactive, and supplementary discontinuous
silk patterning weft floats tied at intervals (*toji*).
GROUND: MAIN WARP: Silk, unglossed; Z twist,
2 ends; *ikat* dyed light blue, ivory; 154 per in.

MAIN WEFT: Silk, unglossed; no twist, X ends; light
blue, ivory; 82 per in.
FLOATING PATTERN: SUPPLEMENTARY WEFT 1:
Gold-leafed paper lamellae; 38 per in.
SUPPLEMENTARY WEFT 2: Silk, glossed; no twist,
X ends; white, orange-red, light red-orange, yellow, yellow-
green, green, dark blue, blue, light blue, purple, pink;
42 per in.

MEASUREMENTS: CENTER BACK LENGTH:
46 ¾", 118.8 cm.
CENTER BACK TO SLEEVE EDGE: 21 ½", 54.7 cm.

Nuihaku with split body (*katamigawari*) design of scattered fans over pampas grass on one side and clematis arabesques on a dark-brown ground on the other. Momoyama period, seventeenth century. Tokyo National Museum.

14

KARAORI
Edo period, early nineteenth century
Fan papers with a background pattern of weeping willows on an orange-red ground
35.480

At first sight this *karaori* with orange-red ground and design of fan papers and weeping willows done in polychrome silk and gold-leafed paper patterning wefts appears unimpressive, but a number of interesting techniques can be found in the execution of the design.

Although the design looks as if it is simply a unit repeat, it has some subtle and sophisticated variations. For example, the way in which the fan papers are scattered over the main back panels differs on the left and right side. This design construction is known as *katamigawari*, or "split body" design. Furthermore, this is reversed at the shoulder line for the front of the garment. The switching of the pattern at the shoulder line, in the middle of a single length of cloth, indicates clearly that the design of the robe was minutely calculated before the actual weaving.

Split-body design (*katamigawari*), designs of alternating blocks (*dangawari*), and pattern changes at shoulder and hem (*katasuso*; cat. no. 22), are frequently seen in Momoyama-period *kosode* (street-wear kimono) and Nō costumes, but all three essentially disappeared from use in *kosode* design after the beginning of the Edo period. On the other hand,

with its emphasis on tradition, the Nō costume continued to exhibit the old styles, primarily *dangawari*, incorporating some changes in the form. *Katamigawari* and *katasuso* are rarer in Edo-period Nō costume design, where generally the dynamic contrasts inherent in these designs have been softened, as is the case here.

While the Momoyama-period *katamigawari* display strongly opposing designs on the right and left of the center back, as in the *nuihaku* shown at left with fans on one side and clematis arabesques on the other, in this robe the *katamigawari* style is employed as a supplementary device to keep the design from appearing overly simple without seriously altering the uniformity of the pattern. Although from a strictly formal design standpoint this robe is a typical *katamigawari*, the design affirms that Momoyama-period *katamigawari* and late-Edo *katamigawari* like this one are fundamentally different.

The effective differentiation of use of the colored weft floats and the wefts bound into the ground is noteworthy. On this robe, the willows that cover the whole garment are depicted with float wefts. The fan papers are flatly rendered in the ground twill weave, but the naturalistically elaborated peonies, chrysanthemums, pines, and bamboo represented on the fan sheets are woven in weft floats that seem to rise out of their background. This pictorial, naturalistic rendering as well as the textural control whereby part of the floating design is flattened by being tied into fabric with a "coarse" twill date this robe to the late Edo period.

A very similar robe is in the collection of the Hayashibara Art Museum, Okayama Prefecture (see fig. 24).

WEAVE STRUCTURE: 1Z2 twill ground; background pattern of supplementary discontinuous silk patterning weft floats; floating pattern of supplementary discontinuous silk and gold-leafed paper patterning wefts tied in 2Z1 twill over 6 warps, 2, 4, and 6 remain inactive, and supplementary discontinuous silk patterning weft floats.
GROUND: MAIN WARP: Silk, unglossed; Z twist, 2 ends; orange-red; 152 per in.
MAIN WEFT: Silk, unglossed; no twist, X ends; orange-red; 80 per in.
BACKGROUND PATTERN: SUPPLEMENTARY WEFT 1: Silk, glossed; no twist, X ends; yellow-green, light light-blue; 40 per in.
FLOATING PATTERN: SUPPLEMENTARY WEFT 1: Gold-leafed paper lamellae; 40 per in.
SUPPLEMENTARY WEFT 2: Silk, glossed; no twist, X ends; white, brown, orange-red, light orange-red, yellow, yellow-green, green, dark blue, blue, light blue, purple, light purple, pink; 40 per in.
SUPPLEMENTARY WEFT 3: Silk, glossed; no twist, X ends; white, orange-red, light orange-red, yellow, green, blue, light blue, light light-blue, purple; 38 per in.
MEASUREMENTS: CENTER BACK LENGTH: 59", 149.9 cm.
CENTER BACK TO SLEEVE EDGE: 25 1/4", 64.2 cm.

15

KARAORI
Edo period, first half of the nineteenth century
Scattered Chinese fans and pine bark diamonds on a
gold background
35.460

On a gold background, the design is brought out
with weft threads of purple, orange-red, yellow,
green, sky blue, medium blue, and white. The colored
wefts of the background within the Chinese fans
(*uchiwa*) and pine-bark diamonds (*matsukawa-bishi*)
are held down to form a stiff ground out of which
rise plum branches, irises, bush clovers, mandarin
ducks, and netted plovers done in polychrome weft
floats. Since the colored weft is comparatively thick
and the length of the float short, the float designs
bulge up. Both these characteristics appear in *karaori*
made after the end of the eighteenth century and
thus suggest a date for the piece.

This type of framed pattern was extremely
popular in the Genroku era (1688-1703) for everyday
kosode (street-wear kimono) styles. One can see
examples of similar designs not only on *kosode*
preserved from the period, but also in fashion books
like the *hinagatabon* (woodblock printed books of
kimono designs that guided wholesalers and pur-
chasers) and ukiyo-e prints of beautiful women
(*bijin-ga*), which have minutely realistic depictions of
clothing. However, in general, the patterns used for
Nō costumes, which tend to adhere strictly to traditional forms, show a certain time lapse before they

Paper wrapper

begin to be influenced by *kosode* fashions. Once a
pattern is incorporated into the repertoire of Nō
costumes, it most often remains for a long time. As a
result it is impossible to decide the date of a costume
purely from the form of its patterns. Although this
garment displays a pattern that reflects late seventeenth-century and early eighteenth-century fashion,
technical considerations and the stylization of the
pattern place it in the nineteenth century.

According to the inscription on the wrapping
paper of this costume, it belonged to the Hirase family, a wealthy banking family during the Meiji period
(1868-1912). In 1886, 1903, and 1906, R. Kamenosuke
Hirase sold much of his private art collection, including costumes and tea-ceremony objects, at auction.
Yamanaka & Company purchased many pieces at
these auctions; this robe and the *kariginu* cat. no. 31
were probably among them, since the firm was the
source for the Aldrich Nō costumes.

WEAVE STRUCTURE: 1Z2 twill ground; background
pattern of supplementary continuous gold-leafed paper
patterning wefts; floating pattern of supplementary discontinuous silk patterning wefts tied in 2Z1 twill over 6 warps,
2, 4, and 6 remain inactive, and supplementary discontinuous
silk patterning weft floats.
GROUND: MAIN WARP: Silk, unglossed; no twist, 2
ends; orange-red; 156 per in.
MAIN WEFT: Silk, unglossed; no twist, 2 ends; orange-
red; 80 per in.
BACKGROUND PATTERN: SUPPLEMENTARY
WEFT 1: Gold-leafed paper lamellae; 42 per in.
FLOATING PATTERN: SUPPLEMENTARY WEFT 1:
Silk, glossed; no twist, X ends; white, beige, orange-red,
light orange-red, yellow-green, green, blue, light blue,
purple, pink; 42 per in.
SUPPLEMENTARY WEFT 2: Silk, glossed; no twist,
X ends; white, beige, light brown, orange-red, yellow-green,
green, dark blue, light blue, light light-blue, purple; 42
per in.
MEASUREMENTS: CENTER BACK LENGTH:
57 3/4", 146.7 cm.
CENTER BACK TO SLEEVE EDGE: 27 1/2", 69.9 cm.

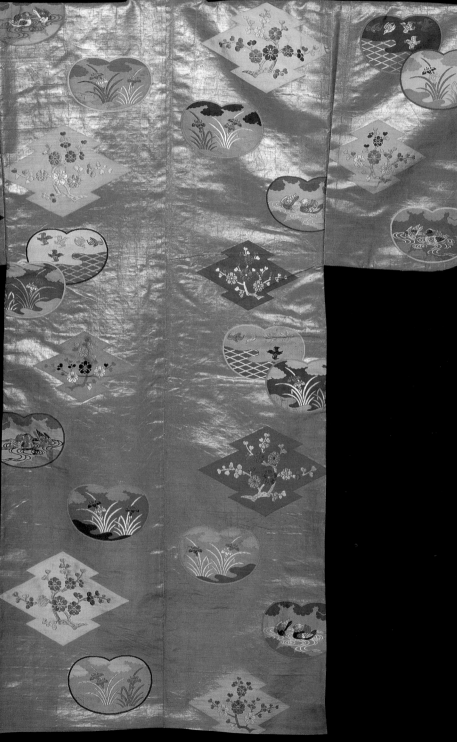

16

KARAORI
Edo period, first half of the nineteenth century
Bamboo grass with a background pattern of pampas
grass on a ground of alternating blocks of orange-
red, green, and white
35.473

Ikat-dyed alternating blocks (*dangawari*) of orange-
red, green, and white form the ground of this three-
layered design. The background pattern, woven in
gold-leafed paper wefts, depicts pampas grasses bent
by a breeze so that they bow their heads to form a
stylized wave pattern (*seigaiha*). The floating pattern
of similarly stylized bamboo grass woven in discontinuous supplementary silk wefts of white, blues,
purple, orange-red, yellow-green, green, yellow, and
brown has a decorative impact set against the gold
metallic background.

Both the pampas grass and the bamboo grass
spill over the edges of each block without being
shackled by them. The bamboo grass, distributed in
two groups of alternating zigzag triangles running
from top to bottom in each block, creates the traditional mountain-path motif, seen in the Momoyama
karaori with design of chrysanthemums and paulownia
flowers over a mountain-path background pattern
owned by the Mōri Museum, Yamaguchi Prefecture
(fig. 47). The free placement of the background and
float patterns, not bound by the blocks, as well as the
stylized expression of the motifs typifies *karaori*
made at the end of the eighteenth century and the
beginning of the nineteenth century. In addition, the
tailoring, which gives a slight flare to the bottom of
the robe, is a characteristic seen frequently in Nō
costumes made after the beginning of the nineteenth
century.

The use of orange-red categorizes this robe as
"with color" (*iroiri*), suitable for a young woman's
role, but the season is undefined.

WEAVE STRUCTURE: 1Z2 twill ground, *ikat* dyed;
background pattern of supplementary continuous and
discontinuous gold-leafed paper patterning wefts tied in
2Z1 twill over 6 warps, 2, 4, and 6 remain inactive; floating
pattern of supplementary discontinuous silk patterning
weft floats.

GROUND: MAIN WARP: Silk, unglossed; no twist,
2 ends; ivory, *ikat* dyed orange-red, green; 152 per in.
MAIN WEFT: Silk, unglossed; no twist, 2 ends; ivory,
orange-red, green; 76 per in.

BACKGROUND PATTERN: SUPPLEMENTARY
WEFT 1: Gold-leafed paper lamellae; 40 per in.

FLOATING PATTERN: SUPPLEMENTARY WEFT 1:
Silk, glossed; no twist, X ends; white, brown, orange-red,
light orange-red, gold, yellow, yellow-green, green, dark
blue, blue, light blue, light light-blue, purple; 40 per in.

MEASUREMENTS: CENTER BACK LENGTH:
57 3/4", 146.7 cm.
CENTER BACK TO SLEEVE EDGE: 25 1/4", 64.2 cm.

17

KARAORI
Edo period, nineteenth century
Scattered roundels of chrysanthemums, clouds, and
flowers containing three swirling comma-shapes
with a background pattern of rushing water on an
orange-red ground
35.490

In this *karaori*, great care has been taken in the choice
of appropriate weaving techniques to best portray
each pattern. The background pattern of rushing
white waves is neatly woven into the structure of the
fabric with continuous and discontinuous supplementary silk patterning wefts using a "coarse" twill.
The floating design of flowers and clouds, executed
in polychrome discontinuous supplementary weft
floats and gold-leafed paper patterning wefts, appears
to be bobbing up and down on the wild waves of an
overflowing river.

    The robe shares the characteristics of other
nineteenth-century pieces. Technically, these include
the short length of the floats and the strong luster of
the gold, while the design is stylized and lacks flow.
Moreover, the motif of a flower with swirling comma-
shapes (*tomoe*) at its center surrounded by half
chrysanthemums and clouds appears on other
karaori and *atsuita* of the period (cat. nos. 38, 40).
Finally, the flare in the construction of the bottom of
the robe marks this garment as being made in the
nineteenth century or later.

WEAVE STRUCTURE: 1Z2 twill ground; background
pattern of supplementary continuous and discontinuous
silk patterning wefts tied in 2Z1 twill over 6 warps, 2, 4, and
6 remain inactive; floating pattern of supplementary discontinuous gold-leafed paper patterning wefts tied in 2Z1 twill
over 6 warps, 2, 4, and 6 remain inactive, and supplementary
discontinuous silk patterning weft floats tied at intervals
(*toji*).

GROUND: MAIN WARP: Silk, unglossed; Z twist, 2
ends; orange-red; 148 per in.

MAIN WEFT: Silk, unglossed; no twist, 2 ends; orange-
red; 80 per in.

BACKGROUND PATTERN: SUPPLEMENTARY
WEFT 1: Silk, glossed; no twist, X ends; white; 40 per in.

FLOATING PATTERN: SUPPLEMENTARY WEFT 1:
Gold-leafed paper lamellae; 40 per in.

SUPPLEMENTARY WEFT 2: Silk, glossed; no twist,
X ends; white, brown, orange-red, light orange-red, yellow-
green, green, blue, light blue, purple, pink; 40 per in.

MEASUREMENTS: CENTER BACK LENGTH:
55 1/4", 140.3 cm.

CENTER BACK TO SLEEVE EDGE: 25 1/4", 64.2 cm.

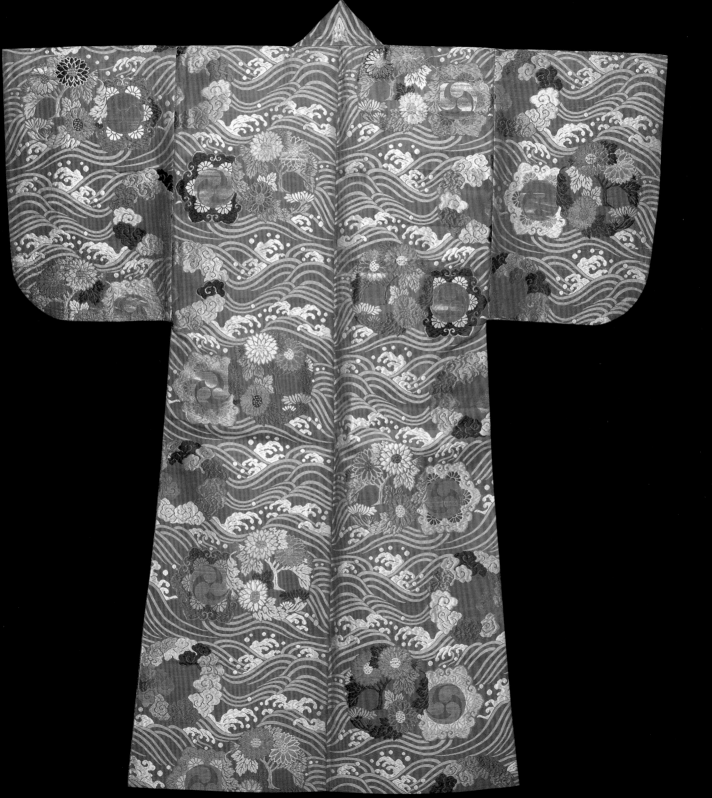

Nuihaku

outer cloak has been stolen. *Nuihaku* may be worn *koshimaki*-style under a *chōken* (cloak) by young women in male attire and entertainers and under *tsuboori*-draped *karaori* by court ladies (see p. 68). Under a *mizugoromo* (cloak) it is the garb of a shrine priestess. Although *nuihaku* are primarily worn as an outer robe for women's roles, they can be worn as an underrobe (*kitsuke*) for certain male roles: emperors, young warriors, young courtiers, young lay priests, and acolytes.

Nuihaku are pliant garments with both embroidery and gold- or silver-leaf stenciled decorations, tailored in box-sleeve *kosode* style. They are usually lined with plain silk in red, purple, or white.

The base fabric of Edo-period and later *nuihaku* is usually satin weave (*shusu*) or figured satin (*rinzu*), but may also be *nerinuki*, a thin plain-weave silk, like Momoyama-period *nuihaku*. All *nuihaku* have stenciled metallic-leaf decoration and are further embellished with embroidery. The metallic patterns are formed by applying an adhesive through a stencil onto the stretched fabric. Gold or silver leaf is then placed on the adhesive and pressed down gently with cotton. When the metallic leaf has been securely affixed, the excess is brushed off with a feather.

The majority of *nuihaku* are a single color; white, red, dark blue, yellow, golden brown, purple, and black are common. Some *nuihaku* have broad horizontal bands of various colors, and others have alternating blocks of color (*dangawari*) similar to *karaori*. Solid gold-leaf backgrounds are known as *dōhaku* and considered particularly aristocratic and elegant.

Embroidery may cover the entire garment or may be confined to the lower area with only sparse patterns above. Early *nuihaku* are often entirely covered with decoration, but those of the Edo period tend to be less densely covered with more naturalistic pictorial patterns, such as birds, flowers, or fans. Scattered roundels on a dark ground are considered appropriate for roles of jealous women.

Nuihaku may either be draped like standard kimono, crossed tightly at the neck, or folded down at the waist so the sleeves hang over the hips in *koshimaki* ("waist wrap") style. As such they form part of a two-piece suit worn by jealous spirits, as in *Dōjōji*, or in *Hagoromo* (*The Feather Cloak*) by the moon maiden whose

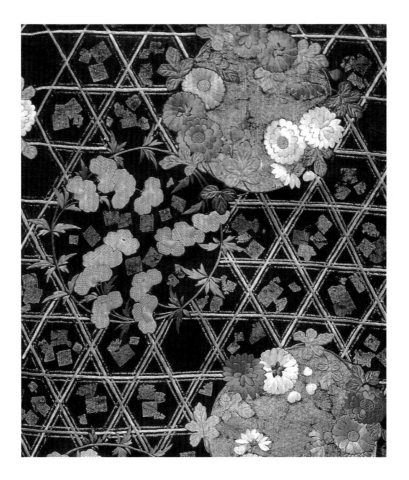

18

NUIHAKU
Edo period, first half of the eighteenth century
Chrysanthemum and patrinia-flower wreaths with a
woven-basket pattern on a black ground
35.461

On a black figured satin ground with woven-basket
(*kagome*) interlace in stenciled gold leaf are elegantly
scattered chrysanthemum and patrinia-flower wreaths
embroidered in silk dyed in subdued colors. The
black, dyed with tannin, enlivens the brightness of
the other colors, but due probably to the iron mordant
used in the dyeing process, the ground cloth is
deteriorating in spots.

The gold leaf has been applied in a variety of
ways: pasted flat in the flower wreaths, as strips to
form the basket-weave pattern, and in scattered
flakes in the background. The finely executed embroidery likewise includes numerous techniques to
supplement the basic satin stitch (*hira-nui*) and stem
stitch (*matoi-nui*, also called *matsui-nui*). The finishing touches lend the piece a stylish grace.

The overall design features an undecorated
area over the left hip in the back view (see cat. no.
25), seen in several *kosode* (street-wear kimono)
designs of the first half of the eighteenth century.
Also, the flower-wreath motif was fashionable from

the end of the seventeenth century to the early eighteenth century. Since the techniques used to make
nuihaku are similar to those used in street-wear
kosode, nuihaku seem to have been directly influenced
by fashion trends more than other Nō costumes.
This piece is a typical example and can probably be
dated to the period when these designs were fashionable, the early mid-Edo period.

A dark-ground *nuihaku* such as this might be
worn by a middle-aged woman, like a mother in search
of her lost child, as in the Nō play *Sumidagawa (The
Sumida River)*, although the embroidered red flowers
would also make it suitable for young women's roles.

WEAVE STRUCTURE: 4/1 warp-faced satin ground
self-patterned in 1Z2 weft-faced twill; stenciled gold leaf;
silk-floss embroidery.

GROUND: MAIN WARP: Silk, unglossed; Z2S; black;
232 per in.

MAIN WEFT: Silk, unglossed; no twist, X ends; black;
104 per in.

EMBROIDERY: THREAD: Silk, glossed; no twist,
X ends; white, orange-red, gold, yellow, dark green, light
green.

STITCHES: Satin stitch (*hira-nui*), stem stitch (*matoi-nui*),
overlay (*norikake-nui*).

MEASUREMENTS: CENTER BACK LENGTH:
57 ½", 146.1 cm.

CENTER BACK TO SLEEVE EDGE: 25 ½", 64.8 cm.

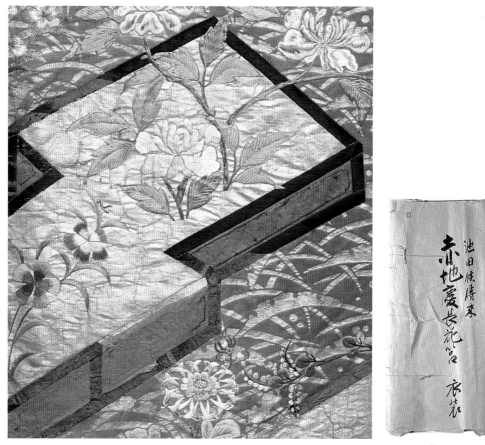

19

NUIHAKU
Edo period, mid-eighteenth century
Peonies and autumn flowers in flower beds with
snow-laden grasses on an orange-red ground
35.458

On a ground of red satin with gold stenciled patterns
of grasses laden with snow are embroidered many-
colored camelias, peonies, and autumn flowers
planted in flower beds. Gold leaf fills the inside of
the flower-bed boxes, bringing out the brilliance of
the exquisitely detailed embroidery. Satin stitch
(*hira-nui*), stem stitch (*matoi-nui*), shading (*bokashi-
nui*), and overlay (*norikake-nui*) are used to render
the autumn flowers, which include two types of chrysanthemums, bush clovers, bell flowers, pinks,
peonies, and camelias.

One of the two types of chrysanthemums has
very thin petals; it is a strain imported to Japan from
China during the Hōei era (1704-1711), after which
it became very popular in Japan. The free use of
intricate and varied techniques to create realistic
designs in embroidery appears after the mid-eighteenth
century. Both of these facts suggest that this work
represents a typical *nuihaku* of the mid- to late
eighteenth century. With the exception of the frames
of the flower boxes, the state of preservation of this
piece is extremely good. Even among the many

beautiful *nuihaku* at the Museum, it stands out by its
magnificence.

On the paper wrapper is inked, "Estate of
Lord Ikeda," implying that this *nuihaku* belonged to
the Ikeda family, who were daimyo in the Bishū area
(present-day Okayama Prefecture) during the Edo
period (see cat. nos. 22, 24, 36, and 37).

Peeping out from under a *chōken* dancing
cloak (see p. 123) and topped by a courtier's cap, a
nuihaku with red completes the costume of a woman
dressed in her lover's robe, such as the patient, loving
wife in *Izutsu* (*Well-Curb*) or the spirit of the iris in
Kakitsubata (*The Iris*). It is also worn by the sisters
Pine Wind and Autumn Rain in *Matsukaze* (*Pine
Wind*).

WEAVE STRUCTURE: 7/1 warp-faced satin ground;
stenciled gold leaf; silk-floss embroidery.

GROUND: MAIN WARP: Silk, unglossed; Z2S;
orange-red; 224 per in.

MAIN WEFT: Silk, glossed; no twist, X ends; 84 per in.

EMBROIDERY: THREAD: Silk, glossed; no twist,
X ends; beige, brown-black, brown, red-brown, orange-red,
yellow-green, green, dark blue, light blue, pink.

STITCHES: Satin stitch (*hira-nui*), satin stitch over paper,
shading in satin stitch (*bokashi-nui*), stem stitch (*matoi-nui*),
overlay (*norikake-nui*).

MEASUREMENTS: CENTER BACK LENGTH:
58 ¼", 148 cm.

CENTER BACK TO SLEEVE EDGE: 28 ½", 72.5 cm.

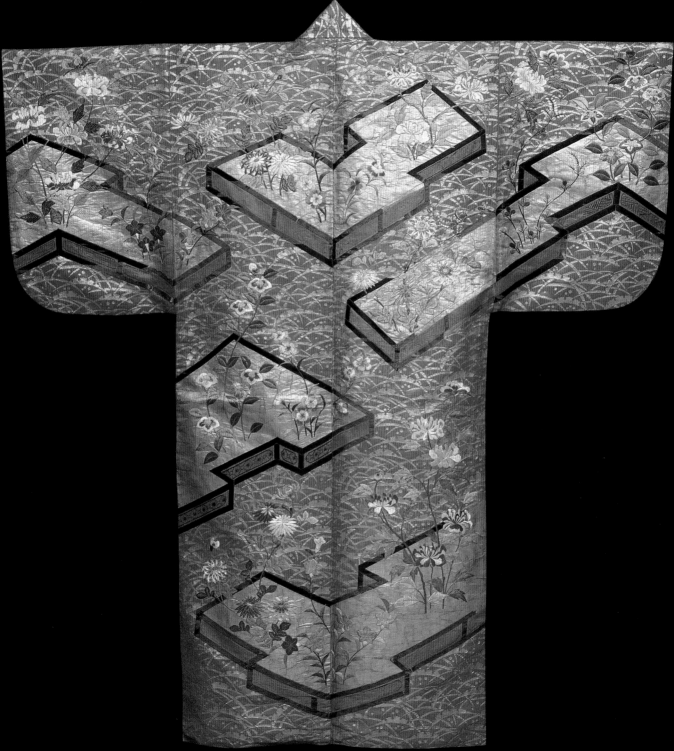

The back of the *nuihaku* displays eight long-tailed birds in various forms, with necks and tails gently curved so that they trace a graceful arc. The form of the long-tailed birds, similar to that seen on late eighteenth-century *karaori*, suggests a date for the Museum's robe. The egrets on cat. no. 10, although not long-tailed, show the same grace and variety, and both can be compared to the long-tailed birds in the *nuihaku*, cat. no. 22.

The robe has a paper wrapper inscribed in ink, "Estate of Lord Maeda," suggesting that this *nuihaku* belonged originally to the Maeda family, who were daimyo in Kaga (now Ishikawa Prefecture) during the Edo period (see p. 60).

The orange-red ground classifies this *nuihaku* as "with color" (*iroiri*), suited to roles of young women.

20

NUIHAKU
Edo period, mid-eighteenth century
Long-tailed birds and clouds on an orange-red ground
35.457

Gold clouds float over a bright ground of "glossed-weft" plain-weave silk (*nerinuki*), in which the warp retains its natural gum for strength, but the weft is degummed ("glossed") to bring out the luster and softness of the silk. Among the clouds fly long-tailed birds in elegant polychrome silk embroidery.

The decorative element is enhanced by alternating flat gold clouds and clouds scattered with such things as gold flakes, gold powder, and gold rice stalks. The birds are realistically portrayed, their breasts given bulk by the use of long and short satin stitch (*sashi-nui*), while in contrast the wing feathers are ingeniously textured by using graduated colors in the embroidery (*bokashi-nui*) and the tail feathers are represented naturalistically with overlay stitch (*norikake-nui*). The number of colors used for the embroidery thread is comparatively small, which lends repose to the design.

WEAVE STRUCTURE: Unbalanced plain-weave ground; stenciled gold leaf; silk-floss embroidery.

GROUND: MAIN WARP: Silk, unglossed; no twist, 2 ends; gold; 108 per in.

MAIN WEFT: Silk, glossed; no twist, X ends; orange-red; 108 per in.

EMBROIDERY: THREAD 1: Silk, glossed; no twist, X ends; white, grey, light grey, brown, orange-red, light orange-red, dark blue, blue, light blue, purple, black.

THREAD 2: Silk, unglossed; S; dark blue.

STITCHES: Long and short satin stitch (*sashi-nui*), shading in satin stitch (*bokashi-nui*), stem stitch (*matoi-nui*), overlay (*norikake-nui*).

MEASUREMENTS: CENTER BACK LENGTH: 56", 142.3 cm.

CENTER BACK TO SLEEVE EDGE: 26 3/4", 68 cm.

The beauty of the work lies in the faithful transposition of keen observation into the design.

The flower diamonds in tortoise-shell hexagon links and the paulownia motif are traditional patterns seen in textiles of the Momoyama and early Edo period, such as the seventeenth-century *atsuita* with design of flower wreaths over a hexagon pattern on a dark-green ground at the Tokyo National Museum (fig. 53). In the Providence robe, however, the breaking up of the linked hexagons with patches of plain color and the difference in tone of the paulownia motifs from those of the earlier period suggest a later date of production.

This *nuihaku* could be worn in waist wrap (*koshimaki*) style for any variety of roles. Only the bottom area would be visible when worn under a traveling cloak (*mizugoromo*) for roles of lower-class women, like the boat woman in the first part of the play *Tamakazura* (*Lady Tamakazura*), or the crazed mother looking for her lost child in *Sumidagawa* (*The Sumida River*), or when worn under a dancing cloak (*chōken*; cat. nos. 26-28) for a similar role in the play *Hyakuman*. A little more of the *nuihaku* would show when worn under another type of dancing cloak (*maiginu*; cat. no. 29), as it would be by the wife of the drum player in *Fuji Taiko* (*Fuji's Drum*), when she dances to the beat of her dead husband's drum.

WEAVE STRUCTURE: 1/7 warp-faced satin ground self-patterned in 2Z1 twill; stenciled gold leaf; silk-floss embroidery.

GROUND: MAIN WARP: Silk, unglossed; Z2S; blue; 384 per in.

MAIN WEFT: Silk, unglossed; no twist, 2 ends; blue; 160 per in.

EMBROIDERY: THREAD 1: Silk, glossed; no twist, 3 ends; white, light brown, orange-red, light orange-red, gold, yellow-green, green, light blue, purple.

THREAD 2: Silk, unglossed; Z-plied cable of 2 Z2S; white, orange-red, gold, yellow-green, green.

STITCHES: Satin stitch (*hira-nui*), stem stitch (*matoi-nui*), couching (*koma-nui*), overlay (*norikake-nui*).

MEASUREMENTS: CENTER BACK LENGTH: 60", 152 cm.

CENTER BACK TO SLEEVE EDGE: 27 ½", 70 cm.

2 1

NUIHAKU

Edo period, second half of the eighteenth century
Sprigs of chrysanthemums and paulownia with tortoise-shell hexagons enclosing flowers on a blue ground
35.468

On a blue figured satin ground scattered with plum blossoms among cracked ice is a gold-leaf stencil pattern of linked hexagons (*kikkō*) containing flower diamonds. Scattered through the broken links of the hexagons spurt sprigs of chrysanthemums and paulownia blossoms rendered in embroidery.

The chrysanthemums and paulownias are embroidered in the standard satin stitch (*hira-nui*), stem stitch (*matoi-nui*), and a variant of couching, overlay stitch (*norikake-nui*), as well as with two special techniques. In the chrysanthemum petals the satin stitch is held down with threads applied in twill weave style, and the paulownia motif is outlined by couching stitch (*koma-nui*) using a twisted colored thread. The effect is of fine work with well-aligned needle holes.

The rendering of the design is realistic. The flowers and leaves of the chrysanthemums – shown not just from the front view, but also from side and back views – are faithfully reproduced, as well as the layering of flower over flower or leaves over flowers.

Paper wrapper

and Nō costumes (see p. 51). It is generally called either *katasuso* ("shoulder and hem") or *koshiake* ("open waist"). This work exhibits a brilliant color sense in the rendering of an old design using refined techniques of the mid-Edo period. The long-tailed birds appear in various forms, and despite its extreme delicacy and stylization, the design is free-flowing. The robe is in a good state of preservation, which enhances its refined appeal.

On the paper wrapper is inked an inscription reading, "Estate of Lord Ikeda," indicating that like cat. nos. 19, 24, 36, and 37, it was once in the collection of the Ikeda family of Bishū (now Okayama Prefecture), who were daimyo during the Edo period.

22

NUIHAKU
Edo period, second half of the eighteenth century
Long-tailed birds with linked good-luck diamonds
on a white ground
35.470

On a white ground of plain-weave silk in which the warp is unglossed silk (with the natural gum left on to preserve its strength) and the weft is glossed silk (making it soft and shiny), the shoulder and hem area are dyed dark brown with a jagged, pine-bark-lozenge (*matsukawa-bishi*) edge. Within the brown area, luxuriant diamond links in gold leaf form a background pattern, except in scattered brown roundels in which long-tailed birds have been embroidered. Embroidery also borders the pine-bark-lozenge edge. The design is exquisitely rendered; the gold leaf is delicately and uniformly applied and the embroidery employs a variety of stitches, such as satin stitch (*hira-nui*), long and short satin stitch (*sashi-nui*), stem stitch (*matoi-nui*), graduated shading (*bokashi-nui*), and overlay (*norikake-nui*). It demonstrates the characteristics of eighteenth century embroidery in its especially well-arranged needle holes and its soft pliability.

The overall design in which shoulder and hem are decorated, but the waist area left blank, is traditional and is seen in Momoyama-period garments

WEAVE STRUCTURE: Unbalanced plain-weave ground, hand-painted; stenciled gold leaf; silk-floss embroidery.
GROUND: MAIN WARP: Silk, unglossed; no twist, 2–3 ends; white; 112 per in.
MAIN WEFT: Silk, glossed; no twist, X ends; white; 92 per in.
EMBROIDERY: THREAD: Silk, glossed; no twist, X ends; white, beige, brown, orange-red, light orange-red, gold, yellow, yellow-green, green, violet.
STITCHES: Satin stitch (*hira-nui*), long and short satin stitch (*sashi-nui*), shading in satin stitch (*bokashi-nui*), stem stitch (*matoi-nui*), overlay (*norikake-nui*).
MEASUREMENTS: CENTER BACK LENGTH: 64″, 161 cm.
CENTER BACK TO SLEEVE EDGE: 24 ½″, 62 cm.

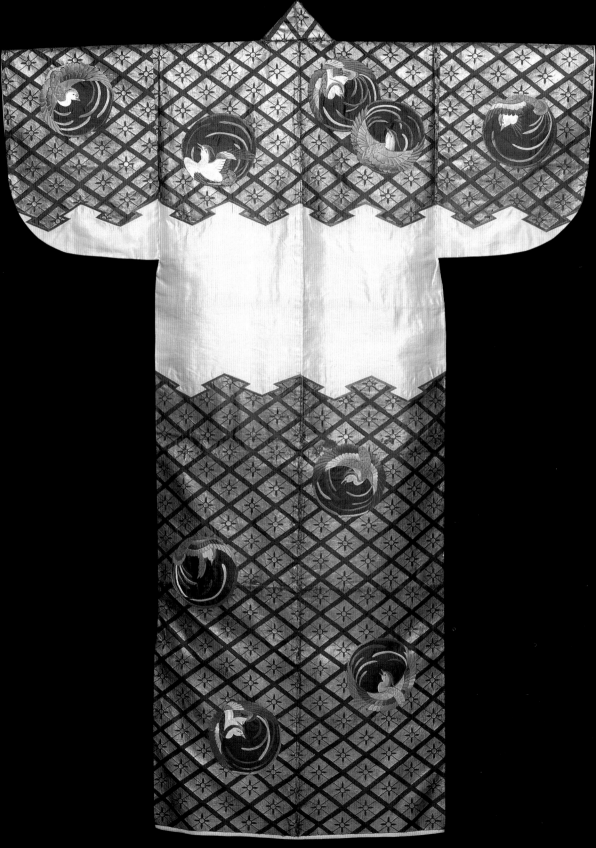

2 3

NUIHAKU
Edo to Meiji period, late nineteenth to early twentieth century
Bamboo blinds and cherry and mandarin-orange branches on a tan ground
55.380

Embroidered on a tan satin ground are bamboo blinds with cherry and mandarin-orange branches. The embroidery is done in gold and tightly twisted colored threads, using couching (*koma-nui*) as the basic stitch and supplementing it with stem stitch (*matoi-nui*), satin stitch (*hira-nui*), long and short satin stitch (*sashi-nui*), and French knots (*sagara-nui*). The tone of the red thread holding down the gold threads, the strong brilliance of the latter, and the twisted paper string (*koyori*) placed under the embroidery threads to add volume are all characteristics seen frequently in embroidery from the late Edo period and later.

Other special embroidery techniques have also been employed. The mandarin-orange leaves are first stitched with twisted colored thread that has been couched in place, then line stitches in another color are superimposed on this couching to suggest the ribs of the leaves. The cords holding the bamboo slats of the blinds together are also realistically portrayed by untwisting the threads and couching them in place.

The trend towards realistic depiction using complex embroidery techniques began at the end of the Edo period and continued into the early Meiji period, suggesting that this piece was produced at that time.

WEAVE STRUCTURE: 1/4 warp-faced satin ground; silk-floss and gold metallic-wrapped-thread embroidery.
GROUND: MAIN WARP: Silk, unglossed; Z2S; tan; 240 per in.
MAIN WEFT: Silk, unglossed; no twist, X ends; tan; 64 per in.
EMBROIDERY: THREAD 1: Gold-leafed paper wrapped silk.
THREAD 2: Silk, glossed; no twist, X ends; white, tan, brown, orange-red, light orange-red, blue.
THREAD 3: Silk; Z single, unglossed, and X ends, glossed, Z-plied together; brown, orange-red, yellow, yellow-green, green.
STITCHES: Couching (*koma-nui*), long and short satin stitch (*sashi-nui*), stem stitch (*matoi-nui*), satin stitch (*hira-nui*), and French knots (*sagara-nui*).
MEASUREMENTS: CENTER BACK LENGTH: 49 1/4″, 125 cm.
CENTER BACK TO SLEEVE EDGE: 24″, 61 cm.

Surihaku

chest area visible under the *karaori* (*kinagashi* style), or the right sleeve of the *karaori* slipped off to expose the *surihaku* sleeve beneath (*nugisage* style).

A satin or warp-faced twill underrobe with gold- or silver-leaf stenciled patterns for women's roles, this *kosode*-style garment is lined with purple, red, navy blue, or white cloth. Satin, twill, or figured satin weaves are standard today, and have been since the mid-Edo period, but very early *surihaku* were made of a thin, plain-weave silk (*nerinuki*). Like *nuihaku*, all *surihaku* have stenciled gold- or silver-leaf designs. The metallic patterns are formed by applying paste through a cut stencil placed on the stretched cloth. Before the paste dries, gold or silver leaf is laid on and pressed gently with cotton to insure adhesion. Once the leaf is securely affixed, the excess gold or silver is brushed away with a feather. *Nui-iri surihaku* (see cat. no. 25) are highlighted with touches of embroidery.

Surihaku may have overall patterns or decoration only in certain areas, like the chest and sleeves. Sometimes the area from the waist down has simplified designs. Common motifs include bamboo grass with dew, interlocked seven-jewels, flower diamonds, floral designs, waves, rice-field patterns, V-twill patterns, and triangle scales. Common colors are white, light blue, light red, or stripes of green, red, and white.

Surihaku are worn as the undermost layer of clothing and may be visible only at the collar in some combinations, as in the first half of the play *Dōjōji*, where the *nuihaku* covers a *surihaku* with a pattern representing reptilian scales (see p. 7). When worn in combination with *nuihaku* in the waist wrap (*koshimaki*) draping style, the entire upper portion of the robe can be seen, as, for example, in the first half of the play *Hagoromo* (*The Feather Cloak*). Generally, however, another garment, like the broad-sleeved dancing cloak (*chōken* and *maiginu*) or the traveling cloak (*mizugoromo*), is worn over it, the glitter of the gold or silver foil being barely noticeable under the gossamer of the outer cloak. *Surihaku* may be worn under *karaori* as well, with the

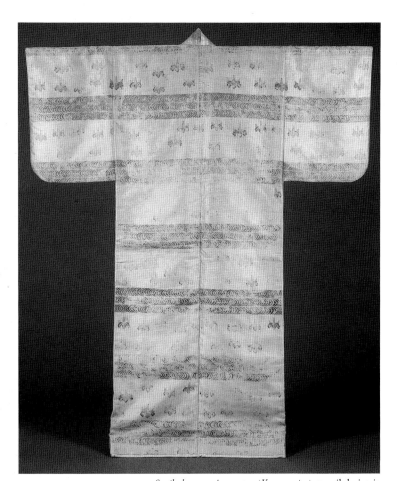

Surihaku, running water (*Kanze mizu*) stencil design in copper foil on a red ground. Edo period, seventeenth century. Tokyo National Museum.

Paper wrapper

24

SURIHAKU
Edo period, second half of the eighteenth century to early nineteenth century
Running water on a striped ground of yellow and blue
35.462

The satin ground is dyed in broad horizontal stripes of blue and yellow. Pale india-ink images of floating chrysanthemums appear stenciled onto the blue ground. Over this, with the exception of the waist area, the entire robe has silver leaf stenciled in a pattern of running water. The running-water motif is very similar to a motif known as *Kanze mizu*, said to have been created by the Kanze family, headed by Kan'ami and his son Zeami (see p. 36) at the time that Nō drama was being given its definitive form, and long established as a symbol of the troupe. The version on the robe is somewhat stiff and formal.

A similar *surihaku* with the same running-water pattern dating from the seventeenth century can be seen in the Tokyo National Museum (see above), but on that robe the stencil pattern of running water falls neatly within the stripe divisions. In contrast, the pattern on this robe extends over the height of two stripes, a freer construction thought to be characteristic of robes dating after the eighteenth century.

On the paper wrapper of the robe is an inked inscription reading "Estate of Lord Ikeda," and indicating that it, like cat. nos. 19, 22, 36, and 37, is from the collection of the Ikeda family of Bishū (now Okayama Prefecture).

WEAVE STRUCTURE: 4Z1 warp-faced satin ground; stenciled India ink and silver leaf.

GROUND: MAIN WARP: Silk, unglossed; Z2S and Z; originally white, dyed yellow and blue; 220 per in.
MAIN WEFT: Silk, unglossed; Z2S; originally white, dyed yellow and blue; 84 per in.

MEASUREMENTS: CENTER BACK LENGTH: 56 ½", 143.5 cm.
CENTER BACK TO SLEEVE EDGE: 27 ¾", 70.4 cm.

eighteenth century and that is also seen in cat. no. 18. The design appears somewhat stylized, but the rendering of the wisteria is free and flowing. Profuse hanging buds of purple wisteria entwined in deep-green pine have been considered particularly beautiful for centuries in Japan, and it is a common motif in painting and craft decoration. In *The Pillow Book* (*Makura no Sōshi*), the Heian authoress Sei Shōnagon mentions in her list of things that are felicitous, "Wisterias flowering in long trailing blossoms of deep shades matched with pines."

This robe has darkened spots along the center back from the collar down. These are from the oil on the long hair of the wig, which was bound at the nape of the neck. The presence of this type of soiling indicates that the robe was worn draped over the shoulders (*kitsuke* style) for a woman's role, rather than folded down over the hips in waist wrap (*koshimaki*) style, as was common for *nuihaku* (robes with both embroidery and metallic-leaf stenciling). For this reason, this robe is characterized as a *surihaku* with embroidery, rather than a *nuihaku*. Very few *surihaku* that were worn *kitsuke*-style remain. Ten other examples are preserved at the Hayashibara Art Museum, previously the property of the Ikeda family of Bishū (Okayama Prefecture).

WEAVE STRUCTURE: 4Z1 warp-faced twill ground; stenciled gold leaf; silk-floss embroidery.
GROUND: MAIN WARP: Silk, unglossed; Z2S; ivory; 350 per in.
MAIN WEFT: Silk, unglossed; no twist, X ends; ivory; 124 per in.
EMBROIDERY: THREAD: Silk, glossed; no twist, X ends; ivory, orange-red, gold, yellow-green, green, dark blue, light blue, purple.
STITCHES: Satin stitch (*hira-nui*), stem stitch (*matoi-nui*).
MEASUREMENTS: CENTER BACK LENGTH: 52 ½", 134 cm.
CENTER BACK TO SLEEVE EDGE: 28", 71 cm.

25

SURIHAKU WITH INCIDENTAL EMBROIDERY (NUI-IRI)

Edo period, first half of the eighteenth century
Pine flowers, wisteria, and cypress-fence diamonds with a pattern of interlocked seven jewels on a white ground
35.463

On the white ground a background pattern of interlocked seven jewels (*shippō-tsunagi*) appears in stenciled gold-leaf. Pine flowers, wisteria, and diamonds filled with cypress-fence patterns are embroidered with colored threads. Gold leaf fills the fence lattice. The embroidery is done in standard satin stitch (*hira-nui*) and stem stitch (*matoi-nui*); none of the special techniques that characterize late eighteenth- and nineteenth-century embroidery are present. The threads are of medium weight, the stitch holes comparatively well-aligned, making for a loose, soft appearance. The fine technique has not lost the open feeling seen in pieces of the late seventeenth century and early eighteenth century.

On the back of the robe the design features an undecorated area over the left hip, a characteristic that it shares with *kosode* from the first part of the

Chōken

The *chōken* is an unlined gossamer dancing cloak with broad, open sleeves, loosely draped front and back panels, and decorative cords on the sleeves and chest; it is usually worn for women's roles. The open, double-width sleeves are longer than they are wide. They are attached to the front and back panels only at the shoulder area for a length of about fifteen centimeters, and there are no underarm or side seams, allowing the sleeves to fall freely. The collar is sewn directly to the three-quarter-length front panels, with no overlap panel. Long round cords are attached next to the collar about ten centimeters below the shoulder with a butterfly bow, and small cords form tassels (*tsuyu*) at the bottom outer corner of the two sleeves.

The most common weave structure for *chōken* is *ro*, a complex gauze often embellished with weft patterning done in gold-leafed paper strips or colored silk. *Chōken* may also be woven in plain gauze (*sha*) with supplementary gold-leafed paper patterning wefts (*kinsha*) or in figured gauze (*kenmonsha*) with gold-leafed paper patterning wefts. A few are of thin plain weave of "glossed" or degummed silk, decorated with embroidery. Colors include white, crimson, purple, light and dark blue, green, yellow, and brown. Cords may be red, yellow, purple, or green.

Typically the upper and lower portions have complementary designs with large patterns above, often crestlike motifs placed in the center back and middle of each sleeve front and back, and scattered small motifs below. Flower baskets, bouquets, fans, or phoenixes commonly appear above, while plant sprigs, swallows, or small geometric motifs are scattered over the bottom area. Variation is considerable however, and some *chōken* have overall even distribution of patterns. Overall patterns tend to combine floral motifs with a geometric grid or arabesque.

Chōken are used as the outer dancing cloak for maidens and female ghosts performing a long dance to instrumental music. They are placed over the shoulders and allowed to fall freely, the left front panel loosely crossing over the right and the cords tied in a large bow at about waist level. Either the *chōken* covers a *koshimaki* outfit, as in the play *Hagoromo* (*The Feather Cloak*), or a *kosode*-style robe (*karaori, surihaku,* or *nuihaku*) worn with broad divided skirts (*ōguchi*). For elegant warrior-courtiers of the legendary Heike clan, the *chōken* draped snugly and belted at the waist may replace an unlined *happi* to suggest armor. To facilitate sword handling, the right sleeve of the *chōken* is slipped off the shoulder, folded, then rolled up and tucked into the belt at the back (*nugisage* style; fig. 30), or both sleeves are hiked up and stitched at the shoulders.

26

CHŌKEN
Edo period, eighteenth century
Fans and maple leaves with good-luck diamonds on
a purple ground
35.495

On a purple gauze ground, gold- and silver-leafed
paper patterning wefts are inserted and then clipped
at the edge of the pattern area, causing the ground to
appear as if embroidered with gold and silver threads
(*nuitori-fū*). Differentiation in the use of gold and
silver complicates the pattern; for example, the fan
papers are executed in gold, the ribs in silver, or
conversely silver is used for the fan papers and gold
for the ribs.

The design of five large emblemlike motifs at
shoulder level and smaller motifs at the bottom of
the sleeves and hem is frequently seen on *chōken* (see
cat. no. 27). Here a unit composed of two fans and
maple leaves is placed on the front and back shoulder
areas and at center back, while a separate design of
good-luck diamonds works upwards from the bottom
of the sleeves and hem. Fan emblems appear on other
chōken, such as an eighteenth-century *chōken* with
fans on a purple ground at the Tokyo National
Museum or another *chōken* with fans and peony
emblems on a purple ground at the Hayashibara Art
Museum, Okayama Prefecture. The simplicity of the
design in the Providence robe suggests a date in the
eighteenth century. The robe gives an impression of

overall refinement: the fan and maple design is fresh
and polished, and the lower diamond design is clear
and sharp.

Purple *chōken*, like this one, may be worn for
a wide variety of roles. They are particularly suited to
women's roles that include performance of the long,
slow Quiet Dance (*jonomai*) or the long, moderately
paced Medium Dance (*chūnomai*), both categorized
as "instrumental dances" (dances accompanied by
music but without song). Examples are the spirit of
the iris in the poetic play *Kakitsubata* (*The Iris*) or the
melancholy sister Pine Wind, who yearns for her
aristocratic lover in *Matsukaze* (*Pine Wind*). In these
cases it would be worn over *nuihaku* in waist wrap
(*koshimaki*) style.

WEAVE STRUCTURE: Complex gauze ground (*ro*), 1/1
gauze of 1 shot alternating with 3 shots of plain weave;
patterned with supplementary discontinuous gold- and
silver-leafed paper patterning wefts tied in plain weave over
4 warps, 2 and 4 remain inactive.

GROUND: MAIN WARP: Silk, unglossed; Z2S; purple;
126 per in.

MAIN WEFT: Silk, unglossed; Z twist, X ends; purple;
42 per in.

PATTERN: SUPPLEMENTARY WEFT 1: Gold-
leafed paper lamellae; 34 per in.

SUPPLEMENTARY WEFT 2: Silver-leafed paper lamellae; 34 per in.

MEASUREMENTS: CENTER BACK LENGTH:
42 1/4", 107 cm.

CENTER BACK TO SLEEVE EDGE: 40 7/8", 104 cm.

27

CHŌKEN
Edo period, second half of the eighteenth century
Bamboo and plum with scattered wildflower sprigs
on a green ground
35.497

The design is woven with discontinuous supplementary wefts in *nuitori-fū* style with white, light-blue, and light-yellow threads on a green gauze ground, which, like the purple of cat. no. 26, is commonly seen. Placed at front shoulders, sleeve backs, and center back are large, round, emblemlike motifs of bamboo with plum, while small wildflower motifs are discretely scattered over the lower area of the sleeves and main panels. The overall design construction of large, crestlike pattern units placed at five spots and small patterns scattered along the bottom of the sleeves and hem can also be seen in cat. no. 26, which has fans, maple leaves, and good-luck diamonds on a purple ground. The motif of bamboo and plum, often combined with pine, is considered auspicious, for all three withstand the winter cold and snow, remaining green or blossoming with red. The *karaori* with young pines and snow-laden bamboo (cat. no. 11) shows another variation.

     This *chōken* is suitable for women's roles that include a long dance to instrumental music (see cat.

no. 26). It may be draped over waist wrap (*koshimaki*) costumes or over broad divided skirts (*ōguchi*) to create a fuller, more imposing figure. In combination with a tall lacquer dancing hat (*eboshi*), the *chōken* might be worn over broad divided skirts (*ōguchi*) by a professional dancer, like Shizuka Gozen in *Yoshino Shizuka* (*Shizuka of Yoshino*). A green *chōken* like this might also be worn by a warrior-courtier, if draped to suggest armor by belting it at the waist and slipping off the right sleeve so that it does not interfere with sword manipulation (fig. 30). For performance, chest cords are attached to the collar, but many extant Edo-period *chōken* lack this feature.

WEAVE STRUCTURE: Complex gauze ground (*ro*), 1 shot of 1/1 gauze alternating with 3 shots of plain weave; patterned with supplementary discontinuous gold-leafed paper and silk patterning wefts tied in plain weave over 4 warps, 2 and 4 remain inactive.

GROUND: MAIN WARP: Silk, unglossed; no twist, 2 ends; green; 80 per in.

MAIN WEFT: Silk, unglossed; no twist, X ends; green; 40 per in.

PATTERN: SUPPLEMENTARY WEFT 1: Gold-leafed paper lamellae; 36 per in.

SUPPLEMENTARY WEFT 2: Silk, glossed; no twist, X ends; white, light yellow, light blue; 36 per in.

MEASUREMENTS: CENTER BACK LENGTH: 41 1/2", 106.6 cm.

CENTER BACK TO SLEEVE EDGE: 39 7/8", 102.2 cm.

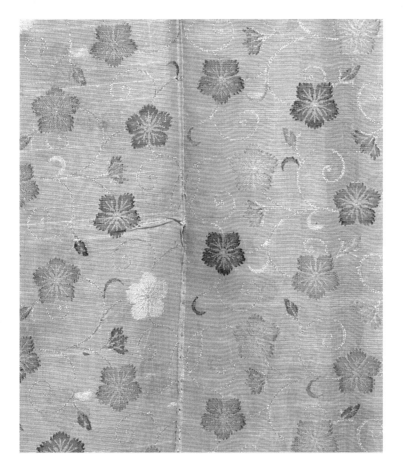

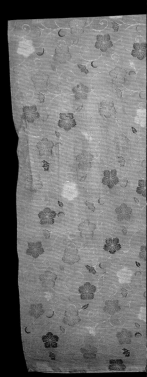

28

CHŌKEN
Edo period, late eighteenth century to early nineteenth century
Evening-glory arabesques on a cream ground
35.498

The design is woven into an ivory *sha* ground (plain gauze in which two warp threads twist around one weft thread) with gold-leafed paper wefts and silk wefts in shades of brown, purple, blue, light blue, and green-yellow. The use of a *sha* ground is rare; many *chōken* employ a *ro* ground (three, five, or seven shots of plain weave with the addition of a single shot of gauze). Also unusual is the use of evening glories in the arabesque motif, rather than the more commonly seen peonies, clematis, and chrysanthemums.

The arabesques are densely spread over the entire robe. The flowers are created with well-balanced soft-hued silk wefts, which interlink gracefully with the vines in gold-leafed paper wefts, giving the robe its calm color harmony. The vines are rendered with a delicacy that complements their gentle flow, forming a wonderful balance with the flowers.

White *chōken* are often chosen for roles of women's ghosts suffering in hell, like the ghost of Princess Shokushi in *Teika* (*Teika Vine*) or the ghost of Unai-otome in *Motomezuka* (*The Sought-for Grave*), although there is no strict rule about this. The white adds dignity, the color being associated with purity and high status, and also indicates the figure's ghostly transparence.

WEAVE STRUCTURE: 1/1 plain gauze ground (*sha*); supplementary discontinuous gold-leafed paper and silk patterning wefts tied in plain weave over 4 warps, 2 and 4 remain inactive.

GROUND: MAIN WARP: Silk, unglossed; Z2S; ivory; 82 per in.

MAIN WEFT: Silk, unglossed; slight Z twist, 7 ends; 32 per in.

PATTERN: SUPPLEMENTARY WEFT 1: Gold-leafed paper lamellae; 32 per in.

SUPPLEMENTARY WEFT 2: Silk, glossed; no twist, X ends; light brown, yellow-green, green, blue, light blue, purple, light purple; 32 per in.

MEASUREMENTS: CENTER BACK LENGTH: 43 ½", 111.4 cm.

CENTER BACK TO SLEEVE EDGE: 41", 104 cm.

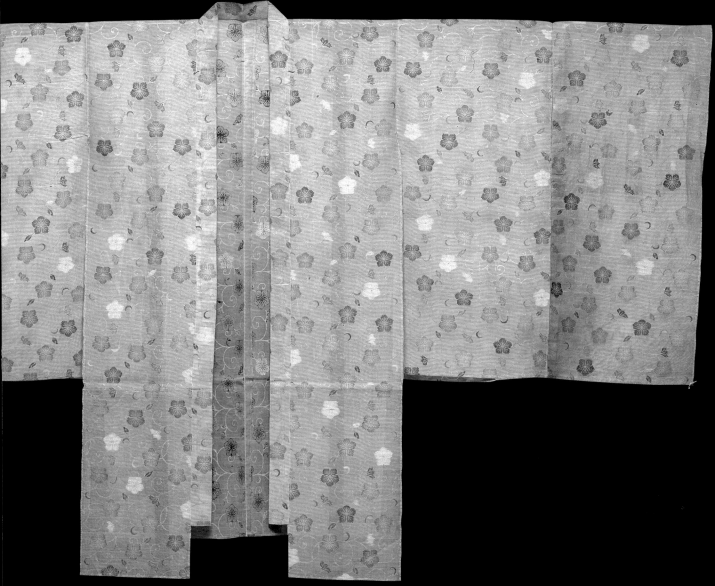

Maiginu

The *maiginu* is a gossamer woman's dancing cloak with broad, open sleeves and overlapping panels in front, without decorative cords. Compared to the *chōken*, the balance between the length of the sleeve panels and the main body panels is more even, with narrower sleeves and a longer main body. Unlike the *chōken*, extra overlap panels are added in the front, and the front and back panels are stitched together part way down the sides. Similarly, the seam joining the sleeves to the main panel at the shoulder area extends farther down, resulting in a "tighter" garment.

Like *chōken, maiginu* may be made of *ro*, a complex gauze with supplementary patterning wefts of gold-leafed paper (*rokin*) or silk; or of a plain gauze with supplementary gold-leafed paper patterning wefts (*kinsha*); or of figured gauze (*kenmonsha*) with gold-leafed paper patterning wefts. Overall patterns predominate, many reminiscent of Heian court patterns like arabesques, medallions with undulating vertical lines, and flower-filled diamond grids. Like the *chōken*, the *maiginu* may be worn for women's roles that include the performance of long dances to instrumental music, either belted over a *koshimaki* suit or draped and bound at the waist over broad divided skirts (*ōguchi*). While *chōken* are allowed to fall freely, *maiginu* are secured so as to lie close to the torso.

29

MAIGINU

Edo period, late eighteenth century to early nineteenth
century
Peonies and dew-topped grass on a purple ground
35.496

Peonies and grasses with dew are woven into a purple
gauze ground with supplementary gold-leafed paper
patterning wefts. The grasses flow freely with a
springy curve of the blades, and the peonies appear
to be riding on top of them. Both motifs are somewhat
stylized, but are not so stiff as to spoil the elegance of
the piece.

The designs of *maiginu* tend to cover the
whole garment uniformly, and one does not find the
crestlike emblems at shoulder level so typical of many
chōken. The round red braided cords attached to the
collar at chest level on this robe are most
probably a later, unorthodox addition, since from
the point of view of construction and pattern, this
piece is indeed a *maiginu* and would not have cords
at the chest.

In the play *Fuji Taiko* (*Fuji's Drum*) the wife
of a drum player who has been killed by a jealous
competitor appears in a *nuihaku* draped in waist
wrap (*koshimaki*) style, *maiginu* cloak, and large performance hat (*tori kabuto*) when beating her dead
husband's drum while dancing. See cat. no. 21 for a
nuihaku suitable for this role.

WEAVE STRUCTURE: Complex gauze ground (*ro*), 1
shot of 1/1 gauze alternating with 3 shots of plain weave;
supplementary discontinuous gold-leafed paper patterning
wefts tied in plain weave over 4 warps, 2 and 4 remain inactive.

GROUND: MAIN WARP: Silk, unglossed; Z twist, 2
ends; purple; 84 per in.

MAIN WEFT: Silk, unglossed; Z twist, X ends; purple;
42 per in.

PATTERN: SUPPLEMENTARY WEFT 1: Gold-
leafed paper lamellae; 32 per in.

MEASUREMENTS: CENTER BACK LENGTH:
59", 149 cm.

CENTER BACK TO SLEEVE EDGE: 44 ¾", 115 cm.

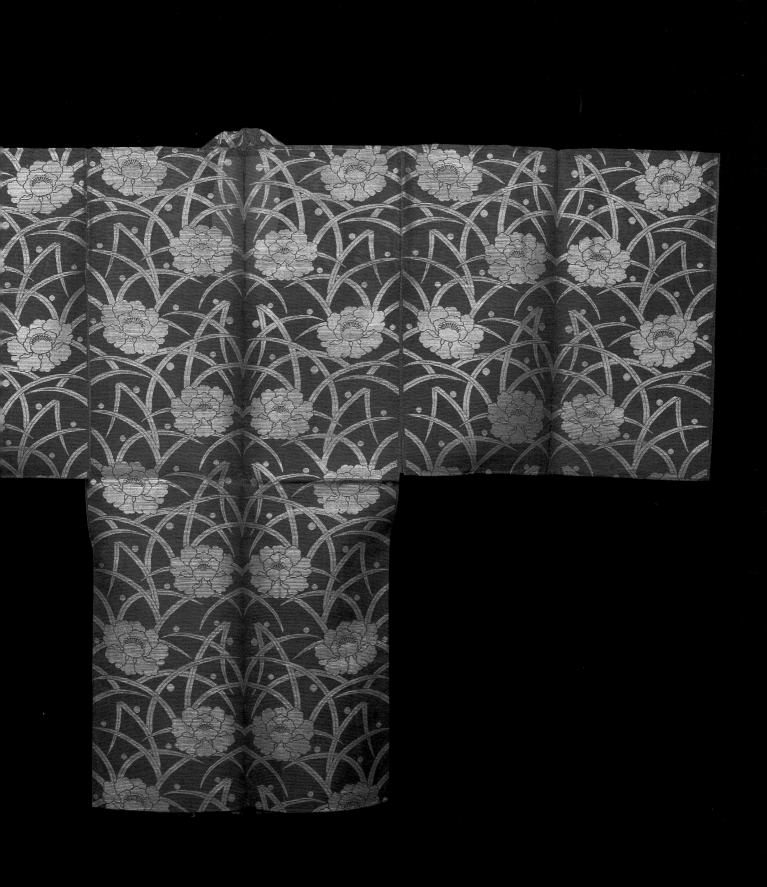

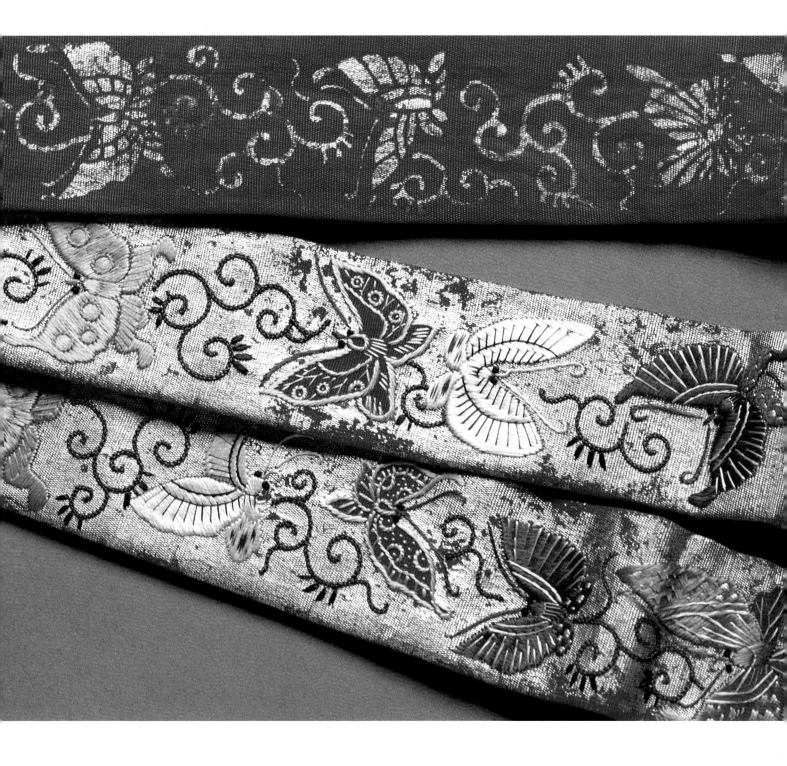

Katsura-obi

A long, narrow band embroidered at both ends and along a central strip, the *katsura-obi* is tied around the forehead under the mask and knotted in a bow at the back of the head. Embroidery decorates only the exposed areas (the center strip shows at either side of the mask), although sometimes the unembroidered areas have a stenciled gold- or silver-leaf pattern. Fabrics include glossed plain weave (*seigō*), twill, satin, and figured satin (*donsu*). While some of the designs are geometric, like triangle scales (*uroko*), many are naturalistic, like flower arabesques. Those with red are worn for roles of young women, and those with copper or gold leaf (*dōhaku*) are used in the most elegant of women's plays (*hon-sanbamme-mono*). The white, undecorated *hachimaki* hair band is reserved for warrior roles and is worn over the mask.

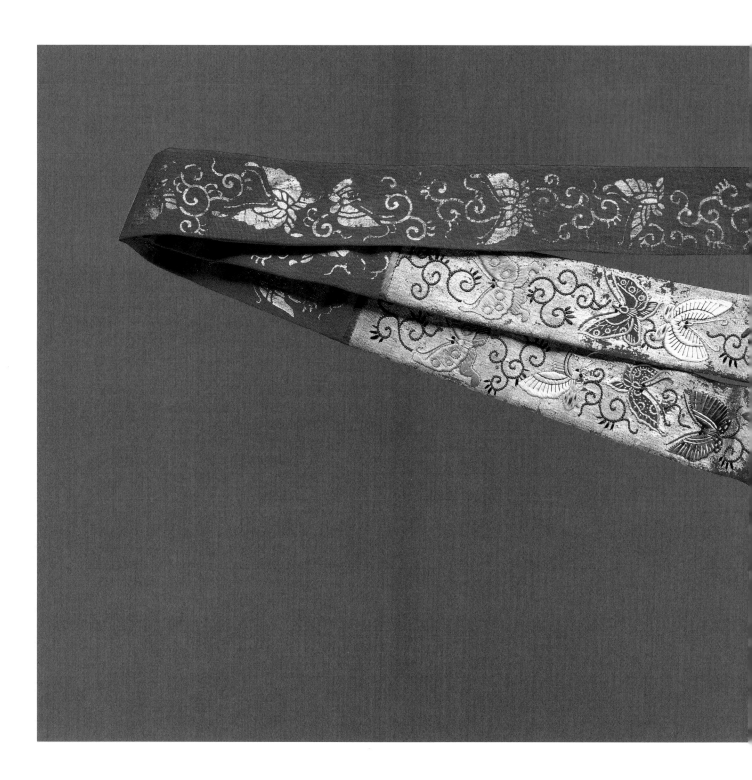

30

KATSURA-OBI
Meiji or Taishō period, late nineteenth to early
twentieth century
Butterflies and arabesques on a gold ground
35.502

The hair band is of orange-red silk woven in ribbed
plain weave or rep with designs of butterflies and
arabesques in embroidery at the ends and in the
center. Gold leaf fills the background. Gold-leaf
stencil patterns of butterflies and arabesques appear
elsewhere.

Katsura-obi became necessary as hair bands at
the time when actors began to wear wigs for women's
roles. The design covering the forehead at the center
of the band is shorter in length than the design at
the two ends, which fall down the actor's back
when worn.

Among the embroidery threads are some
which appear to be dyed with aniline colors, indicating
that the piece may well have been made in the late
nineteenth or early twentieth century.

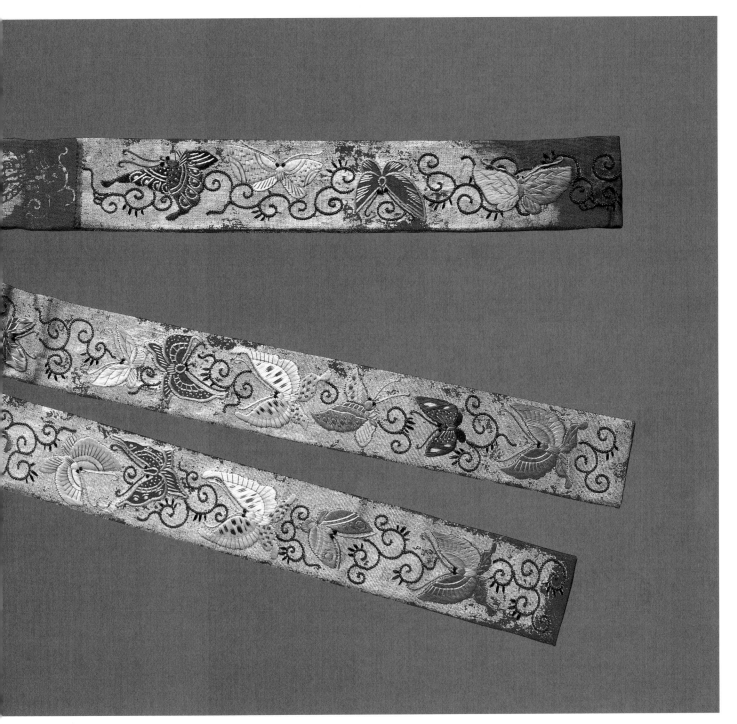

WEAVE STRUCTURE: Plain-weave ground, rep;
stenciled gold-leaf; silk-floss embroidery.

GROUND: MAIN WARP: Silk, unglossed; no twist,
X ends; orange-red; 116 per in.

MAIN WEFT: Silk, unglossed; slight Z twist, X ends;
orange-red; 48 per in.

EMBROIDERY: THREAD 1: Silk, glossed; no twist,
X ends; white, beige, blue-green, green-blue, blue, purple,
pink, black.

STITCHES: Overlay (*norikake-nui*), stem stitch (*matoi-nui*), French knot (*sagara-nui*); satin stitch (*hira-nui*).

THREAD 2: Silk; Z single, unglossed, and X ends,
glossed, Z plied together; green-blue.

STITCHES: Couching (*koma-nui*).

MEASUREMENTS: LENGTH: 94", 239 cm.
WIDTH: 1 ½", 4 cm.

Kariginu

A broad-sleeved outer cloak with round over-lapping collar, the *kariginu* is worn for male roles of nobles and gods. Its open sleeves are double width, approximately square, and sewn to the front and back panels, which are not sewn to each other below the sleeves. The stiffened round collar stands up about two centimeters and is fastened on the right side with tying cords. Round braided cords (often double) decorate the edge of the sleeves. Some *kariginu* are lined (*awase*) and some unlined (*hitoe*).

Lined *kariginu* may be of lampas with satin or twill ground, supplementary silk warp, and supplementary gold-leafed paper and silk patterning wefts tied in plain weave (may be *kinran, nishiki*); figured satin (*donsu*); or double-cloth of two interacting plain-weave structures (*fūtsu*).

Unlined *kariginu* may be of complex gauze (*ro*) with supplementary patterning wefts of gold-leafed paper (*rokin*) or silk and gold-leafed paper; patterned gauze; plain-weave ground with gauze patterning (*kenmonsha*); plain gauze with supplementary silk patterning wefts (*monsha*); plain weave with no supplementary pattern (*shike*); or unbalanced plain weave (*yore*).

Lined *kariginu* have solid grounds of white, scarlet, navy blue, grayish blue, and bottle green with large-scale bold designs. The *Okina kariginu*, worn only in the sacred play *Okina*, has a special pattern of linked hexagons and squares known as *shokkō* (see cat. no. 41). Unlined *kariginu* have solid grounds of white, light blue, navy, or light green decorated with soft, pictorial patterns or with elegant patterns derived from Heian imperial court textiles (*yūsoku*). *Shike* and *yore kariginu* have earthy color combinations of browns and dull greens. The tying cords may be red, olive green, or white.

The broad-sleeved hunting cloak called *kariginu* was originally an informal gown worn by Heian courtiers; in its adaptation for Nō costume, it is used as an outer garment for roles of high status, worn belted and draped over broad divided skirts (*ōguchi* or *hangire*). Lined *kariginu* are worn by ministers, powerful gods, and goblins (*tengu*) in such plays as *Tsurukame* (*The Crane and the Tortoise*), *Takasago* (*Takasago Pine*), *Chikubushima* (*The Isle of Chikubu*), and *Kurama Tengu* (*The Goblin of Mount Kurama*). Unlined *kariginu* are used for roles of ministers and elegant courtiers in plays like *Tōru*, *Unrin'in* (*Temple Unrin*), and *Suma Genji* (*Genji at Suma*), as well as for the spirits of old trees like the willow in the play *Yūgyō yanagi* (*Yūgyō and the Willow*) (see cat. no. 31). *Shike* and *yore kariginu* are the garb of minor god-kings such as the *shite* in *Kasuga Ryūjin* (*The Dragon God of Kasuga*).

Paper wrapper

31

KARIGINU
Edo period, first half of the nineteenth century
Swallows and willow trees with trailing branches on
a blue ground
35.459

The design of swallows and willow trees, woven in a
style that resembles embroidery (*nuitori-fū*), with
discontinuous gold-leafed paper and white silk
patterning wefts on a blue gauze ground, has great
dignity and style. The design is extremely large, with
a single pattern covering the front and the back, quite
different from the repetitive unit designs that usually
characterize weaving. This piece is outstanding, for
Nō costumes rarely display such painterly designs on
so large a scale.

While the roots and trunk of the willow are
rendered in a style similar to that seen in Nō costumes
of the Momoyama and early Edo periods, the treatment is antiquarian, suggesting that it dates from a
revival movement of the first half of the nineteenth
century, the end of the Edo period. Generally, revival
works degenerate into stereotypes, but in the present
case, the imitation of the older style is far more
expansive, attaining a special painterly expression.

Although the willow-tree-and-swallows motif is a set
combination, the rendering is free from stiffness and
stylization. The swallows flit swiftly and lightly in
various forms.

With its graceful, gnarled willows the robe
seems almost as if it were made for the role of the
spirit of the old willow in the god play *Yūgyō yanagi*
(*Yūgyō and the Willow*).

The cloak has a paper wrapper with an ink
inscription reading, "Owned by the Hirase family,"
who also owned cat. no. 15.

WEAVE STRUCTURE: Complex gauze ground (*ro*), 1
shot of 1/1 gauze alternating with 3 shots of 2/1 warp gauze;
supplementary discontinuous gold-leafed paper and silk
patterning wefts tied in plain weave over 4 warps, 2 and 4
remain inactive.

GROUND: MAIN WARP: Silk, unglossed; Z2S; indigo
blue; 126 per in.

MAIN WEFT: Silk, unglossed; no twist, X ends; indigo
blue; 40 per in.

PATTERN: SUPPLEMENTARY WEFT 1: Gold-
leafed paper lamellae; 36 per in.

SUPPLEMENTARY WEFT 2: Silk, glossed; no twist,
X ends; white; 36 per in.

MEASUREMENTS: CENTER BACK LENGTH:
64 3/4", 163 cm.

CENTER BACK TO SLEEVE EDGE: 40", 102.3 cm.

Paper wrapper

32

KARIGINU
Edo period, first half of the nineteenth century
Pine, ginko-leaf, and hawk-feather roundels over a
cypress-fence pattern on a purple ground
35.494

The outer fabric is lampas with purple satin ground
and a cypress-fence pattern woven with supplementary
gold-leafed paper wefts tied with a supplementary
silk warp. The lining is purple plain-weave silk. The
decorative cords that accompany *kariginu* have been
preserved with this costume. There are round red
braided cords (*maruuchi*) for securing the overlap
panel to the right side of the collar, and similar red
cord runs around the outer edge of the sleeves.
Scattered over the cypress-fence pattern are roundels
composed of pine trees, ginko leaves, and hawk
feathers. The well-balanced arrangement of the
roundels creates a rhythm that rescues the simple
woven pattern from tediousness.

 This *kariginu* with its dark purple ground and
richly glittering gold would be well suited for the
weighty and majestic role of the god of Sumiyoshi,
the spirit of the Sumiyoshi pine tree and protector of
the Imperial House, in the play *Takasago* (*Takasago
Pine*).

 The cloak has a paper wrapper with an ink
inscription reading, "Mark Yu, number 73, crests
over a cypress fence on a purple ground."

WEAVE STRUCTURE: Lampas: 8/1 warp-faced satin
ground weave, plain-weave pattern weave.

GROUND: MAIN WARP: Silk, unglossed; Z2S; purple;
240 per in.

MAIN WEFT: Silk, unglossed; Z twist, X ends; purple;
80 per in.

PATTERN: SUPPLEMENTARY WARP 1: Silk,
unglossed; no twist, 1 or 2 ends; light gold; 60 per in.

SUPPLEMENTARY WEFT 1: Gold-leafed paper
lamellae; 40 per in.

MEASUREMENTS: CENTER BACK LENGTH:
56", 142 cm.

CENTER BACK TO SLEEVE EDGE: 41 1/2", 105.5 cm.

Paper wrapper

33

KARIGINU
Edo period, nineteenth century
Feather fans and clouds on a dark-blue ground
35·493

The outer fabric is lampas with a twill ground and a pattern created by supplementary gold-leafed paper wefts with small additional highlights in white, light blue, beige, and yellow silk patterning wefts at the center of the fans, tied with a supplementary silk warp. The color of the gold-leafed paper lamellae appears to be different from those seen in other Nō costumes. The pattern, with its widely spaced fans of hawk feathers and densely packed cloud patterns filling the ground between, is also quite different from the patterns generally seen on *kariginu*. The motif of circular fans and clouds gives a distinctly Chinese impression and might have been intended for a role representing a Chinese emperor such as Gen-so in the Nō play *Tsurukame* (*The Crane and the Tortoise*). Feather fans like those represented here are carried by long-nosed goblins (*tengu*) in plays like *Kurama Tengu* (*The Goblin of Mount Kurama*), in which the goblin wears a lined *kariginu* similar to this one. Along the outer edge of the sleeves is a round red braided cord (*maruuchi*). The body has a lining of plain-weave purple silk, while the lining of the sleeves is light-brown plain-weave silk.

Probably the light-brown is the original, the purple a replacement.

This cloak has a paper wrapper with an ink inscription reading, "Mark Yu, number 77, clouds and feather fans on a dark-blue ground."

WEAVE STRUCTURE: Lampas: 4/1 warp-faced satin ground weave, plain-weave pattern weave.
GROUND: MAIN WARP: Silk, unglossed; Z2S; dark blue; 160 per in.
MAIN WEFT: Silk, unglossed; no twist, X ends; dark blue; 88 per in.
PATTERN: SUPPLEMENTARY WARP 1: Silk, unglossed; no twist, 1 or 2 ends; beige; 68 per in.
SUPPLEMENTARY WEFT 1: Gold-leafed paper lamellae; 48 per in.
SUPPLEMENTARY WEFT 2: Silk, unglossed; no twist, X ends; white, beige, yellow, light blue; 44 per in.
MEASUREMENTS: CENTER BACK LENGTH: 59 3/8", 151 cm.
CENTER BACK TO SLEEVE EDGE: 37", 94 cm.

Happi

The *happi* is a broad-sleeved outer cloak for men
with straight collar and cloth strips connecting
the front and back panels at the hemline. Unique
to the Nō stage, the *happi* has double-width open
sleeves that form a square. They are attached to
the main panels only at the shoulders. A strip of
cloth six to seven centimeters wide – the distinguishing characteristic of this garment –
connects the front and back body panels. Since
there are no overlap panels in front, the collar
hangs straight down. *Happi* may be lined
(*awase*) or unlined (*hitoe*).

The weave structure and decorative
techniques are essentially the same as for *kariginu*
(see p. 139). The lined version is of satin weave
with gold patterning wefts (*kinran* and *nishiki*),
or more rarely embroidery, while the unlined is
of gauze either of a solid color or with colored
silk or gold patterning wefts. Lined *kariginu*
have large bold patterns, often geometric or of
Chinese origin, like dragons and clouds, on
backgrounds of white, dark or light blue, olive,
purple, brown, or black. The unlined variety
has more delicate patterns like floral arabesques,
insects, or undulating lines on backgrounds of
white, blue, or purple.

Happi are worn over broad, divided skirts
(*hangire* and *ōguchi*) and are belted at the waist.
Lined *happi* may be worn over an *atsuita* and
hangire by ghosts and demons, while the warriors
who vanquish them wear *happi* over *ōguchi*.
With the sleeves hiked up, the lined *happi* may
be used to suggest armor for victorious warriors.
Unlined *happi*, which have less bold designs,
are worn by defeated warriors with aristocratic
sensibility; here the *happi* form an alternative to
chōken.

34

HAPPI
Edo period, late eighteenth century to early
nineteenth century
Scattered Chinese flowers with lightning on a dark
green-blue ground
35.492

On a dark green-blue ground, Chinese flowers
woven in gold-leafed paper lamellae appear in
staggered rows. Between them are embroidered
lightning patterns in yellow-green, green, gold,
and white.

    The embroidery is executed in satin stitch
(*hira-nui*), and where the threads have broken, bits
of reinforcing paper peep out. When the satin stitch
float is very long, additional overlay stitches (*norikake-
nui*) are used to hold the threads in place. Since the
embroidery threads are fine and tightly worked in,
they give an impression of a flat surface, at first glance
appearing as if they were woven. It is possible that
the embroidery was applied before the tailoring of
the garment, but such examples are very rare, except
when broken wefts have been repaired, and it is
possible that the embroidery here is a later addition.

    The motif of lightning is most appropriate to
lined *happi*, which may be used to represent military
garb. Lightning motifs with crooked lines (*inazuma*)
like these are rarely seen in textiles. If indeed the

lightning is original to the robe, this design is extremely
rare and most interesting.

WEAVE STRUCTURE: Lampas: 7/1 warp-faced satin
ground, plain-weave pattern weave; silk-floss embroidery
over paper.
GROUND: MAIN WARP: Silk, unglossed; Z2S; green-
blue; 200 per in.
MAIN WEFT: Silk, unglossed; no twist, X ends; green-
blue; 76 per in.
PATTERN: SUPPLEMENTARY WARP 1: Silk,
unglossed; no twist, 1 end; gold; 60 per in.
SUPPLEMENTARY WEFT 1: Gold-leafed paper
lamellae; 48 per in.
EMBROIDERY: THREAD: Silk, glossed; no twist,
X ends; white, gold, yellow-green, green.
STITCHES: Satin stitch (*hira-nui*), overlay (*norikake-nui*).
MEASUREMENTS: CENTER BACK LENGTH:
41 1/4", 105.5 cm.
CENTER BACK TO SLEEVE EDGE: 37 1/4", 94.5 cm.

35

HAPPI
Edo period, first half of the nineteenth century
Circles containing three swirling comma-shapes with
triangle scales on a blue ground
35.491

The outer fabric of this *happi* is lampas woven with a
twill ground with a pattern created with supplementary gold-leafed paper wefts tied with a supplementary
silk warp. The lining is purple plain-weave silk. This
robe has a blue ground on which triangle scales
(*uroko*) appear as a ground pattern, scattered with
large circles composed of three swirling comma-
shapes (*tomoe*). A peculiarity of the robe is that the
triangles that make up the scale pattern are not all
facing the same direction. Generally, scale patterns
have triangles with their apexes facing either all up
or all down. Robes like this with triangles facing at an
angle to the upper right or lower left are extremely
rare. The fact that the back panels consist of four
lengths rather than the standard two make it likely
that the garment has been retailored.

   The boldness of the pattern on this lined *happi*
makes the robe suitable for powerful characters, like
the dragon god in *Chikubushima* (*The Isle of Chikubu*),
Kasuga Ryūjin (*The Dragon God of Kasuga*), and
Iwafune (*The Stone Boat*). It could also be worn by
the robber-warrior in *Kumasaka*.

WEAVE STRUCTURE: Lampas: 1Z3 twill ground weave,
plain-weave pattern weave.

GROUND: MAIN WARP: Silk, unglossed; Z2S; blue;
144 per in.

MAIN WEFT: Silk, unglossed; no twist, 3 ends; blue; 56
per in.

PATTERN: SUPPLEMENTARY WARP 1: Silk,
unglossed; no twist, 1 end; orange-red; 48 per in.

SUPPLEMENTARY WEFT 1: Gold-leafed paper lamellae; 26 per in.

MEASUREMENTS: CENTER BACK LENGTH:
40 ½″, 103 cm.

CENTER BACK TO SLEEVE EDGE: 45 ½″, 114.5 cm.

Paper wrapper

36

HAPPI
Edo period, first half of the nineteenth century
Paulownia arabesques on a white ground
35.471

The outer fabric of this *happi* is lampas with a figured
twill ground and a pattern of large arabesques of
paulownia in supplementary gold-leafed paper wefts
tied with a supplementary silk warp. The lining is a
plain-weave purple cloth. The paulownia arabesque
that sprawls over the outer fabric is thought to be a
variation on a standing paulownia tree. It lacks the
rhythm and free flow characteristic of arabesque
patterns. The vines have a branchlike stiffness, and
the rendering of the flowers and leaves is stylized.
There is almost no empty space in the design, a
characteristic seen often in weaving of the nineteenth
century, yet the robe still has the feeling of power
and strength appropriate for such roles as the brave
warrior Yoshitsune, who gallops out to sea in the
middle of a battle in the play *Yashima (Arrow Isle)*.
In such a case it would be worn with the right sleeve
slipped off, or else with both sleeves hiked up and
sewn at the shoulder, effectively eliminating the
encumbering broad sleeves and suggesting the stiffness of armor.

On the paper wrapper is an inscription reading
"Estate of Lord Ikeda." The *happi* presumably
belonged to the Ikeda family, daimyo in Bishū (now
Okayama Prefecture) during the Edo period (see
cat. nos. 19, 22, 24, and 37).

WEAVE STRUCTURE: Lampas: 3Z1 broken twill
ground weave, plain-weave pattern weave.

GROUND: MAIN WARP: Silk, unglossed; S, 2 ends;
ivory; 112 per in.

MAIN WEFT: Silk, unglossed; no twist, X ends; ivory;
88 per in.

PATTERN: SUPPLEMENTARY WARP 1: Silk,
unglossed; no twist, 1 end; light gold; 56 per in.

SUPPLEMENTARY WEFT 1: Gold-leafed paper lamellae; 40 per in.

MEASUREMENTS: CENTER BACK LENGTH:
48 3/4", 117 cm.

CENTER BACK TO SLEEVE EDGE: 39 1/4", 100 cm.

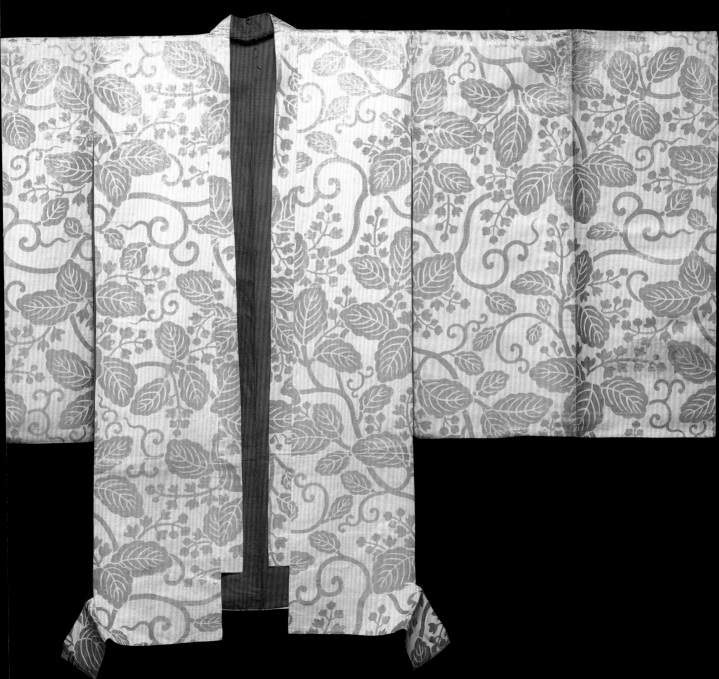

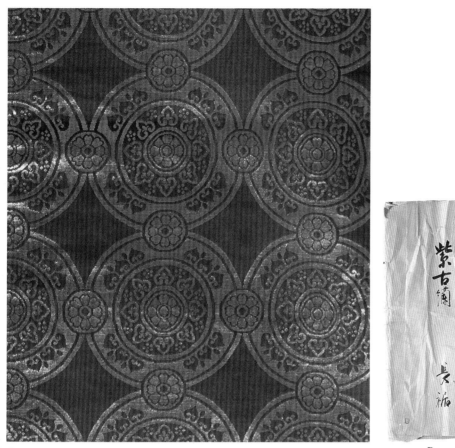

池田候苗裔
紫古繍

長袖

Paper wrapper

37

HAPPI
Edo period, nineteenth century
Linked circles on a purple ground
35.469

The outer cloth is lampas with a purple satin ground and supplementary gold-leafed paper wefts tied with a supplementary warp to form a pattern of interlocking circles. The lining is of purple plain-weave silk.

Motifs of three concentric circle patterns create a flowerlike medallion. The smallest circle contains a flower motif and acts as the center of a large-petaled flower surrounded by another circle. Within the petals of the large flower are Chinese-style cloud patterns and between them plum patterns. Surrounding the second concentric circle and contained within the outermost circle are four cloud patterns placed diagonally across from each other. Between these on the vertical and horizontal axes are small circles that link the large circle motifs to each other. The general construction seems similar to the *shokkō* pattern (cat. no. 41), which was popular during the Ming period (1368-1644) in China, but true *shokkō* patterns are composed of four, six, or eight-sided figures, not circles as in this *happi*. Probably with the passage of time only the basic concept of the *shokkō* pattern, interlocking geometric figures in an overall design, was retained, while the

finer points were lost. Still, despite obvious modification, the pattern shows no sign of being mixed with Japanese motifs. The exclusive use of Chinese motifs in the composition and the formal, abstract rendering of the design strongly suggest that the cloth was produced in China.

On the paper wrapper is an ink inscription reading, "Estate of Lord Ikeda," indicating that this robe, like cat. nos. 19, 22, 24, and 36, belonged to the Ikeda family of Bishū (now Okayama Prefecture).

WEAVE STRUCTURE: Lampas: 7/1 warp-faced satin ground weave, plain-weave pattern weave.

GROUND: MAIN WARP: Silk, unglossed; S twist, 1 end; purple; 232 per in.

MAIN WEFT: Silk, unglossed; no twist, 2 ends; purple; 80 per in.

PATTERN: SUPPLEMENTARY WARP 1: Silk, unglossed; no twist, X ends; orange-red, gold; 56 per in.

SUPPLEMENTARY WEFT 1: Gold-leafed paper lamellae; 40 per in.

MEASUREMENTS: CENTER BACK LENGTH: 42", 106.5 cm.

CENTER BACK TO SLEEVE EDGE: 38 ½", 98 cm.

Atsuita

panel crossing over the right. *Atsuita* appear under broad-sleeved jackets and cloaks like *happi, kariginu, chōken,* and *mizugoromo* for roles of gods, demons, warriors, old men, monks, and ghosts. When the sleeves of the jacket or cloak are hiked up or slipped off one shoulder, the *atsuita* becomes more visible. *Atsuita* are also worn tucked into pantaloons by servants (*kyōgen*).

Weft-patterned, box-sleeved, *kosode*-style garments, worn for male roles under a cloak, *atsuita* have bold, masculine designs, often geometric, the content and quality of the design motifs being the feature that distinguishes *atsuita* from *karaori*.

During the Muromachi and Momoyama periods many of the textiles used for garments of the upper class were imported from China, wrapped around boards for transport. The thin satins and flexible figured cloths were rolled onto thin boards (*usu-ita*) and the stiffer weft-patterned textiles and tightly woven twills were wrapped around thick boards (*atsu-ita*). Of these heavier fabrics, it is said that those without patterning wefts but with densely set warp threads were particularly stiff and boardlike and were therefore known as *atsuita*. The name of the textile was then applied to garments made of that cloth. Today the textiles used to make the Nō costume *atsuita* include a wide variety of weaves, twill and twill patterned with supplementary-weft techniques being most common.

The latter is similar in weaving technique to that of *karaori*, and often has an additional background pattern of gold- or silver-leafed paper strips tightly bound into the structure of the fabric using a "coarse" twill. In addition to stripes and checks, the ground pattern may be based on alternating blocks (*dangawari*) created by *ikat*-dyeing the warp or on triangles (*uroko*) evoking reptilian scales. Motifs lean towards geometric patterns and symbolic figures of Chinese origin, such as dragons with clouds, lions with peonies, and temple gongs (*umpan*), as well as those with distinctly masculine flavor, like hatchets, torches, or arrows. Motifs tend to be boldly displayed with strong color contrasts.

Atsuita are the basic *kosode*-style garments for male roles, worn as *kitsuke* undergarments draped to fit the body snugly, with left front

38

ATSUITA
Edo period, late eighteenth century to early
nineteenth century
Alternating blocks of clouds containing circles of
swirling comma-shapes on orange-red and gold
grounds and checks on a white ground
35.465

For the ground of alternating blocks (*dangawari*),
the warp threads are *ikat* dyed in orange-red, gold,
and white and the ground weft woven in to match. In
the white area the pattern is of regular checks; in the
orange-red and gold blocks are clouds around fire
circlets containing circles of three swirling comma-
shapes (*tomoe*). This well-preserved garment combines
the clarity of checks with the majesty of bold, large-
scale, weft-patterned motifs. An *atsuita* with a very
similar *tomoe* pattern is housed in the Tokyo
National Museum (fig. 23).

WEAVE STRUCTURE: Ground of alternating *ikat*-dyed
blocks of 1Z5 twill and blocks of 5Z1 and 1Z5 twill color
and weave-effect check; floating pattern of supplementary
discontinuous silk patterning wefts tied in 2Z1 twill over 6
warps, 2, 4, and 6 remain inactive, and supplementary
discontinous patterning weft floats.
GROUND: MAIN WARP: Silk, unglossed; Z2S; originally white, *ikat*-dyed light brown, orange-red, gold, green,

dark blue; 158 per in.
MAIN WEFT: Silk, unglossed; no twist, 2 ends; white,
orange-red, yellow-green, dark blue; 89 per in.

FLOATING PATTERN: SUPPLEMENTARY WEFT 1:
Silk, glossed; no twist, X ends; white, light orange-red,
yellow, yellow-green, blue, light blue, pink; 45 per in.
SUPPLEMENTARY WEFT 2: Silk, glossed; no twist,
X ends; white, beige, light brown, orange-red, gold, yellow,
yellow-green, dark blue, blue, light blue, pink; 45 per in.

MEASUREMENTS: CENTER BACK LENGTH:
56 ¾", 144.5 cm.
CENTER BACK TO SLEEVE EDGE: 27 ½", 70 cm.

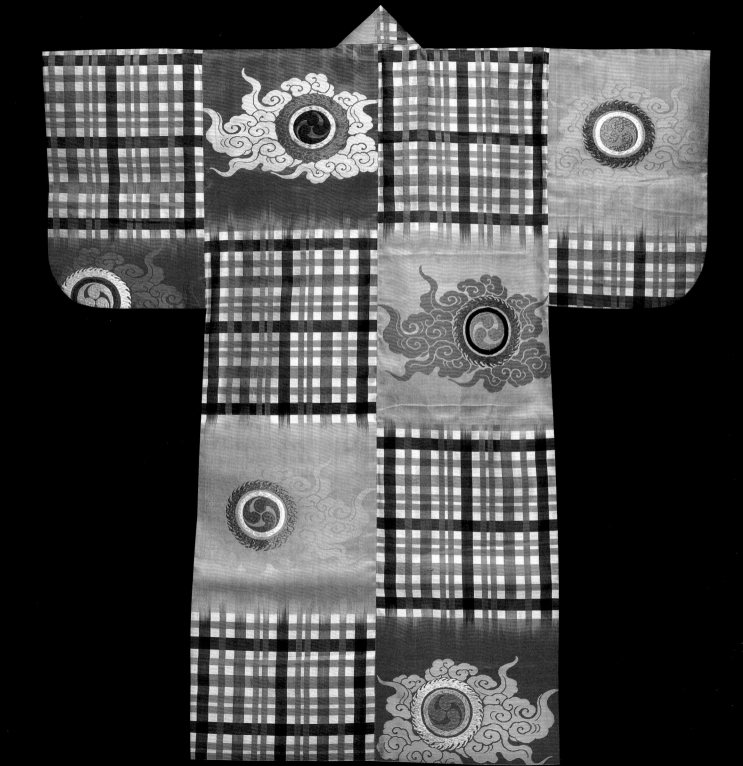

39

ATSUITA
Edo period, late eighteenth century to early
nineteenth century
Genji wheels and dragon roundels with a background
pattern of pine-bark diamonds on a ground of alternating blocks of orange-red and green
35.464

Ikat-dyed warp threads form a ground of alternating
orange-red and green blocks (*dangawari*). Continuous
and discontinuous supplementary wefts form the
background pattern of pine-bark diamonds (*matsukawa-bishi*) in light orange-red on the orange-red
ground and in silver on the green ground. Discontinuous patterning wefts of various colors create the
scattered dragon roundels and Genji wheels, with
gold-leafed paper-lamellae highlights.

    Scattered circles or diamonds on top of a
small-repeat ground motif appear in textiles of the
seventeenth century, but the triple-layer construction
of ground (*ji*), background pattern (*jimon*), and
floating pattern (*uamon*) became popular only at the
end of the eighteenth century.

    The colors have a martial flavor and would be
appropriate for an *atsuita* worn under a *chōken*
or *happi* draped to suggest armor for the role of a
warrior-courtier. The robe is finished with finesse,

using silver lamellae only in the empty spaces of the
ground repeat and gold as an occasional accent.

WEAVE STRUCTURE: 1Z5 twill ground, *ikat* dyed;
background pattern of supplementary continuous silver-
leafed paper and continuous and discontinuous silk
patterning wefts tied in 2Z1 twill over 6 warps, 2, 4, and 6
remain inactive; floating pattern of discontinuous gold-
leafed paper and silk patterning wefts tied in 2Z1 twill over
6 warps, 2, 4, and 6 remain inactive.

GROUND: MAIN WARP: Silk, unglossed; Z2S; *ikat*
dyed orange-red and blue-green; 152 per in.

MAIN WEFT: Silk, unglossed; no twist, X ends; orange-
red and green; 80 per in.

BACKGROUND PATTERN: SUPPLEMENTARY
WEFT 1: Silver-leafed paper lamellae; 40 per in.

SUPPLEMENTARY WEFT 2: Silk, glossed; no twist,
X ends; light orange-red; 40 per in.

FLOATING PATTERN: SUPPLEMENTARY WEFT 1:
Gold-leafed paper lamellae; 40 per in.

SUPPLEMENTARY WEFT 2: Silk, glossed; no twist,
X ends; white, brown, orange-red, gold, yellow, yellow-
green, dark blue, blue, light blue, purple; 40 per in.

MEASUREMENTS: CENTER BACK LENGTH:
25 1/2", 134.5 cm.

CENTER BACK TO SLEEVE EDGE: 26 3/4", 64.5 cm.

40

ATSUITA
Edo period, late eighteenth century to early
nineteenth century
Scattered flower medallions with a background
pattern of cobblestones on an orange-red ground
35.475

A checkerboard background design of cobblestones
is woven in gold-leafed paper wefts on an orange-red
ground. Within the orange-red squares are flower
patterns that can be thought of as variations on good-
luck diamonds (see cat. nos. 22, 26). Over these are
placed staggered six-sided flower patterns enclosing
half-flower motifs and circles of three swirling comma-
shapes (*tomoe*). In contrast to the background design,
in which both the gold-leafed paper wefts and the
colored silk wefts are tightly anchored in the warp to
form a stiff ground, the floating pattern of six-sided
flower motifs rises above the ground weave, except
where it is woven with gold-leafed paper.

Despite the stiff rendering of both the background and floating patterns, their geometric conception is appropriate to this garment for male roles.
The robe is in good condition, its colors still bright.

Like *karaori, atsuita* with red in the pattern or
ground (*iroiri*) are reserved for youthful roles. This
robe could be worn by the young boy Kagetsu carried
away from his home by a long-nosed goblin (*tengu*)
and brought up at Kiyomizu Temple in Kyoto in the
play *Kagetsu*.

WEAVE STRUCTURE: 1Z2 twill ground; background
pattern of supplementary continuous and discontinuous
gold-leafed paper and discontinuous silk patterning wefts
tied in 2Z1 twill over 6 warps, 2, 4, and 6 remain inactive;
floating pattern of supplementary discontinuous silk
patterning weft floats tied at intervals (*toji*).

GROUND: MAIN WARP: Silk, unglossed; no twist,
X ends; orange-red; 144 per in.

MAIN WEFT: Silk, unglossed; no twist, X ends; orange-
red; 80 per in.

BACKGROUND PATTERN: SUPPLEMENTARY
WEFT 1: Gold-leafed paper lamellae; 40 per in.

SUPPLEMENTARY WEFT 2: Silk, glossed; no twist,
X ends; white, orange-red, yellow, yellow-green, green,
dark blue, blue, light blue, purple, pink; 40 per in.

FLOATING PATTERN: SUPPLEMENTARY WEFT 1:
Gold-leafed paper lamellae; 40 per in.

SUPPLEMENTARY WEFT 2: Silk, glossed; no twist,
X ends; white, orange-red, yellow, yellow-green, green,
dark blue, blue, light blue, light light-blue, purple, pink;
40 per in.

MEASUREMENTS: CENTER BACK LENGTH:
43 ¼", 110 cm.
CENTER BACK TO SLEEVE EDGE: 37 ¼", 94.5 cm.

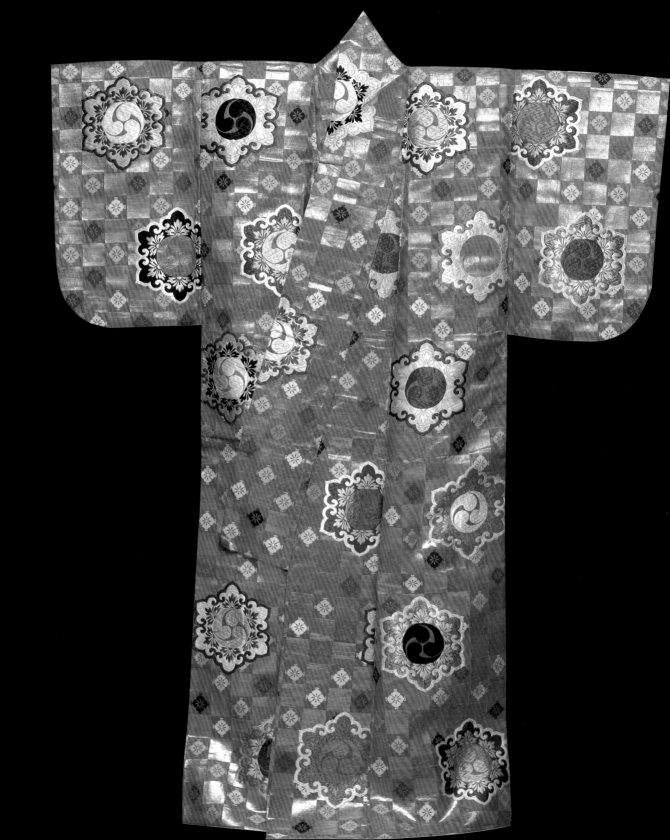

41

ATSUITA
Edo period, late eighteenth century to early
nineteenth century
Tortoise-shell hexagons linked with flower roundels
on an orange-red ground
35.467

The design, in lampas woven with white and green
silk and gold-leafed paper wefts on an orange-red
satin ground, is of linked tortoise-shell hexagons
enclosing phoenix birds with a flower roundel of
peonylike blossoms at every second hexagon cross.
The entire pattern belongs to the category of *shokkō*
designs, which appear in weft-patterned textiles
(*nishiki*) also called *shokkō* and generally have either
linked hexagons only or linked octagons alternating
with squares. *Shokkō* silks originated in China in the
area of Shi-tsien (Shisen in Japanese), where geometric
patterns woven on a red ground were particularly
popular. The Chinese have woven these silks since
the Sui (589-618) and Tang (618-907) periods, but
only after the beginning of the Ming period (1368-
1644) were large quantities imported to Japan. It is
thought that around the mid-eighteenth century this
type of textile began to be produced in Japan as well.
Compared to the Chinese version, the Japanese
fabrics are less solemn and give an impression of
moderation and quiet calm. The naturalistic additions

of phoenixes and peonies within the geometric tor-
toise-shell-hexagon patterns and the flower-roundel
links in this *atsuita* suggest that it was produced
in Japan after the mid-eighteenth century. In Nō
costumes, the *shokkō* pattern appears on *kariginu*,
and it occasionally appears on jackets (*happi*) and
sleeveless jackets (*sobatsugi*), but it is rarely found on
atsuita. The shoulders, hem, and sleeve bags of
this *atsuita* seem to have been retailored. Judging
from its frayed condition, the lining may be original
to the *atsuita*.

WEAVE STRUCTURE: Lampas: 1/5 warp-faced satin
ground weave, plain-weave pattern weave.

GROUND: MAIN WARP: Silk, unglossed; Z2S;
orange-red; 160 per in.

MAIN WEFT: Silk, unglossed; no twist, 2 ends; orange-
red; 84 per in.

PATTERN: SUPPLEMENTARY WARP 1: Silk,
glossed; no twist, 1 end; orange-red; 58 per in.

SUPPLEMENTARY WEFT: 1: Gold-leafed paper
lamellae; 40 per in.

SUPPLEMENTARY WEFT 2: Silk, glossed; no twist,
2 ends; white, yellow, green; 41 per in. (at times wefts
doubled in shed).

MEASUREMENTS: CENTER BACK LENGTH:
57", 145 cm.
CENTER BACK TO SLEEVE EDGE: 27 ½", 70 cm.

tively large motifs is a traditional design seen in *atsuita* and *karaori* after the seventeenth century. In this robe the extremely stylized rendering of the Buddhist wheels and the use of gold-leafed paper lamellae, almost never seen in seventeenth-century *karaori* and *atsuita*, also suggest that this *atsuita* was produced much later, in the nineteenth century.

WEAVE STRUCTURE: 1Z2 twill ground; background pattern of supplementary discontinuous silk patterning wefts tied in 2Z1 twill over 6 warps, 2, 4, and 6 remain inactive; floating pattern of supplementary discontinuous gold-leafed paper patterning wefts tied in 2Z1 twill over 6 warps, 2, 4, and 6 remain inactive, and supplementary discontinuous silk patterning weft floats tied at intervals (*toji*).
GROUND: MAIN WARP: Silk, unglossed; Z2S; green-blue; 164 per in.
MAIN WEFT: Silk, unglossed; no twist, X ends; blue; 84 per in.
BACKGROUND PATTERN: SUPPLEMENTARY WEFT 1: Silk, glossed; no twist, X ends; white; 45 per in.
FLOATING PATTERN: SUPPLEMENTARY WEFT 1: Gold-leafed paper lamellae; 44 per in.
SUPPLEMENTARY WEFT 2: Silk, glossed; no twist, X ends; white, orange-red, gold, yellow, yellow-green, green, dark blue, blue, light blue, light light-blue, purple, light purple, pink; 44 per in.
MEASUREMENTS: CENTER BACK LENGTH: 54 ¼", 138 cm.
CENTER BACK TO SLEEVE EDGE: 25 ¾", 65.3 cm.

42

ATSUITA
Edo period, first half of the nineteenth century
Buddhist ritual-implement wheels with a background pattern of triangle scales on a white ground
35.466

The background motif of scales (*uroko*) is woven in white and blue. Large and small Buddhist wheel motifs (*rimbō*) are scattered over the entire robe. The Buddhist wheel represents one of the seven jewels that the exemplary magistrate of ancient India, King Tenrin, is said to have owned. It is a common motif for decorating utensils, particularly Buddhist implements, but for textiles, with the exception of religious garments like priests' robes (*kesa*), it is seen only on Nō costumes for male roles, such as the *atsuita* (cat. no. 44), *happi*, and the sleeveless *happi* (*sobatsugi*). The two most commonly seen Buddhist motifs are these wheels and cloud-shaped gongs (*umpan*) hung at the corner of a temple and rung to announce dinner. On the other hand, the scale pattern (*uroko*) composed of linked triangles appears on many Nō garments, not only on *atsuita*, but also on women's robes like the *surihaku*, where it is used to symbolize female jealousy, and on hair bands and waist sashes.

The pattern of irregularly scattered, compara-

Atsuita with a design of mallet wheels over a background pattern of triangle scales on a ground of alternating blocks. Edo period, early nineteenth century. Tokyo National Museum.

43

ATSUITA
Edo period, first half of the nineteenth century
Clouds with a background pattern of triangle scales on a dark green-blue ground
35.476

The background design of triangles of alternating colors suggesting scales (*uroko*) is woven in a "coarse" ground twill using weft threads of light orange-red on a dark green-blue ground. The floating pattern of clouds is woven in shades of yellow, green, blue, brown, purple, and red supplementary weft floats intermixed with gold-leafed paper lamellae tied into the ground structure.

The scale design is frequently seen as a background pattern for *atsuita* (cat. nos. 42, 44). Typical accompanying floating patterns are mallet wheels (*tsuchiguruma*; see above), half-circle wheels (*katawaguruma*), Buddhist implement wheels (*rimbō*; cat. no. 42), and clouds. The cloud motif appears often on *atsuita* by itself and in combination with other motifs, such as circles enclosing swirling comma-shapes (*tomoe*). In their shape and the execution of the drawing, most such cloud motifs are very similar to those seen here. This may well have been a fashion-

able style of the second half of the eighteenth century into the first half of the nineteenth century.

The pattern on this *atsuita* would be appropriate for supernatural roles, such as the mountain crone who inhabits lofty heights in *Yamamba* (*The Mountain Crone*; fig. 33). The cloud pattern is partially cropped on the left and right sides of the robe, however, indicating that this *atsuita* was tailored to a small size and must have been used as a costume for a child actor. Roles for child actors include not only characters who are indeed children, but also characters who are of too high a class to attempt to represent them realistically, as for instance the emperor in the play *Kuzu* (*The Emperor in Hiding*) or the revered warrior Yoshitsune in *Funa Benkei* (*Benkei in the Boat*).

WEAVE STRUCTURE: 1Z2 twill ground; background pattern of supplementary discontinuous silk patterning wefts tied in 2Z1 twill over 6 warps, 2, 4, and 6 remain inactive; floating pattern of discontinuous gold-leafed paper patterning wefts tied in 2Z1 twill over 6 warps, 2, 4, and 6 remain inactive, and supplementary discontinuous silk patterning weft floats tied at intervals (*toji*).
GROUND: MAIN WARP: Silk, unglossed; Z2S; dark green-blue; 152 per in.
MAIN WEFT: Silk, unglossed; no twist, X ends; dark green-blue; 80 per in.
BACKGROUND PATTERN: SUPPLEMENTARY WEFT 1: Silk, glossed; no twist, X ends; orange (now faded); 40 per in.
FLOATING PATTERN: SUPPLEMENTARY WEFT 1: Gold-leafed paper lamellae; 40 per in.
SUPPLEMENTARY WEFT 2: Silk, glossed; no twist, X ends; white, red-brown, orange-red, gold, yellow, yellow-green, green, dark blue, blue, light blue, dark purple, light purple; 40 per in.
MEASUREMENTS: CENTER BACK LENGTH: 53 5/8", 136.3 cm.
CENTER BACK TO SLEEVE EDGE: 25 3/4", 65.5 cm.

each color. The cloth for the two garments was clearly woven separately, but the similarity of pattern conception hints that they had a very close connection. For example, it is possible that at the same workshop the draft sketch for one formed the basis from which the other was drawn. Among extant *karaori* one also finds robes whose designs suggest that a number of garments were made using the same line drawing, or that the line drawing was altered somewhat and then used again for other robes (see pp. 40-43).

WEAVE STRUCTURE: 1Z2 twill ground; background pattern of supplementary continuous gold-leaf paper patterning wefts tied in 2Z1 twill over 6 warps, 2, 4, and 6 remain inactive; floating pattern of supplementary discontinuous gold-leafed paper and silk patterning wefts tied in 2Z1 twill over 6 warps, 2, 4, and 6 remain inactive, and supplementary discontinuous silk patterning weft floats tied at intervals (*toji*).
GROUND: MAIN WARP: Silk, unglossed; Z twist, 2 ends; *ikat* dyed orange-red, green; 148 per in.
MAIN WEFT: Silk, unglossed; no twist, X ends; orange-red, green; 80 per in.
BACKGROUND PATTERN: SUPPLEMENTARY WEFT 1: Gold-leafed paper lamellae; 40 per in.
FLOATING PATTERN: SUPPLEMENTARY WEFT 1: Silk, glossed; no twist, X ends; orange-red, light orange-red, gold, light gold, yellow-green, green, blue, light blue, dark purple, light purple; 40 per in.
SUPPLEMENTARY WEFT 2: Silk, glossed; no twist, X ends; white, dark orange-red, orange-red, light orange-red, gold, light gold, yellow-green, green, dark blue, blue, light blue, dark purple, light purple; 40 per in.
MEASUREMENTS: CENTER BACK LENGTH: 54 ¼", 138 cm.
CENTER BACK TO SLEEVE EDGE: 25", 63.8 cm.

44

ATSUITA
Edo period, first half of the nineteenth century
Clouds and arrows in standing screens with a background pattern of triangle scales on a ground of alternating blocks of orange-red and green
35.477

On an *ikat*-dyed ground of alternating blocks (*dangawari*) of orange-red and green appears a triangle-scale pattern (*uroko*) in supplementary gold-leafed paper wefts. Two units make up the floating pattern: clouds containing Buddhist implement wheels (*rimbō*) and arrows in standing screens.

It is noteworthy that there is an *atsuita* with almost identical design in the Tokyo National Museum (fig. 23). It, like this piece, has alternating blocks of red and green with a background pattern of scales over which are clouds and arrows in standing screens; it can be said to be essentially the same except that within the clouds, instead of Buddhist implement wheels, there are circles containing three swirling comma-shapes (*tomoe*) and at certain places around the arrows in screens small cloud patterns appear. The biggest difference between the two robes is that while the Providence robe has its motifs placed symmetrically left and right of the back seam, the layout for the Tokyo National Museum robe has the motifs in alternating blocks matching one motif to

Hangire

Hangire are divided skirts, pleated in front and having back panels stiffened with an interfacing of straw (*goza*). Although they look like skirts from the front, in fact they have a low-set crotch and are divided into pant legs. In order to make the broad back panels bulge out over the buttocks, round braided cords of the same color as the *hangire* are threaded through holes, pulled tight, and tied to form a large central back pleat. This is hiked over a forked wooden prong at center back. Unlike the similarly shaped *ōguchi*, which have waistbands of the same fabric as the skirts, *hangire* generally have waistbands of plain white silk.

Hangire are usually woven with a satin (*shusu*) base patterned with large, dynamic designs of a single color, often gold-leafed paper (*kinran*) or silver-leafed paper (*ginran*). Ground colors tend to be strong, clear shades like white, red, green, purple, dark blue, brown, or black.

Hangire are worn for male roles of gods, demons, goblins, and warriors.

45

HANGIRE
Edo period, first half of the nineteenth century
Chrysanthemums and undulating vertical lines on a
purple ground
35.500

These *hangire* of lampas have a purple ground with a
design rendered in gold that combines the traditional
Heian-period imperial court motif (*yūsoku*) of
undulating vertical stripes (*tatewaku*) containing
chrysanthemum arabesques with the Edo-period
motifs of chrysanthemum and pine medallions in the
bulges created by the stripes.

     The tailoring is standard for *hangire*: pleats in
front, broad panels in back stiffened by an interfacing,
a round braided cord (*maruuchi*) of matching color
threaded through the waist, and a flat, white, plain-
weave silk band at the waist. The classical motifs of
this *hangire* suggest a Heian warrior-courtier role or
perhaps the Chinese Emperor Gen-so in the play
Tsurukame (*The Crane and the Tortoise*), in which it
would be worn in combination with a *kariginu*.

WEAVE STRUCTURE: Lampas: 4/1 warp-faced satin
ground weave, plain-weave pattern weave.
GROUND: MAIN WARP: Silk, unglossed; Z2S; purple;
140 per in.

MAIN WEFT: Silk, unglossed; no twist, X ends; light
gold; 72 per in.
PATTERN: SUPPLEMENTARY WARP 1: Silk,
unglossed; no twist, 1 or 2 ends; gold to orange-red; 52
per in.
SUPPLEMENTARY WEFT 1: Gold-leafed paper
lamellae; 32 per in.
MEASUREMENTS: WIDTH AT WAIST: 31 ¾",
80.8 cm.
CENTER BACK LENGTH: 41", 104.2 cm.

46

MEASUREMENTS: WIDTH AT WAIST: 32 ³/₈",
82.4 cm.
CENTER BACK LENGTH: 38 ³/₄", 98.7 cm.

HANGIRE
Edo period, first half of the nineteenth century
Branches on a green ground
35.499

Leafy gold branches and arabesques alternate directions on a green twill ground. The rendering is very
stylized and the variety of plant unidentifiable. The
cut is standard for *hangire*, but the round green
braided cord (*maruuchi*) at the waist and the green
crepe waistband are not. The form is similar to that
of plain-colored divided skirts (*ōguchi*), but the
round braided cords for *hangire* ought to be the same
color as the ground fabric and the flat waistband
should be white plain-weave silk. Presumably the
green crepe waistband was added later.

WEAVE STRUCTURE: Lampas: 1Z3 twill ground weave,
plain-weave pattern weave.
GROUND: MAIN WARP: Silk, unglossed; Z2S; green;
224 per in.
MAIN WEFT: Silk, unglossed; slight Z twist, 3 ends;
green; 80 per in.
PATTERN: SUPPLEMENTARY WARP 1: Silk,
unglossed; slight Z twist, 1 or 2 ends; light gold; 52 per in.
SUPPLEMENTARY WEFT 1: Gold-leafed paper
lamellae; 36 per in.

Koshi-obi

The *koshi-obi* is a long, embroidered sash tied in front, used to belt broad-sleeved cloaks like *kariginu, happi*, and *mizugoromo* for male roles, as well as female costumes worn in waist wrap (*koshimaki*) style. The two ends and a central section visible at the back are made of stiff, decorated cloth, generally a satin or figured satin weave. Between these are strips of soft, flat, plain-weave silk in white, light blue, brown, or grey. The ground color of the embroidered area tends to be red, yellow, green, blue, or brown. The designs divide into two types: those with three rounds similar to family crests and those with designs that cover the entire area, such as triangle scales or arabesques.

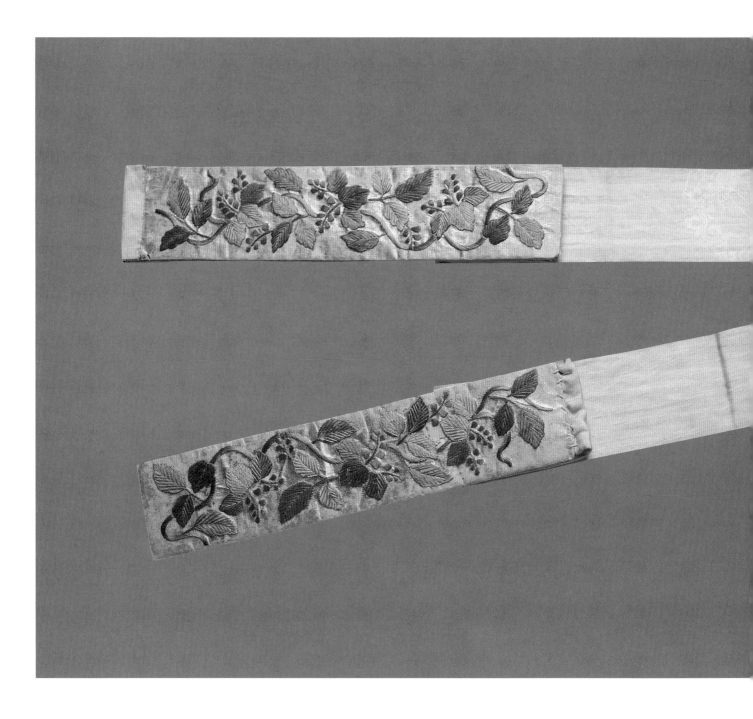

47

KOSHI-OBI
Edo period, eighteenth century
Paulownia arabesques on a gold-leafed ground
35.501

This white belt is of plain weave with twill patterning, to which sections of satin weave embroidered with paulownia arabesques over a gold-leafed ground have been sewn at the ends and center.

The embroidery stitches include satin stitch (*hira-nui*), stem stitch (*matoi-nui*), and overlay (*norikake-nui*). The execution of the paulownia arabesques is comparatively freely done, despite the limitations of the narrow width of the belt.

Koshi-obi are belts worn wrapped around the waist and tied in front on top of such garments as *kariginu, happi,* or *mizugoromo* to hold them in place. The design appears at the center back and on the front panels, where it is visible to the audience.

WEAVE STRUCTURE: Center and ends: 4/1 satin ground; stenciled gold leaf; silk-floss embroidery.

GROUND: MAIN WARP: Silk, white; too abraded to count.

MAIN WEFT: Silk, white; too abraded to count.

EMBROIDERY: THREAD: Silk, unglossed; no twist, X ends; brown, orange-red, yellow-green, green, blue.

STITCHES: Satin stitch (*hira-nui*), overlay (*norikake-nui*), stem stitch (*matoi-nui*).

MEASUREMENTS: LENGTH: 87 7/8″, 223.5 cm.

WIDTH: 2 3/8″, 6 cm.

Glossary

Atsuita – A stiff *kosode*-style robe with checks and/or geometric designs generally worn under a cloak for male roles.

Atsuita-karaori – A robe worn for young male courtier-warrior roles that combines characteristics of the *karaori* and *atsuita*.

Aya-ori – Twill or, most often, figured twill weave.

Background Pattern – See *Jimon*.

Bokashi-nui – See Shading in Satin Stitch.

Chōken – Lightweight dancing cloak with broad, open sleeves, loosely draping front and back panels, and decorative cords. Often made of gauze.

Complex Gauze – See Gauze Weave and *Ro*.

Continuous Supplementary Weft – A nonstructural patterning weft that passes from one edge of the cloth to the other without interruption. Continuous supplementary wefts that are composed of metallic-leafed paper strips are clipped at or near each selvedge due to their lack of pliability, while continuous supplementary silk wefts pass through the selvedge and double back.

Couching – Embroidery stitch in which one thread or a number of threads are held to the surface of the fabric by stitching over them with a second thread. See *Koma-nui*.

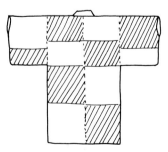

Dangawari – *Ikat*-dyed ground pattern of alternating blocks.

Discontinuous Supplementary Weft – A nonstructural patterning weft that operates only in discrete areas. Discontinuous supplementary silk wefts double back at the edges of each motif, while discontinuous supplementary wefts composed of metallic-leafed paper strips are usually clipped at the edges of each motif because of their lack of pliability, although in cat. no. 12 the gold-leafed paper strips double back at the edges of each motif. Above: cat. no. 2, back of fabric.

Dōhaku – *Nuihaku* with gold-leafed stenciled ground for roles of upper-class women.

Donsu – Figured satin damask in which the pattern, often created with warp and weft of differing colors, appears reversed on the back and front of the fabric.

Float – The segment of a warp or weft thread that crosses at least two yarns between points of binding into the ground.

French Knot – An embroidery stitch created by knotting the thread in the surface of the fabric, then taking the loose end to the back of the fabric to hold the knot down.

Futsu – A double weave with two interacting plain-weave structures.

Gauze Weave – A weave with warp ends arranged in sets, one end of which is carried alternately to the right then the left of the others and held in place by the weft. In plain gauze, *sha*, this pattern is repeated; in complex gauze the pattern is varied (see *Ro*). Above: cat. no. 28.

Ginran – Textile with weft-patterning in silver, usually silver-leafed paper lamellae made by affixing silver leaf to paper, then cutting it into strips.

Glossed Silk – *Neriito*, silk yarns in which the natural gum has been removed. Also known as "soft silk."

Ground – See *Ji*.

Hakama – General term for divided skirts. See *Hangire, Ōguchi, Sashinuki*.

Hangire – Divided skirts pleated in front with back panels stiffened with an interfacing of straw mat (*goza*). Tailored of weft-patterned silks with gold- or silver-leafed paper patterning wefts. Also called *hangiri*.

Happi – Three-quarter-length broad-sleeved outer cloak for men's roles.

Hira-nui – See Satin Stitch.

Hirosode – See *Ōsode*.

Hitatare – A lined matched suit of stencil-dyed hemp or ramie worn by samurai officials. The broad-sleeved cloak is tailored from the same fabric as the *hakama* pants, which may be either ankle length or so long that they trail behind the wearer (*nagabakama*).

Ikat – *Kasuri*, a method of creating a reserved pattern by tie-dyeing the warp or weft yarns before weaving.

Iroiri – Garments with red or orange-red in ground or pattern, suitable for roles of young persons.

Ironashi – Garments without red or orange-red in ground or pattern, suitable for roles of older persons.

Ji – The ground structure of the fabric, created by the main warp and weft. In the microphotograph below, the ground *ji* is a 1Z2 twill in green silk (cat. no. 2).

Jimon – The background pattern of a fabric. In *karaori, atsuita,* and *atsuita-karaori* it is often woven of supplementary gold- or silver-leafed paper lamellae or silk patterning wefts (see above). For *nuihaku* and *surihaku*, it is stenciled metallic leaf.

Kamaito – Unglossed silk thread for embroidery.

Karaori – A stiff *kosode*-style robe worn for women's roles, decorated with "feminine" patterns such as flowers, shells, fans, baskets, and fences.

Kariginu – Long, broad-sleeved, round-necked "hunting cloak" for male roles.

Kasuri – See *Ikat*.

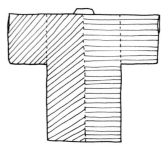

Katamigawari – Split-body patterning in which designs differ on the right and left sides of the garment.

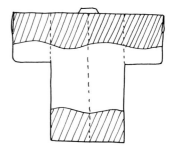

Katasuso – Shoulder-hem patterning in which the shoulder and hem areas are filled, but the area between is left blank. Also called *koshiake*.

Katsura-obi – A long, narrow headband embroidered at both ends and along a central strip. It is tied around the forehead under the mask and knotted in a bow at the back of the head.

Kiito – See Unglossed Silk.

Kinagashi – Style of draping for *karaori* as an outer robe. It lies snugly at the hip but is open at the neck to reveal the undergarment.

Kinran – Cloth with woven-in pattern of gold, usually gold-leafed paper lamellae made by affixing gold leaf to paper, then cutting it into very thin strips.

Koma – Pattern-repeat block for weft-patterned weaving. Textiles that have no repeat across the width of the fabric from selvedge to selvedge have one *koma*, those with the same pattern left and right have two *koma*.

Koma-nui – A variation of the embroidery stitch called couching, in which a thread is laid onto a surface of the fabric and held down with small stitches of another thread.

Koshimaki – Waist-wrap style of draping a *kosode*-style garment, creating the effect of a two-piece suit in which an outer robe is worn slipped off the shoulders and wrapped around the waist fastened by the sash, revealing the underrobe on the upper part of the body.

Koshi-obi – A long, embroidered sash used to belt broad-sleeved cloaks and *nuihaku* in waist-wrap draping.

Kosode – "Small sleeve" garment whose wrist-length sleeves have sewn-up outer edges to form small openings for the wrist (compare to *ōsode* and *hirosode*). The principal outer garment for all classes since the sixteenth century. It was the precursor of the kimono and is similar in cut and construction.

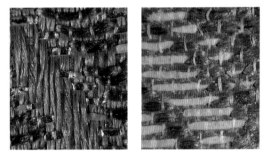

Lampas – Figured textile in which a pattern composed of supplementary wefts bound by a supplementary warp is combined with a ground fabric formed by a main warp and a main weft. Above: lampas with a satin ground (cat. no. 41). Left: front of fabric. Right: back of fabric.

Long and Short Stitch – *Sashi-nui*, a variation of satin stitch in which the inside of a motif is divided into several areas that are filled in with alternating long and short stitches. Used in realistic depiction or for effects such as animal hair and petals.

Maiginu – A lightweight women's dancing cloak, generally made of gauze. It has broad, open sleeves and overlapping panels in front, with no decorative cords.

Matoi-nui – An outline stitch. Also called *matsui-nui*. See Stem Stitch.

Mizugoromo – "Traveling cloak," an unlined outer cloak for roles of priests, monks, and old men (of plain colors), old women (of mesh fabric), Yamabushi priests (striped), and traveling women.

Mokuito – Several strands of different colored silk twisted together to form a polychrome embroidery thread for reeds and grasses.

Name – Figured satin.

Neriito – Silk yarns in which the natural gum has been removed. Often referred to as "glossed" or "degummed." See also Unglossed Silk.

Nerinuki – A plain-weave silk in which the warps are unglossed and the wefts are glossed, used extensively in the sixteenth century.

Nishiki – General term for silk fabrics with either warp- (*keikin*) or weft-patterning (*ikin*) in polychrome silk or metallic-leafed paper strips, including *karaori, atsuita, kinran, ginran,* and other textile weaves.

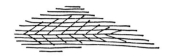

Norikake-nui – Overlay stitching. A variation of couching used for creating minor details like the veins of leaves or the stamens of flowers.

Nōshi – A courtier's broad-sleeved cloak.

Noshime – A plain-weave-silk *kosode*-style undergarment. The waist area may be unpatterned and undyed, or the garment may have broad horizontal stripes.

Nugisage – Style of draping in which the right sleeve is slipped off the shoulder to reveal the robe beneath.

Nuihaku – A combined technique of embroidery and *surihaku* (applied metallic leaf). Also refers to Nō robes decorated in that technique.

Nui-iri – Incidental embroidery, sometimes used on *surihaku*, which are then called *nui-iri surihaku*.

Nuitori-fū – Discontinuous supplementary patterning wefts that double back at the edge of the motif, or in the case of gold-leafed paper patterning wefts, are clipped on the back of the fabric along the edges of the motif.

Obi – Sash.

Ōdon – Satin weave with silk warps and cotton wefts and additional silk or gold patterning wefts (see fig. 35).

Ōguchi – Broad-backed, ankle-length pleated divided skirts whose backs are stiffened during the weaving process with thick, ropelike threads creating a rib. Usually red, white, or pale green. Compare to *Hangire*.

Ōsode – Classical Japanese court garment with broad, open sleeves, worn in many layers that were visible at the open cuff. See *Hirosode*.

Patterning Weft – Weft supplementary to the main weft, used to create a pattern or enrich the main weft.

Plain Weave – Basic weave structure in which the weft interfaces over one warp and under one warp. Also known as tabby.

Rinzu – Figured satin in which the pattern is created by a monochrome main warp and weft and is visible only on the surface of the fabric.

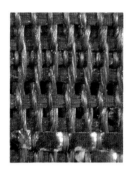

Ro – Gauze in which plain weave alternates with insertions of gauze. Above: cat. no. 26.

Sagara-nui – See French Knot.

Sashi-nui – See Long and Short Stitch.

Sashinuki – Divided skirts with pleats front and back, bound at the ankle to look like pantaloons. Worn over *ōguchi*, which give them fullness, as formal attire by noble characters.

Satin Stitch – *Hira-nui*, an embroidery stitch in which long stitches are taken parallel to one another to fill in large or small areas.

Satin Weave – Warp-faced weave in which the warp threads pass under one and over more than three weft threads. The points at which the warp passes under the weft threads are never lined up as in a twill weave, but are distributed so that the warp floats produce a shiny, smooth surface on the face of the fabric.

Sha – See Gauze Weave.

Shading in Satin Stitch – *Bokashi-nui*, a variation of satin stitch in which colors are graduated in order to shade an area with color hues from light to dark.

Shike – Plain-colored plain-weave raw silk.

Shite – The main actor in a Nō play.

Shusu – See Satin Weave.

Sobatsugi – "Vest," a sleeveless *happi* worn for roles of Chinese women and men and for unmasked samurai.

Stem Stitch – *Matoi-nui*, an embroidery stitch used for rendering lines.

Suō – An unlined matched suit of stencil-dyed hemp or ramie worn for male roles of commoners. See *Hitatare*.

Supplementary Warps or Wefts – Nonstructural warps or wefts used to create a pattern.

Surihaku – A method of metallic-leaf decoration. Paste is applied to the fabric and gold and/or silver leaf is pressed on. After the paste has dried, the excess leaf is rubbed off. Also refers to a Nō robe in which this method of decoration is used.

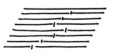

Toji – Binding thread, the individual warp thread that binds a supplementary weft to the surface of the fabric.

Tsuboori – A style of draping in which a *karaori* or *atsuita* is worn folded up and tucked in at the waist like a jacket. It can be draped either over *koshimaki* or over broad divided skirts.

Tsure – The companion actor to the main actor (*shite*) in a Nō play.

Twill Weave – Weave with parallel diagonal pattern produced by passing the weft over one and then under two or more warp threads, or vice-versa, instead of over one and under one as in plain weave. The notation 1/2 indicates the number of warps the weft passes first under, then over. The addition of Z or S indicates the direction of the diagonal as in 1Z2, in which the diagonal is to the right.

Uamon – Floating pattern that sits atop the ground of the textile. It is woven with discontinuous weft floats; gold-leafed paper and silk wefts tied to the ground in a twill weave may be included to add textural variety. See illustration of "Discontinuous Supplementary Weft."

Unglossed Silk – *Kiito*, silk yarns from which the gum has not been removed. Also known as hard silk.

Waki – The secondary actor who generally opens a Nō play, often a traveling priest.

Wakitsure – The companion of a *waki* or secondary actor.

Ware-nui – A variation of satin stitch in which two sides of a bilaterally symmetrical motif such as a leaf or feather are embroidered in satin stitch at an oblique angle, creating a V-shape. Because of the differential way the stitches catch the light, *ware-nui* creates the appearance of two different colors.

Warp – The longitudinal threads of a textile, as strung on a loom. A single thread of warp is called an end.

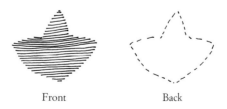

Front   Back

Watashi-nui – A variation of satin stitch. Embroidery stitch used in the sixteenth century, in which long stitches appear on the front of the fabric, but only tiny stitches are used on the back so there is no build-up behind. The result is a soft, flexible cloth.

Weft – The transverse threads of a textile, those that pass through the warp as inserted by the weaver. They can be continuous and pass from selvedge to selvedge, or discontinuous and traverse only the patterned area.

Weft-patterned – A textile in which a pattern is formed or the ground enriched by the use of a patterning weft.

Yore – Mesh fabric with a loose plain weave that is then pulled out of shape.

Yūzen – A method of surface decoration using resist paste applied through a funnel or stencil to define different colored pattern areas, to create fine white outlines, and to protect pattern areas from the background color. Various colors are brushed onto the unresisted areas of the cloth to create polychrome pictorial designs.

Selected References
for Further Study

Bethe, Monica, and Karen Brazell, *Dance in the Nō Theater*, 3 vols. Ithaca: China-Japan Program, Cornell University, 1982.

———, *Nō as Performance: An Analysis of the Kuse Scene of Yamamba*, Cornell University East Asian Papers. Ithaca: China-Japan Program, Cornell University, 1978.

Goff, Janet, *Noh Drama and the Tale of Genji: The Art of Allusion in Fifteen Classical Plays*. Princeton: Princeton University Press, 1991.

Hare, Thomas Blenman, *Zeami's Style: The Noh Plays of Zeami Motokiyo*. Stanford: Stanford University Press, 1986.

Ishimura, Hayao, and Nobuhiko Maruyama, *Robes of Elegance: Japanese Kimonos of the 16th-20th Centuries*. Raleigh: North Carolina Museum of Art, 1988.

Keene, Donald, compiler and ed., *Anthology of Japanese Literature from the Earliest Era to the Mid-Nineteenth Century*. New York: Grove Press, Inc., 1955.

———, *Nō and Bunraku: Two Forms of Japanese Theatre*. New York: Columbia University Press, 1966 (reprinted 1990).

———, *Nō: The Classical Theater of Japan*. Tokyo and Palo Alto: Kodansha International, 1966 (rev. ed. 1973).

———, ed., *Twenty Plays of the Nō Theater*. New York and London: Columbia University Press, 1970.

Kennedy, Alan, *Japanese Costume: History and Tradition*. Paris: Éditions Adam Biro, 1990.

Konishi, Chu'nichi, *Zeamishū*, vol. 8 of *Nihon no shisō*. Chikuma Shobo, 1970.

Konparu, Kunio, *The Noh Theater: Principles and Perspectives*. New York: Weatherhill/ Fankosha, 1983.

Levy, Ian Hideo, trans., *The Ten Thousand Leaves: A Translation of the Manyōshū, Japan's Premier Anthology of Classical Poetry*, vol. 1. Princeton: Princeton University Press, 1981.

McCullough, Helen Craig, trans., *Kokin Wakashū*. Stanford: Stanford University Press, 1985.

———, trans., *Tales of Ise: Lyrical Episodes from Tenth-Century Japan*. Stanford: Stanford University Press, 1968.

Meech, Julia, and Gabriel P. Weisberg, *Japonisme Comes to America: The Japanese Impact on the Graphic Arts 1876-1925*. New York: Harry Abrams, 1990.

Minnich, Helen Benton, *Japanese Costume and the Makers of Its Elegant Tradition*. Tokyo: Charles E. Tuttle Co., 1986.

Mizoguchi, Saburo, trans. and adapted by Louise Allison Cort, *Design Motifs*, vol. 1 of *Arts of Japan*. New York and Tokyo: Weatherhill/ Shibundo, 1973.

Morris, Ivan, *The World of the Shining Prince: Court Life in Ancient Japan*. Great Britain: Oxford University Press, 1964 (reprinted in the United States by Alfred A. Knopf, Inc., 1964, and Peregrine Books, 1969; reprinted Penguin Books, 1979).

Nakamura, Yasuo, trans. Don Kenny, *Noh: The Classical Theater*. New York and Tokyo: Walker/Weatherhill, 1971.

Nippon Gakujutsu Shinkōkai, *Japanese Noh Drama: Ten Plays Selected and Translated from the Japanese*, 3 vols. Tokyo: Nippon Gakujutsu Shinkōkai, 1955-60.

———, trans., *The Manyōshū: One Thousand Poems*. New York and London: Columbia University Press, 1965.

Nishimura, Hyōbu, Jean Mailey, and Joseph S. Hayes, Jr., *Tagasode: Whose Sleeves... Kimono from the Kanebo Collection*. New York: Japan Society, Inc., 1976.

Okochi, Sadao, trans. and adapted by Louise Allison Cort and Monica Bethe, *Tokugawa Collection of Nō Robes and Masks*. New York: Japan Society, 1977.

Priest, Alan, *Japanese Costume; An Exhibition of Nō Robes and Buddhist Vestments*. New York: Metropolitan Museum of Art, 1935.

Rimer, J. Thomas, and Masakazu Yamazaki, *On the Art of the Nō Drama: The Major Treatises of Zeami*. Princeton: Princeton University Press, 1984.

Rodd, Laurel Rasplica, with Mary Catherine Henkenius, trans., *Kokinshū: A Collection of Poems Ancient and Modern*. Princeton: Princeton University Press, 1984.

Stinchecum, Amanda Mayer, *Kosode, 16th-19th Century Textiles from the Nomura Collection*. Tokyo: Japan Society and Kōdansha International, 1984.

Ueda, Makoto, *Literacy and Art Theories in Japan*. Cleveland: The Press of Case Western Reserve University, 1967.

_____, *The Old Pine Tree and Other Noh Plays*. Lincoln: University of Nebraska Press, 1962.

Waley, Arthur, *The Nō Plays of Japan*. New York: Grove Press, Inc., 1911.

Yasuda, Kenneth, *Masterworks of the Nō Theater*. Bloomington and Indianapolis: Indiana University Press, 1989.

Zeami Motokiyo, trans. Sakurai Chu'ichi et al., *Kadensho*. Kyoto: Sumiya-Shinobe Publishing Institute, 1968.